THE ENTIREPRENEUR

In this groundbreaking book Bill Bolton and John Thompson present a completely new take on the conventional domains of entrepreneur, leader and manager. They argue that in today's turbulent and uncertain world, businesses no longer have the time for a business cycle that begins with an entrepreneur, hands over to a manager and finally brings in a strategic leader when things are flagging. The 'New Normal' that now prevails requires that these things run together and calls for a new kind of all-rounder.

Bolton and Thompson give us a new word to describe such a person:

'The ENTIREPRENEUR'

'The entirely competent person, able to discern aright and make things happen.'

Drawing upon the successful person-centred approach of their books on 'entrepreneurs' they first tell the stories of over 40 **entrepreneurs**, demonstrating clearly that such people do exist. After discussing the 'New Normal' context they present a fascinating analysis that goes below the surface to describe the key Talent, Temperament, Technique and Discernment attributes that explain the **entirepreneur**. Readers have the opportunity to make a self-evaluation of their own attribute strengths, concluding with a final '**entirepreneur**' score.

This fascinating and insightful look at the **entirepreneur** is a clear pointer to what will be demanded of those who would succeed amid the vicissitudes of the 'New Normal'.

Bill Bolton has spent his working life in industry (as Technical Director of a Swedish Multinational), in academia (at the University of Cambridge) and as an international consultant.

John Thompson has experience in retailing and the steel industry as well as spending many years as an academic. He is a Professor of Entrepreneurship but he has also taught strategy extensively.

This is the fifth book they have written together.

If you are in senior management or aspire to be then this book is essential reading. It will help you to understand how to succeed as an entrepreneur, manager and leader—all at the same time. In this hands-on book you will find the key person-attributes in which you need to be strong and most importantly how they can be measured.

Jill Garrett, Executive Director Tentpeg Consulting and formerly Managing Director of Gallup Europe

In this book, Thompson and Bolton have not only developed their own ideas, but really moved forward the whole discourse on the interrelationship between entrepreneurship, leadership and management. Full of good theory, explained through well chosen case studies.

Dan Corlett, CEO, Farming and Countryside Education, UK

Bolton and Thompson challenge the conventional wisdom that entrepreneurs generally do not make effective leaders and rarely become strong managers. The authors present an integrative framework for business people to become entrepreneur, leader and manager for the 'New Normal' facing business today. A must read for both entrepreneurs and managers alike.

Jeff Cornwall, Jack C. Massey Professor of Entrepreneurship, Belmont University, Nashville, USA

This book on the entirepreneur is unlike any other books about entrepreneurship, from which it emerges. It is a direct and tangible reflection of what is being demanded by the challenges of the 'New Normal'; and it is interspersed with good, concrete examples which bring an academic subject into the realm of reality. I think anyone who will read this, will either want to start his/her own business at the end of it, or reflect upon their existing style and approach, fuelled with enthusiasm and drive emanating from this book.

Patrick van der Vorst, Founder, valuemystuff.com, UK and USA

A very pleasant read which brings attention to the significance of the 'New Normal' in start-up and established organizations. Successfully balancing directional and operational excellence is the challenging role of the entirepreneur.

Simon S. Mak, Professor of Practice in Entrepreneurship, Cox School of Business, Southern Methodist University, Dallas, USA

The negativity toward entrepreneurial thinking has been reversed in the last ten years—in many ways due to the work of Bill Bolton and John Thompson. In their latest book, *The Entirepreneur*, they explore the relationship between the entrepreneur, leader and manager and show how these three threads need to be woven together. They also highlight the need, constantly, to explore the social and economic horizon and not get caught by the urgency of the immediate. This is an important book, not just for those in the business world, but also for those who want to make a difference to society and approach the future with imagination and creativity.

Rev. Canon Chris Neal, Mission Consultant, UK

THE ENTIREPRENEUR

The all-in-one entrepreneur-leader-manager

Bill Bolton and John Thompson

Routledge
Taylor & Francis Group

LONDON AND NEW YORK

First published 2015
by Routledge
2 Park Square, Milton Park, Abingdon, Oxon OX14 4RN

and by Routledge
711 Third Avenue, New York, NY 10017

Routledge is an imprint of the Taylor & Francis Group, an informa business

© 2015 Bill Bolton and John Thompson

British Library Cataloguing in Publication Data
A catalogue record for this book is available from the British Library

Library of Congress Cataloging in Publication Data
Bolton, Bill.
The entirepreneur: the all-in-one entrepreneur-leader-manager / Bill
Bolton and John Thompson. – 1 Edition.
pages cm
Includes bibliographical references and index.
1. Entrepreneurship. 2. Leadership. 3. Management–Employee
participation. I. Thompson, John L. II. Title.
HB615.E5778 2015
658.4'09–dc23
2014045870

ISBN: 978-0-415-85865-6 (hbk)
ISBN: 978-0-415-85866-3 (pbk)
ISBN: 978-0-203-79828-7 (ebk)

Typeset in Bembo
by Swales & Willis Ltd, Exeter, Devon, UK

Printed and Bound in Great Britain by Ashford Colour Press Ltd., Gosport

CONTENTS

List of figures   vii
List of tables   viii
The cover story   ix
Preface   xi
Introduction   xiii

PART ONE
Entirepreneur stories   **1**

1 Stories of entirepreneurs and entirepreneurship in action   3

PART TWO
The entirepreneur and the 'New Normal'   **67**

2 The 'New Normal' world of business   71

3 Conventional wisdom: a commentary and critique   78

4 Dealing with the 'New Normal'   97

5 Growth and sustainability   104

PART THREE
The person dimension 111

6 The 3Ts—explained 115

7 Talent—applied 139

8 Temperament—applied 157

9 Technique—applied 172

10 Discernment—applied 183

11 The final score 203

Notes 208
Bibliography 215
Index—a quick guide to the entirepreneur attributes 217
Subject index—main references 219
Entirepreneurs index—main references 221
About the authors 223

FIGURES

5.1	The growth-cycle challenge	107
6.1	The person dimension	116
6.2	Temperament model	128
6.3	The 3Ts plus triangle	136
7.1	The talent attributes	140
7.2	The creativity group	140
7.3	Focus	147
7.4	Operations	150
8.1	Temperament model	157
9.1	The technique elements	172
9.2	Teams plus	173
9.3	The Gallup performance model	178
10.1	The elements of discernment	184
10.2	Vision	185
10.3	Values	189
10.4	Perception	197
11.1	Diagrammatic framework—person B	205
11.2	Diagrammatic framework—your personal profile	206

TABLES

3.1   Personal styles   93
11.1 Entirepreneur scores   204
11.2 The direct score tabulation   205
11.3 Converting your score   207
11.4 Your hand of cards   207

THE COVER STORY

The title of this book introduces a new word into the English language

The entirepreneur.

Our sub-heading defines an **entirepreneur** as the 'all-in-one' person who possesses and combines the attributes of the entrepreneur, the leader and the manager.

In today's world of the 'New Normal' the traditional singular approach which separates these roles is not enough. At the highest level companies need the attributes of all three within the one person.

We use the metaphor of a deck of cards on the cover of the book to illustrate how our 'attributes' approach works.

There are four key points here:

First we all possess attributes of one kind or another. As the cover illustrates, these can be placed into four groups or suits.

♦ Diamonds represent the Talent attributes that are of great value.

♥ Hearts correspond to the Temperament attributes that define who we are as people.

♣ Clubs are about Technique that we hone by constant practice.

♠ Spades cover the Discernment attributes that give us wisdom and sound judgement.

Our second point is illustrated by the upturned cards, whose values are not yet known. In this book we turn the cards over and help you to discover where your strengths lie and what the cards in your metaphorical hand are.

Third, we show a winning hand, where 'Aces are high'. It is the hand of the **entirepreneur**.

Our final point is that though we use the card metaphor we do not subscribe to the view that success in life depends upon the cards that we are dealt. If you doubt that then simply read some of the stories of the **entirepreneurs** we present in this book. Many have succeeded against amazing odds. It is where you finish that matters and not where you start.

As is often said 'success is not so much about the cards we are dealt as it is about how we use them'.

PREFACE

As we put the finishing touches to this book we were struck by two headlines that really tell our story. Both are from the same issue of the *Financial Times*, November 2014:

1. 'John Chen: can he create a new generation of BlackBerry addicts?'
2. 'Start-ups break through billion-dollar fundraising barrier.'

Our book weaves together two themes. The first is in the title—*The Entirepreneur*. Until now, entrepreneurs, leaders and managers have been seen as separate entities. Here we challenge this conventional wisdom and argue that we need people who can successfully integrate the contributions of all three into a seamless entirety.

We start with the term 'entire' because **entirepreneurs** are entrepreneurs, leaders and managers—and more—rolled into one. We join 'entire' with 'preneur', from the French verb 'to take', because '**entirepreneurs**' take action. They are thus 'entirely competent' and they 'get things done'.

John Chen, at the age of 59, has come out of his retirement to try and turn around the company behind the once-dominant BlackBerry mobile phone. In mid-2007 it had nine million subscribers with three million being added every three months. It was the 'must have' business phone. In 2008 the company had a valuation of $80 billion.

Today BlackBerry is in deep trouble. Its global market share is below 1 per cent and it has been written off by many. The challenge facing Chen calls for more than just a turnaround specialist: it needs someone who can rebuild a business and handle a difficult legacy. As the headline above puts it, he has to 'create a new generation of BlackBerry addicts'.

Mr Chen's task is enormous, but if he is an **entirepreneur** he will be able to call upon his entrepreneurial creativity, his strategic leadership and his management skills to rebuild the business and create a following.

Our second theme is the 'New Normal' that is taking us from the reasonably predictable and certain to the unknown and turbulent. Heralded by the financial turmoil of 2008–2012, the abnormal has become the normal. We must learn to live with change and the unexpected.

We may be anxious about the new and its unpredictability, but it is not all bad news. As the title of Tom Peters' book *Thriving on Chaos* implies, there are huge new opportunities out there. The second *Financial Times* headline is about exactly that. Having been involved some years back in an early seed-capital fund to promote research-based spin-outs from the University of Cambridge, we find it truly remarkable that start-up businesses can now attract billion-dollar funding. Clearly the world is a different place, with opportunities beyond our imagining.

This book is presented in three parts. In Part One we tell the stories of real-life **entirepreneurs** to show that these amazing people really do exist, and have for a long time. We hope their stories will inspire you and allow you to contextualise our later analysis.

In Part Two we consider the environment in which the **entirepreneur** operates. Specifically, we describe the 'New Normal' and critique the extent to which the conventional approach is able to deal with its challenges.

Part Three looks in detail at the **entirepreneur** as a person, and at what it takes to hold one's own in the 'New Normal' where markets can come and go almost overnight, as BlackBerry found. Roller coaster rides are not for everyone, nor indeed is bungee jumping, but some people thrive in such environments. **Entirepreneurs** welcome the 'New Normal' and are not phased by it. Indeed, they are its children.

A special feature of our book is that we take a person-centred approach which enables you to evaluate yourself as an **entirepreneur**. We don't look at what you've done or might do, but at who and what you are. We seek to identify potential. We do this by describing the four key areas of Talent, Temperament, Technique and Discernment in which the **entirepreneur** has to have real strengths. We then give you the opportunity to evaluate your own strengths in these areas and decide whether you might have what it takes to be an **entirepreneur**.

INTRODUCTION

It is conventional to call people in business entrepreneurs, leaders or managers, often depending on the story we are telling and the point we are making, but we have come to the conclusion that these are no longer adequate terms for describing the people who are able to deal with the challenges posed by the 'New Normal'.

Having failed to find an adequate alternative amongst the common vocabulary for this person and his or her contribution, we created one.

An entirepreneur.

Entirepreneurs are essential if we are to deal with the challenges of our so-called 'New Normal' world. We might be the first people to use this word and we certainly hope we won't be the last!

A new perspective

The declared mission of Babson College in Massachusetts is to 'shape entrepreneurial leaders who create economic and social capital everywhere'. Babson is recognised as one of the leading centres in the world for entrepreneurship education, and we endorse and support their ambition.

In September 2013, Professor Patricia Greene, of Babson, explained to the International Entrepreneurship Educators' Conference (IEEC) in the UK that these entrepreneurial leaders 'organize resources and provide leadership to act on opportunities to create value'. She went on to say that this involves thinking—people need an entrepreneurial mindset—and passion. People have to think and believe they can change things. She quoted the late Steve Jobs:

> It is a seminal moment when you realise the world is as it is because of the things that people no smarter than you have done... . You too can transform something.

Andrew Hamilton, Vice-Chancellor of the University of Oxford, reinforced her message, saying:

> The leadership challenges today can best be met with skills that we commonly associate with entrepreneurs: perceiving opportunity where others see challenge, creativity in motivating people, skills at marshalling scarce resources, and an urge to create change.
>
> *From the brochure for the* Entrepreneurial Leaders Programme,
> *National Centre for Entrepreneurship in Education (NCEE), 2013*

All of these comments summarise the core message of this book.

However, we believe that if we continue using contemporary terminology that separates entrepreneurs from leaders and managers (although sometimes using 'entrepreneurial' as a prefix for both) and sometimes uses the terms interchangeably, we fail to capture the essence and contribution of the individuals who find and seize opportunities and champion change, and on occasion transform the way we think about and do things. These individuals have shown they are able to integrate the skills and capabilities that we typically associate with entrepreneurs, leaders and managers into a seamless totality. They possess the attributes that contemporary wisdom separates into individual roles.

We now want to challenge the contemporary wisdom that separates the entrepreneur, leader and manager roles—we prefer to take a wider perspective and integrate them, calling them **entirepreneurs**.

That said, whether '**entirepreneur**' actually becomes an everyday term is immaterial—the real issue is whether we can close identified gaps in our understanding and provide greater insight into those people who combine the key attributes of entrepreneurs, leaders and managers into a powerful ability to achieve both directional and operational excellence.

The challenge of the 'New Normal'

We have invented the word '**entirepreneur**' because we believe people need to think unconventionally if the challenge of today's 'New Normal' world is to be grasped properly.

After some years thinking and writing about a similar word—entrepreneur—we find that there has been a major shift in context so that a broader term is now required. That context is well captured by the term the 'New Normal'.

Over 30 years ago Alvin Toffler foresaw that the world of the twenty-first century was going to be quite a different place. In *The Third Wave* (1980) he made this observation:

a new civilisation is emerging in our lives … (bringing) with it new family styles; changed ways of working, loving and living; a new economy; new political conflicts; and beyond all this an altered consciousness as well. The dawn of this new civilisation is the single most explosive fact of our lifetimes.

Toffler then struggles to find words that adequately describe this new civilisation, admitting that 'none of these terms even begins to convey the full force, scope and dynamism of the changes rushing towards us'.

The 'New Normal' is perhaps the term he was searching for, although it had not been invented then. What Toffler describes as the 'deepest social upheaval and creative restructuring of all time' is now something that, though certainly 'new', must be seen as 'normal'; as the way things are now. It is an uncertain and turbulent 'normal', inherently ambiguous, unpredictable and unstable. But it cannot be ignored; the challenges it poses have to be met.

In recent years, for example, the memory capacity of computers has grown exponentially whilst the machines themselves have become smaller, lighter and readily transportable. Relatively recent changes in communications, fuelled in part by the Internet, mean information can be transferred instantly and shared all around the world. This has not been the case in the past, so there are new expectations of speedy reactions and instant decisions—the impact is of a magnitude many of us struggle to grasp. Given the potential of these changes, businesses have had to reinvent themselves; business models have been transformed; new opportunities have been abundant. It is now perfectly feasible to run a £1 million business from a spare bedroom.

Indeed, some businesses are now of a size where their actions have a serious impact on societies and economies. Wal-Mart's turnover equates to some 3 per cent of America's gross domestic product (GDP). Nokia might be a much smaller business, and part-owned by Microsoft, but at its height it accounted for 20 per cent of Finland's GDP. The people who head these businesses are powerful, both nationally and internationally. It is important that they behave responsibly and ensure their businesses are entirepreneurial; their survival and growth matters.

In our earlier books we have argued that this kind of business environment is the natural habitat of the entrepreneur. The very turbulence makes it a generator of opportunities for entrepreneurs to spot and exploit. They thrive on chaos.

However, as the 'New Normal' becomes a way of life with the stance of the entrepreneur, something more is needed if both our businesses and societies are to grow and prosper. That something includes the ability to envision the future and apply deep strategic insights to know how to get there.

At the same time, it is necessary to operate effectively on day-to-day issues with productivity, doing more with less, fully embraced. Changes of direction at short notice are part of the 'New Normal', and need to be handled effectively.

Opportunity, strategy, execution and performance must be combined seamlessly and work in synthesis and harmony. In this book we use the terms 'directional' and 'operational' to capture this. Simply, **entirepreneurs** deliver directional and operational excellence.

Taken together, these requirements take us beyond the entrepreneur into unnamed territory, which is why we have come up with the word **entirepreneur**. It suggests the idea of complete competence to handle the many demands of the swirling world of the 'New Normal'. It encompasses both the 'thriving on chaos' promoted by Tom Peters and the mastery of a business advocated by Jim Collins in *Built to Last*. The **entirepreneur** is at home in both these worlds. It is not a case of which approach is right and which is wrong, but rather that both are needed. This synthesis is not easy, but we believe it can be done.

Karren Brady is an **entirepreneur**. In her biography *Strong Woman: Ambition, Grit and a Great Pair of Heels* it is clear that she is a born entrepreneur who had to learn about being a leader. She comments that as a team leader 'you can't be this hugely competitive individual anymore, protecting your own glory. You have to bring out the best in everyone else'. Brady had to learn how to teach people her values, how to develop a vision and have faith to let her team help her to deliver it. She ends the chapter by saying that her team enjoys 'the structure and the freedom, which is an unusual combination but a winning one'.

It is exactly that combination that the **entirepreneur** brings to an organisation.

The entirepreneur

This book on the **entirepreneur** is in many ways an inevitable development from our previous books on the entrepreneur. It has developed from our earlier study of entrepreneurs and our attempt to make sense of who they are and what they do.

We began our research for this book by asking, are our organisations and the people who run them truly 'fit for purpose' in today's 'New Normal' world? We studied numerous stories, read and reread numerous books, and talked to a variety of 'actors' in order to guide our thinking. We concluded we needed to develop a fresh perspective. This book is the result. There is however nothing new, per se, in our core findings. **Entirepreneurs** have always been around, as we show in our stories in Part One. It is just that we have not thought of them in this way. Hopefully this book will help you understand them better.

We chose, and we stand by, a definition for the entrepreneur that is more limiting than the way many people would generally understand and use the word— regardless of any academic debate. Many people associate an entrepreneur with anyone who starts a business, however small and humble this business might stay. We have never dismissed the importance and potentially significant contribution that can be made by such enterprising people and by micro-businesses and from self-employment, but we have argued that we should reserve the term entrepreneur for people who 'habitually create and innovate to build something of recognised value around perceived opportunities'. The implication is that entrepreneurs make a discernible difference through what they do.

In our previous books we have told the stories of various entrepreneurs since 'time immemorial'—for entrepreneurs have always been evident in the world. We went beyond the world of business, as entrepreneurial people are to be found in all walks of life, although, again, many people instinctively associate them with just business. In every case 'opportunity' is evident. Those concerned have seen opportunities, sometimes significant opportunities and sometimes ones that were staring others in the face. We have talked about this as an advantage attribute, and it is an essential attribute for an entrepreneur. In our stories we have often selected and featured those entrepreneurs who have made very significant and lasting contributions; those who have built substantial organisations and left a legacy. In their cases the scale of the opportunity implied significant difference or advantage, and it was executed very well to create an outstanding organisational performance. Some initiatives and businesses will never be able to achieve as much as others, but the opportunity and action-driven approach will always matter.

As well as the opportunity aspect, those concerned have first been able to envision something significantly new and/or different, something that might well be possible, and then deliver on the promise. There is an intuitive ability to see into the future and believe something different can be brought about. This is rarely the outcome of detailed market research, and it provides direction. The visionary attribute is often linked to strategising and sometimes described as an ability to see clearly the 'big picture' that others can be persuaded is a positive improvement on what has gone before. This ability has more typically—and justifiably—been thought of as a key attribute possessed by some successful leaders. In addition, operational strengths in execution and performance require attention to detail and, again with real justification, these are typically seen to be an important attribute for an effective manager.

In reality these people have re-formed perceptions, opinions and behaviours through a process of transformation, which conventional wisdom largely overlooks— although, to be fair, the term 'reformer' has sometimes been used, especially for people associated with social change. Transformers might appear to be saying to the world that they are going to do something that nobody has done before and the world is going to be different. More realistically, they start out with a vision for how they would like to change things and 'adjust course' in an emergent, effectual way as they learn from what works out and what doesn't. There is a systemic element in what happens: changes in one aspect will have impacts elsewhere in an organisation, and not always predictably. Inclination, intent and actuality are not always synonymous.

Conventionally, transformers—people who have a vision, an idea of how they want to pursue that vision (their strategy) and an ability to rally people around that vision and the direction they want to go—are treated as leaders. Whilst not unreasonable, this is not an adequate explanation of leadership.

Managers, conventionally, have expertise in executing the vision and/or implementing the strategy by organising resources, including people.

Entrepreneurs are seen to be more closely aligned with leaders because of the opportunity and risk elements we associate with them—but as well as the tendency to see anybody who starts a small business as an entrepreneur, for some people there is a dubious element to entrepreneurship. For them, the fictional characters Arthur Daley and Derek Trotter are archetypal entrepreneurs.

Our argument is that many transformational people add directional and operational attributes to their opportunity-driven approach, and the typical role-driven terminology of entrepreneur-leader-manager fails to explain the entirety of their contribution. It is for this reason we feel there is a need for a new term—the **entirepreneur**.

In essence, **entirepreneurs** successfully combine the attributes we conventionally associate with entrepreneurs, leaders and managers. They make an all-round contribution. Significantly, they appreciate the needs of different circumstances and challenges and flexibly adjust their style and approach. Sometimes they behave in a way we would conventionally describe as entrepreneurial; on other occasions they exhibit conventional leadership; at other times they are 'managerial'.

In our previous books we have included stories of these significant people and described them as entrepreneurs, because at heart that is what they are: they do build something of recognised value around perceived opportunities. But we always knew there was something additional that singled them out. They are more than entrepreneurs—which is why we are now calling them **entirepreneurs**.

The ability to have 'big picture' vision, to appreciate how to fulfil this vision (by discerning what to do and what not to do), to see opportunities and to run a business (or other organisation) that captures the promise and potential of the vision and opportunities—and performs well—demands a particular set of attributes. People who possess all these attributes at a significant level appear to be relatively unusual, perhaps even exceptional, suggesting they are in a minority rather than a majority. Yet the demands of the 'New Normal' that organisations must deal with mean such individuals are going to be required in increasing numbers.

Our earlier work on the entrepreneur had a clear person focus, which we developed from an examination of the entrepreneur process, and we again take this approach with our consideration of the **entirepreneur**. We describe a person with a particular talent set of attributes and technique set of skills, but there is more to the **entirepreneur** then an extension of abilities to a kind of omni-competence. Like the entrepreneur, the **entirepreneur** has a temperament dimension that has passion and commitment at its heart with an endurable motivation. We thus retain the Talent, Temperament, Technique (3Ts) framework we used in our earlier books, but add an important fourth dimension—Discernment—which is a critical discriminator for the **entirepreneur**.

It is important to identify ways in which you might improve and seek to hone certain skills and capabilities. Deliberate practice can be valuable for developing expertise; looking back, you will find many experts and outstanding performers who practiced extensively in a focused and deliberately targeted way. But looking forward, it is questionable whether anyone can claim: 'If I practice for long enough with a good coach I can be amongst the best in the world.'

The ability to take an entire perspective, and the desire to make a more holistic contribution, needs to become more aspirational—and an appropriate expectation for success in the 'New Normal' world. As we said earlier, **entirepreneurs** have always been around, but our language has failed to capture it. We must not forget, though, that the theme of entirety and completeness, the perspective and attitude of mind that these people have, is sometimes more important than the ultimate level of achievement.

We have written this book to draw attention to this challenge, to allow you to re-evaluate yourself and hopefully to aspire to become a true **entirepreneur**.

> Everyone thinks of changing the world, but no-one thinks of changing himself.
>
> *Leo Tolstoy*

> People need to be outwardly and inwardly aware ... of ...
> What they want to achieve and why
> How they make decisions
> How they execute decisions, and
> How they relate to others.
>
> *Erica Ariel Fox*

Bibliography and endnotes

Parts One and Two of this book comprise a number of case stories, together with a commentary and critique to set the scene for Part Three, which is more empirical and is where we present the findings of our research.

We have used a number of sources for the material in Parts One and Two, including several websites. We have taken ideas from a number of books but some of the comments are our own observations. We have included a bibliography of the key sources which will allow you to track those authors we have deliberately cited, but we have not set out to reference the chapters using a conventional format. We want the book to be as readable as possible.

We recognise there is a clear need to be more rigorous with referencing in Part Three, but, wishing to maintain the general readability, we have opted to include a set of endnotes to enable you track the reference sources should you wish.

We also felt it was more appropriate to present the bibliography and endnotes at the end of the book, not at the end of each chapter.

PART ONE
Entirepreneur stories

PART ONE

Entrepreneur stories

1

STORIES OF ENTIREPRENEURS AND ENTIREPRENEURSHIP IN ACTION

	Introduction	5
1.1	Entirepreneurs whose products changed the world	10
	Steve Jobs and Apple	*10*
	Akio Morita and Sony	*11*
	Howard Schultz and Starbucks	*13*
	Ray Kroc and McDonald's	*14*
	Josiah Wedgwood	*16*
	Terence Conran	*17*
	George Davies	*18*
	James Dyson	*19*
	Henry Ford	*19*
	George Eastman	*19*
	Walt Disney	*20*
	Juan Trippe	*20*
	Herb Kelleher	*20*
	Richard Branson	*20*
1.2	Entirepreneurs whose services changed the world	21
	George Soros	*21*
	Paul Soros	*22*
	Jeff Bezos and Amazon	*22*
	M-Pesa	*23*
	Stephanie 'Steve' Shirley	*25*
	Gerard Pelisson and Paul Dubrule	*26*
	Club Med	*26*

1.3 Three retail entirepreneurs   28
    Ingvar Kamprad and IKEA   28
    Sam Walton and Wal-Mart   29
    Maxine Clarke and Build-A-Bear Workshop   30

1.4 Transformations in transportation   32
    George Stephenson   32
    Malcolm McLean   33
    Edward Stobart   34
    Fred Smith and FedEx   35
    Sam Shoen and U-Haul   36
    The Pony Express   37

1.5 Organisational transformers   39
    Jack Welch   39
    Lou Gerstner   40

1.6 Behaviour and communications transformers   41
    Tim Berners-Lee   41
    Mark Zuckerberg and Facebook   42
    Jack Dorsey, Evan Williams and Twitter   43

1.7 Community entirepreneurship   45
    Silicon Valley   45
    The knife-makers of Laguiole   45

1.8 Social transformers   47
    Anita Roddick and The Body Shop   47
    Mohammed Yunus   48
    David Bussau   49
    Florence Nightingale   51
    William and Catherine Booth   52
    Harish Hande and SELCO   53
    Michael Young   54
    Ebenezer Howard   56

1.9 Sports entirepreneurs   58
    Sir Alex Ferguson   58
    Kerry Packer   59
    Russell Coutts, Ben Ainslie and the America's Cup   60

1.10 Entertainment entirepreneurs   63
    Gerald Durrell   63
    Guy Laliberté and Cirque du Soleil   63
    P.T. Barnum   64

*This chapter consists entirely of stories of **entirepreneurs** and entirepreneurship in action. We include these stories early in the book to illustrate and justify our thesis with examples. We want you to realise that conventional terms such as entrepreneur, leader and manager might be defensible, but individually they are inadequate for truly explaining the people involved in changing the way that others think and behave. We do not believe the role-driven terms that we use conventionally truly explain the entirety of the people and their behaviours and accomplishments. In these stories we show why they are **entirepreneurs** and should be examined through a new lens. In our short introduction to these stories we cross-refer to the forthcoming parts of this book, where we explain our arguments in more detail and fully reveal the **entirepreneur** to you. You might wish to think of these outline arguments, and how they might apply, as you read through the stories.*

Introduction

These stories feature some exceptional people—because outstanding **entirepreneurs** are exceptional people. In some way or another they are 'game changers'. They rewrite the rules. Their stories are encapsulated within stories of the organisations, businesses, products and services where entirepreneurship has been evident, but the real stories are about the people behind the events. Some of our stories feature contemporary **entirepreneurs**, but some go back a long way. A study of history will reveal many **entirepreneurs**—some loved, some feared or treated warily because of their willingness to challenge the status quo. Our stories only scratch the surface, but they provide evidence to support our arguments. All the people we feature made a difference. They all possess attributes which made them all-in-one entrepreneurs, leaders and managers.

Some of our **entirepreneurs** have genuine 'star quality'—they are instantly recognisable for their achievements; they have changed the world in some way by envisaging (and delivering) something that has altered the way others think and behave. They are thus catalysts and enablers of major, sometimes transformational, changes. Naturally many **entirepreneurs** demonstrate more modest achievements, but in a humble way they still affect how others think and behave. One critical issue in understanding potential **entirepreneurs** is whether they themselves are thinking in this way—and what drives them.

Tim Smit conceived and built an innovative and futuristic eco-tourist attraction, the Eden Project, in Cornwall, England. Outside is a sign declaring: 'We are a charity. We are ordinary people trying to change the world'. Whilst the Eden Project is generally and widely regarded as a success story, the original expectations of the costs involved were an underestimate, particularly as fresh ideas led to additional elements being added. In turn this led to fundraising challenges, but Smit's determination prevailed.

Entirepreneurs are people who are driven to achieve and create change. They want to improve things for other people—in some cases for the world—and, ideally, leave a legacy. Recognition for their achievement and contributions is often important to them, and they may thrive on the status and visibility their success brings them. But this is not a prerequisite; some are perfectly happy just to do it. They measure their success in a more personal way. Some **entirepreneurs**, but certainly not all, become wealthy. That said, it is more likely that the wealth and status are enjoyable rewards rather than the original driving force. As you read these stories you might like to reflect upon the motivation of the **entirepreneurs** involved and why they behave as they do.

You will see how people have used their experiences and acquired knowledge and skills alongside their natural attributes. When anyone starts a new business they are in a position to build on three things: who they are (their talent and temperament), what they know and are able to do (knowledge and skills—techniques they have learned) and who they know (the network of contacts they have built up, helped by both their background and experience). A person's background, and the situations and circumstances they have to deal with, affect how they exploit their talents and contacts and manage their temperament. In some cases it will come across that they appear to be the right person in the right place at the right time. Regardless, they still have to accept the challenge and do something—and persist if their initial efforts are received with only lukewarm support and enthusiasm, or resistance, and also when setbacks occur. It is easy to look back with hindsight and say 'great idea' when something succeeds, but how sceptical might we have been at the outset when everything looked far less certain? The ultimate measure of success, of course, will always be what people accomplish—and **entirepreneurs** always look for opportunities from which they can gain.

> The slightest advantage in one being, at any age or during any season, over those with which it comes into competition, or better adaptation in however slight a degree to the surrounding physical conditions, will turn the balance.
> *Charles Darwin*, On the Origin of Species, *1859*

You will come to appreciate that **entirepreneurs** are determined individuals who believe in both themselves and their ideas. Rarely can they see or predict how things will evolve and emerge once the metaphorical start-line has been crossed, but they accept the risks and uncertainty and deal with the setbacks. They know they could lose something if it doesn't work out but they accept the challenge. They are typically helped by drawing in others who not only support them but who come to believe in what they are attempting to do. They learn all the time, developing new insights, capabilities and skills.

Many of the people discussed here are familiar names. They are people whose stories could readily be (and often have been) told in 'conventional wisdom' books on entrepreneurship (because they started out as an entrepreneur) and books on leadership (because they exhibited leader attributes that allowed them to grow and sustain something significant). And it would also be possible to show that they have demonstrated an ability to manage, whatever style and approach they might have adopted. Books on leadership are popular because being recognised as a leader is conventionally more popular than being seen as an entrepreneur or a manager. If we were to go with conventional wisdom it would be defensible to look at these individuals as entrepreneurs, leaders or (sometimes, but less frequently) managers. It would be better to think of them as entrepreneurs *and* leaders *and* managers. But really, none of these are truly adequate, as we argue in Chapter 3 when we critique conventional wisdom. These role-based terms compartmentalise people—and we have come to believe we must look at the complete, entire person—and the scope and entirety of their achievements. Looking at them as **entirepreneurs** embraces that they are individuals who have seen and seized opportunities in the context of a clear strategy and 'big picture' for what they are trying to achieve, alongside an ability to deliver efficient and effective performance through getting to grips with the 'little picture' activities and details. In other words, at heart they are people we would readily cite as entrepreneurs, but who have additional attributes that help explain why they are able to conceptualise something outstanding and different that changes the way people think and behave—and deliver on the promise of the opportunities they spot. They can make sense of the 'New Normal' world. They are also able to gather, organise and influence the support and supporters they need.

Being able to effectively balance directional and operational excellence should not be underestimated, in part because each requires different, but complementary, philosophies. Direction, especially where there is a visionary aspect, often involves conviction and passion for something an individual can articulate clearly; it is this conviction that encourages **entirepreneurs** to take that 'giant leap' and set off. Operations, on the other hand, often involve compromise and flexibility to ensure things get done; there are accommodations with others. Put simply, inflexible dogma can be a serious inhibitor of progress—but so too can directionless action.

Alongside the most outstanding **entirepreneurs** we also feature examples of people who exhibit similar attributes and champion change, albeit at a more modest level. Some of our stories feature **entirepreneurs** whose values have been a significant and driving influence. In the stories of social transformation a strong faith element also comes through. Some individuals are motivated by a cause, and their actions are, in effect, their strategy for fulfilling their cause-driven purpose. They again seek out opportunities and look to make things happen.

Part Two of the book explores the context of entirepreneurship. **Entirepreneurs** understand and make sense of the world in which they live and how they could improve something. They find opportunities, act on them and make things happen. They deliver results. They gather supporters and build something with real momentum and positive, beneficial, appreciated outcomes. Sometimes they see a clear path through the uncertainty of our turbulent world and provide an option that provokes a reaction of 'Why didn't I think of that?'. On other occasions they actually contribute to the dynamism and uncertainty by stirring things up. They disrupt. They introduce something that makes us see our existing practices, products and services as 'old hat', or yesterday's choice. What **entirepreneurs** are good at, and what they contribute, extends beyond starting something for short-term gain. They appreciate the need for sustainability, with the inherent and constant innovation and improvement this requires. In the beginning they may well be very hands-on and lead by example, but they grow as the organisation grows. They harness their various characteristics and attributes (themes we explore in Part Three). In effect, they retain ownership of the 'big picture' and work *on* the business while keeping a watchful eye *inside* the business and making sure the details—the 'little picture' elements that deliver performance—are not neglected.

The BBC television programme *Masterchef* provides an excellent insight into the notion of 'entirety'. For readers who are not familiar with the format, the programme is a lengthy search for a chef with outstanding ability and a real desire to enter or progress in this challenging and competitive world. Generally they are people with only limited experience at the outset, but with the potential to grow and improve. People are eliminated before the televised element in an introductory round, and then in quarter- and semi-finals. Three amateur chefs contest the final. Competition is intense and the winner demonstrates all the attributes we associate with the **entirepreneur**.

Over the course of the programme the contestants are set various challenges, and in every case they are working against the clock. They have to be very organised and focused. They will sometimes be asked to invent and cook dishes of their choice from a set of ingredients they are given; more often they will be given the opportunity to cook anything they like (a completely free choice) but with time acting as a constraint on their freedom of choice. On other occasions they will be given a finished dish—which they do not see being prepared—and, without a menu or directions, they must select the required ingredients and re-create the dish. To succeed in this, they need excellent taste (to discern what is actually in the dish) and insight into how it might have been put together. At times their efforts are judged by the programme's two presenters on their own; at other times professional chefs, professional critics and past winners of the programme will offer their opinions. A variety of 'experts' with different tastes, expectations and standards must all be convinced. These challenges generally take place inside a studio kitchen. But other challenges include mass catering (where the contestants work in teams rather than individually at some external location) and cooking in prestigious restaurants where they are working under the direction of the chef in charge of the kitchen. Both 'everyday' and fine dining are thus involved.

We can see how the programme demands an ability to both discern and create new tastes: combining ingredients in an innovative way to produce a distinctive taste and dish is a key requirement. The ability to imagine something new and different is important. But so too is the ability to deliver perfect food in a tight timescale. Sometimes they choose the menus; at other times they must work under direction. Everything must come together and be plated up in an attractive way. When a meal comprising two or three dishes in total is asked for, balance throughout is also important. Good food presented poorly won't win. Attractively presented food that doesn't have a stimulating taste won't win either. Not being on time is unacceptable performance. In every round the contestants are presented with opportunities and choices. They are required to stretch themselves and improve their level in each round, always dealing with the risk that being too ambitious could mean they fail to deliver a good, attractive dish on time. It is a balance of bravery, imagination and delivery. The ultimate winner deserves to win: they have been truly tested both emotionally and as a chef.

There seems to be no obvious pattern to the backgrounds of the winners. So can 'anyone' win *Masterchef*? In one sense, yes; in another, no. The winner requires motivation and passion to bring out and exploit underpinning capabilities. Typically, and in part linked to ongoing learning, their manifest abilities improve week by week as they enjoy, and thrive on, the challenge and opportunity to work at something they enjoy. At the end of the challenge they are more capable than at the start. They have created a marriage of vision and skills.

Interestingly, there are different *Masterchef* competitions for the general public (the main programme), professional chefs and celebrity chefs. The format is the same, but the extent of the challenge (the number of different demands) and the expected level of attainment vary from the outset.

We now present over 30 stories of **entirepreneurs** and entirepreneurship. We encourage you to look for the following themes as you read through them:

- Their impact. The nature and extent of the transformations we discuss, and whether they 'changed the world' or achieved something more modest, albeit still very significant. How they impacted the world: whether they found new opportunities in the 'New Normal' world or acted as a disturbance. Whether they affected thinking or behaviour, or both.
- Temperament themes. What motivated them to start in the first place and how their ambitions changed as things emerged and developed. We also evaluate how much we might have expected people to appreciate the potential of what they were starting. You might add the extent to which some of them have been attributed 'star quality' or celebrity status for their contribution, and whether this might have been important to them, either before or after the event.
- Examples of key talent attributes. For example, seeing and believing in a different future and then making it happen. Ted Turner foresaw the potential for 24-hour broadcast news and created CNN; now both the BBC and Sky offer a rival service and it is something we take for granted, especially when we travel overseas. Broadly, you are looking for evidence of the directional and operational themes we have already discussed in this introduction.
- Specific choices, and the decisions people took—reflecting their discernment attributes.
- The team element. Some of the stories of entirepreneurship in action emphasise this, as well as the importance of personal values.
- Succession and sustainability issues. How the things **entirepreneurs** start can continue after they are no longer active in the organisation.

1.1 Entirepreneurs whose products changed the world

Steve Jobs and Apple

The words Steve Jobs used to persuade John Sculley to leave PepsiCo and take over as CEO of Apple in the early 1980s sum up his business philosophy. He asked, 'Do you want to spend the rest of your life selling sugared water or do you want a chance to change the world?' Steve Jobs changed the world and left a phenomenal legacy.

The Apple website has included the words 'Apple changes everything ... again. Apple leads and reinvents by designing revolutionary, magical products'. Steve Jobs started Apple in a garage in California in 1976, working with his co-founder Stephen Wozniak. 'Woz' understood computers; Jobs was never 'technical', per se, in the same way. Instead, he imagined what he felt should be possible (over time his ability to envision became stronger, more ambitious and more aspirational) and challenged and cajoled Wozniak, and later others, to build it. Woz did, and by 1983 Apple's turnover from its personal computer reached $1 billion. Their PC was not the first to market; it was simply more attractive and more functional than any of its rivals. But Jobs and Wozniak had a business disagreement and Wozniak left the company.

As the business grew rapidly Jobs became increasingly frustrated with the detail and the bureaucracy, and opted to work on new products with a team of designers he established. The result, in 1984, was the Apple Macintosh, which was always a premium-price niche product that became and remained the favourite of designers. It was ambitious, and featured an illustrated screen (which Jobs had been allowed to copy from developments he had seen at Xerox's Palo Alto Research Centre, or PARC, and was something Xerox themselves were not pursuing) and a mouse. Again, the mouse was not an Apple invention. It had been designed and patented by a computer scientist, Doug Engelbart, who ran his own research laboratory and claimed he 'wanted to change the world'. The licence fee was $40,000. Engelbart is also credited with early work on both email systems and word processing, but he was not an **entirepreneur**—realistically he wasn't an entrepreneur either—and others reaped the financial benefits of these important developments.

As Apple became increasingly 'corporate', Jobs was ousted by Sculley—who was just the first of a number of CEO casualties as Apple's fortunes went up and down in the 1980s and 90s. Jobs established NeXT Software (and it was using a powerful NeXT machine that Tim Berners-Lee would create the World Wide Web) and then Pixar, which Disney bought to boost its capability in animation. When Apple bought NeXT at the end of 1996, Jobs returned to run the company again. Bill Gates (and Microsoft) invested $150 million to keep Apple afloat, and from then on Jobs 'never looked back'. His approach the second time around was both similar and different. He remained passionate about design and recruited Jonathan Ive to lead this; he also realised the importance of operational capability and supply chain management and recruited Tim Cook as Chief Operating Officer (and his eventual successor).

A string of successes followed Jobs' return. The success, though, was never the result of Apple being first to market with a concept. But it always 'got there in time', and invariably with products that improved on the early pioneers. Apple also learnt the significance of not launching until all the necessary supply and support systems were properly in place.

The Macintosh led to the iMac, with an integrated computer and monitor; the MacBook is a compact and lightweight laptop. They utilise Apple operating systems, not Windows, although the two have become compatible.

MP3 players appeared in 1998, and the first iPod was launched in 2001, supported by the iTunes software which enabled Apple to seize market dominance. The iPod had another significant advantage—it was an attractive and therefore desirable product. Apple drove the market and, over time, changed the way people buy and listen to music.

The iPhone, launched in 2007, was not meant to be the best mobile phone on the market; nor was its camera the best available, and so on. But the design and the range of apps available made it again the most desirable alternative on the market for many people. Most of the applications, of course, have been created by third parties who want to become associated with Apple. The value and strategic significance of apps also contributed in no small way to the rapid success and popularity of the iPad from the moment it was launched in 2010.

Without doubt Steve Jobs was an entrepreneur at heart. He found, seized and exploited opportunity after opportunity—but this barely explains the entirety of his achievements. He foresaw future possibilities and brought them to fruition by harnessing the talents of others that he both inspired and cajoled. He was a visionary who made things happen with help from others with different sets of expertise. He came to realise the strategic significance of supply chain management and timing, as well as the fact that, in the end, 'the devil is in the detail'. In this respect he had to overcome the insult of being sacked from the company he founded by someone with a 'corporate' philosophy who simply did not have his visionary capability. Critically, he seemed to instinctively appreciate what people would want to buy and own if it were made available to them in a convenient and attractive format. When Jobs died in 2011—after which Tim Cook replaced him as CEO of Apple—Cook was quoted in *Fortune* magazine saying, 'Steve drilled in all of us over many years that the company should revolve around great products and that we should stay extremely focused on few things rather than try to do so many that we did nothing well'.

Steve Jobs is an archetypal **entirepreneur** for whom neither the term entrepreneur, nor leader, nor manager, comes close to capturing his contribution—quite simply, he was all of them at the same time.

Akio Morita and Sony

Akio Morita was a co-founder of Sony, which, and with a different name, started life in an abandoned building in Japan in 1946. At that time Japan was reeling after the end of the Second World War. His partner and wartime colleague, Masaru Ibuka, had 'gathered a group of engineers to develop some sort of electronics laboratory or enterprise'. The rise and prosperity of Sony is an excellent illustration of how a business can grow in an emergent, effectual manner if it is able to find and exploit opportunities—and deliver products people want to buy. Ibuka was an engineer; so too was Morita, although, and partly the result of him being a member of a family sake brewing business, he had a broader business background and some experience in both finance and marketing.

The company's first product was an electric rice cooker, which wasn't particularly successful. The first breakthrough product came when they were able to build a consumer-size tape recorder, taking ideas from large American machines the occupying forces had brought over with them. This was later followed by their first truly significant product, the transistor radio in 1971. As the company developed skills in miniaturisation the radios became smaller and smaller, until they were pocket-sized. By this time Morita had relocated with his family to America, on the grounds that Sony needed to understand much more about their key target market. Morita is quoted as saying, 'I knew we needed a weapon to break through to the US market, and it had to be something different. Something nobody else was making'.

Televisions, cassettes and video recorders followed. With video, though, Sony favoured quality over 'adequacy' and learnt a harsh lesson when the market preferred the VHS format over the more expensive, but of superior quality, Sony Betamax.

Morita's most notable contribution came in 1979 (he was 58 years old), with the Sony Walkman, which, by providing a new way of listening to music, 'changed the lifestyle of a generation'. The first Walkman was a compact cassette player with personal earphones. Radio, CD and video options came later; as did waterproof and sand-proof versions. Within ten years of launch, Sony had sold ten million sets. Morita was interested in sport and walking as well as being a fanatical golfer; he also knew young people enjoyed listening to music a lot of the time, wherever they were and whatever they were doing. He envisaged something that allowed people to listen to anything they wanted, at the volume of their choice, without disturbing others. He demanded his engineers blend their electronics and miniaturisation skills to build his 'dream machine'. They did, but they were sceptical about its prospects. There was no serious market research before the launch—in Morita's words, 'The public does not know what is possible, but we do'. Morita envisioned what was possible and then used his power and influence to seize what he personally (and correctly) believed was a great opportunity.

It is interesting, though, that it was Steve Jobs and Apple that brought the next listening transformation—the iPod—and not Sony. By the 1990s, when the MP3 player came on the market, two important developments had happened. Morita, not enjoying the best of health since he turned 70, had moved to Hawaii and was much less involved in the business. Sony was increasingly focused on the PlayStation, which came late to market but still became the market leader. Following the same strategic approach that made Jobs so successful, Sony's PlayStation was only launched when there was a good selection of games to accompany it, some developed in-house, others by outside games designers. Interestingly, Sony had originally avoided this market opportunity, but one of its executives won a Nintendo machine in a competition, become hooked on using it and asked Sony's engineers to work on an alternative.

Today, Sony remains successful but is no longer the force in the electronics industry that it once was. We will never truly know how much was dependent on individuals—in particular Akio Morita. In Morita we see a visionary who was strategic, opportunistic and willing to back his own judgement. Under his leadership, Sony's products were technologically excellent and reliable.

Howard Schultz and Starbucks

Starbucks has grown from a single store on the Seattle waterfront to a worldwide chain, spawning competitors in the US and elsewhere. The company, though, has never made headway in Italy, which many see as the home of decent coffee bars. Schultz succeeded because he found the right way to blend sales of top-grade fresh coffee beans with sales of cups of coffee to drink.

Coffee bars have existed for a very long time, but rarely have they featured the strong and distinctive aroma found in stores that sell fresh coffee. The individual drinks in Starbucks are relatively expensive, but they are individualised and made to order. There is a wide range of piping-hot and ice-cold variants to choose from. Customers include shoppers and workers from local stores and offices, who stop by at lunchtime and teatime or on their way home. Many customers take time to relax and converse over their coffee, while others pop out from work when they have a short break, largely because Starbucks' coffee is perceived to be superior to the instant type that they might otherwise have to drink. Outlets can also be found at airport terminals and in bookstores where people go to browse and relax. Essentially, Starbucks 'sells an emotional experience' and not just a commodity product. It thus adds value.

The success comes down to Howard Schultz, the son of a blue-collar worker from Brooklyn. Schultz became a salesman, and when he was working for a houseware products company he visited Seattle and was introduced to the Starbucks Coffee Company, a business that sold imported coffee beans. Its founders loved coffee; they had 'no ambitions to build a business empire'. He joined the business in 1982, when it was around ten years old, with the title of Marketing Director. Enthused by espresso bars he visited on a business trip to Italy, and convinced that a similar concept could be developed for the US, he attempted to sell the idea to his bosses. The family declined to go along with him and he left to start up on his own. He managed to raise enough money to open one outlet, which he called Il Giornale, and within two years he was in a position to buy out Starbucks. 'I became CEO of Starbucks in 1987 because I went out, as an entrepreneur, and convinced investors to believe in my vision for the company'.

'Vision is what they call it when others can't see what you see... . I saw Starbucks not for what it was but for what it could be... . I realised it could reinvent an age-old commodity and appeal to millions' (Schultz). Globally Starbucks now has a 33 per cent market share for coffee bars—in the UK this is slightly less, trailing Costa Coffee (together they have 70 per cent of the UK market). It has been estimated that on average people now drink 21 cups of coffee a week, with 50 per cent at home, 25 per cent at work and 25 per cent from coffee bars, including take-outs. This growth is largely down to Schultz, who, working with a strong team of managers, built an international business. He commented that as Starbucks grew his biggest challenge was 'reinvention whilst at the same time becoming an ever-more professional manager'. One new idea was the Frappuccino, a blended and chilled coffee drink, different from hot brewed coffee cooled with ice. The suggestion came from an employee; initially Schultz was sceptical, but he agreed to trial it. Although coffee to drink is very much the leading product, fresh coffee beans and a range of related products, such as cakes, biscuits, mugs, coffee makers and special Starbucks music CDs, are also now on offer. Starbucks is the third largest retailer of fresh coffee beans in the US, mostly through supermarkets.

At the same time, Starbucks is a values-driven business. Schultz claims that his mission has always been to 'educate consumers everywhere about fine coffee'. Customers who visit Starbucks should feel relaxed and enjoy 'a sense of wonder and romance in the midst of their harried lives'. People will pay 'arguably outrageous prices' for their coffee as long as it is seen as an indulgence. If this is to be achieved, staff attitudes and behaviours are critical. Service, therefore, is everything. Schultz has created Starbucks as 'living proof that a company can lead with its heart and nurture its soul and still make money'. Employees are seen as partners, and they all enjoy free health insurance, stock options (known as bean stock), training programmes and wages above the industry average. Although many employees are young, fit students who will not stay long enough to earn stock options and may not need health care, they feel valued and consequently deliver the desired service. They matter. In addition, all unsold beans over eight days old are given away free to local food banks. Nevertheless, the company has also been criticised for exploiting cheap labour in coffee-growing countries.

Ray Kroc and McDonald's

Ray Kroc has been described by *Time* magazine as 'one of the most influential builders of the twentieth century'. Few children refuse a McDonald's burger, and the company's golden arches logo symbolises American enterprise. Kroc was a truly opportunistic and focused **entirepreneur** who built an organisational network of dedicated franchisees. Yet his contribution began late in life, and the McDonald's chain of hamburger restaurants was certainly not his own invention. Like other **entirepreneurs**, he saw—though really this time he stumbled upon—an opportunity where others missed the true potential for an idea. Once he saw the opportunity, he rigorously applied business acumen and techniques to his vision in order to focus on providing value for his customers. By standardising his product, his restaurants and his operating systems he was able to guarantee high and consistent quality at relatively low cost. There are a number of parallels with our previous story on Howard Schultz, but some significant differences. Starbucks' margins are high, linked to premium pricing, but McDonald's is a 'penny-profit business' with tight margins. Cost control and sales are both essential.

In 1955, at the age of 52, Kroc had completed 30 years as a salesman, mainly selling milkshake machines to various types of restaurants across America, including hamburger joints. His customers included the McDonald brothers, who, having moved from New Hampshire to Hollywood but failing to make any headway in the movie business, had opened a small drive-through restaurant in San Bernardino, California. They offered a limited menu, paper plates and plastic cups—and guaranteed the food in 60 seconds. When their success drove them to buy eight milkshake machines instead of the two their small size would logically suggest, Kroc's interest was alerted and he set off to see the restaurant. Kroc's vision was for a national chain that could benefit from organisation, systems and business techniques. Rival products often beat the McDonald's burger in taste tests, and yet McDonald's is the real success story. Kroc bought out the McDonald brothers and set about building a global empire. After he officially retired from running the business and until his death in 1984, Kroc stayed on as President and visited two or three different restaurants every week. He saw himself as the 'company's conscience', checking standards against his 'QSCV' vision: Quality food, fast and friendly Service, Clean restaurants and Value for money.

McDonald's has always been a focused business, never straying from fast foods. For many years its products were the same everywhere they were served, but local variations have developed. Success depends on a strong supply chain, careful control over production and employee engagement. Many employees are young part-timers, but they must still deliver a high quality service enthusiastically. 'Our competitors can copy many of our secrets, but they cannot duplicate our pride, our enthusiasm and our dedication for this business' (Kroc).

It would be a mistake to underestimate the contribution of Kroc's franchise and supply 'partners', who have always been encouraged to contribute their ideas and expertise. The Big Mac (1968), Egg McMuffin (early 1970s) and Chicken McNuggets (early 1980s) all originated this way, and each of them opened up new opportunities for McDonald's.

One interesting development in recent years—but not in every country—is McCafé, the McDonald's equivalent of Starbucks coffee, which is more competitively priced. Another interesting parallel can be seen in Subway, which focuses on sandwiches and perceived healthier offerings. Subway was started by teenager Fred Deluca in 1965 with a single outlet; there are now more branches in America than there are McDonald's. Deluca shared Kroc's vision for a global empire built substantially on franchises and standardisation.

The fortunes of McDonald's have varied since Kroc's death and there have been critics and periodic setbacks to deal with, but Kroc's legacy is a business built on solid foundations and principles, which has outlived its founder.

Josiah Wedgwood

Josiah Wedgwood, born into a family of potters in 1730, arguably became the most famous potter of all time. He was able to blend developments in the science and technology of pottery with art and design, transforming something perceived as 'functional' into something far more desirable and collectable. He found and created opportunities; he built and left a substantial business.

Josiah left school at the age of nine to work. He was weakened physically by smallpox when he was 11 and became more absorbed in pottery, experimenting all the time with glazes and colours. He was a self-taught chemist and scientist. Using Cornish clay he developed cream and white glazes, which he used for teapots, plates and crockery, thus making them more attractive to discernable middle-class buyers. In 1754 he went to work for England's most renowned potter of the time, Thomas Whieldon, but within six years he had started his own business. His marriage to a relatively wealthy distant cousin was instrumental to his success, as was his partnership with Thomas Bentley, a successful merchant.

In 1765 he entered (and won) a competition to design and make a tea service for Queen Charlotte, the wife of George III. His design featured 22-carat gold on a white glaze. He became a celebrity figure as a result and gained access to a much wider and seriously wealthy market. He would never look back. Perhaps here one can see parallels with popular television business programmes. However, in 1768 he lost a leg, a throwback to the smallpox. Soon after this, once he was properly able to work again, he started to produce 'more decorative' vases and other items of pottery which were sold through the leading retailers in London and other major cities. He packed up examples of his work, especially copies of vases that had been found in the ruins of Pompeii and Herculaneum, and posted them to the great houses of Europe. It was a form of direct marketing: people were invited to pay if they liked the goods or simply return them. This was seen to be very brave at the time—in hindsight, he has been credited with inventing modern marketing techniques.

On the back of his success he built a major new factory in Burslem, Stoke-on-Trent, Staffordshire. It was called Etruria and would stay open for 180 years. He sought 'artistic perfection on an industrial scale'. The working conditions were excellent for the time, and he built houses for his workers. A religious Unitarian, he believed people really mattered; later in his life he was an active campaigner against the slave trade. He produced ceramic medals which he gave away to anyone, anywhere in the world, who supported his cause. After Bentley died, Wedgwood continued on his own, innovating and improving. This led to perhaps his most famous work.

He developed his famous and world-renowned blue ceramic porcelain (using a patented formula) to which he added white relief decoration; he called it Jasperware. At this time he was networking and sharing knowledge and ideas with an important circle of friends, which included James Watt and Matthew Boulton (who, together, improved the steam engine) and the chemist Joseph Priestley, best remembered for discovering oxygen. Wedgwood pioneered the building of the Trent and Mersey Canal, which improved the distribution of his goods.

In 1790 he finally succeeded with a personal challenge: he reproduced the first-century-BC Portland glass vase in a china ceramic. Technically this was seen as his most outstanding achievement, and it came five years before his death. When he died in 1795 his personal fortune was the equivalent of half a billion pounds sterling in today's terms. His business continued with his direct descendants—his enquiring scientific mind was inherited by his grandson, Charles Darwin.

As an **entirepreneur**, Wedgwood was able to combine science, design and true business acumen—something others have found more challenging, as our next story demonstrates.

Terence Conran

Terence Conran is certainly a habitual, serial entrepreneur, given that design has been a key element of all his businesses and activities, but would we describe him as an **entirepreneur**? He is both rich and successful from business, but he will be remembered more for his creative design talents than for his business acumen. The Design Museum comments that 'he has had more impact than any other designer of his generation on everyday life in contemporary Britain through a series of parallel careers'. Conran is an innovator who has applied his talents to furniture making, designing, retailing, publishing and restaurant management. He has had many successes and some notable setbacks. He is still active with design work at over 80 years old.

Born in Surrey in 1931, his background and upbringing were middle class. Interested in crafts from an early age, he set up a workshop at home. As a young boy he spent some considerable time at a local pottery and at school he specialised in chemistry, engineering and art. Encouraged by a friend, he then went to college and studied textile design, where he became intrigued by the possibilities of screen printing. In partnership with an architect, he also started making furniture of his own design, mainly for his friends.

Conran's story is perhaps best told as a timeline. In addition to his furniture, Conran opened a café-cum-soup kitchen in 1953; having built this into a small chain, he sold it. Next came exhibition stands before he formed a consultancy offering architecture and interior design services in 1956. In 1964 he opened the first Habitat store, which sold his own domestic furniture and other designs for the home. In 1973 came the first up-market Conran store in London. A series of lifestyle books followed this before he floated Habitat, acquired Mothercare and Heals (furniture stores) and merged with British Home stores to form Storehouse, of which he was CEO. He left in 1989, buying out just his Conran store, which is now one of a small chain in leading cities around the world. Since the 1980s he has continued to open up a constant stream of exclusive restaurants, mostly in London.

In this story we can see clear evidence that Terence Conran has many qualities of an **entirepreneur**: he is creative, innovative and dedicated to design; he has a strong ego and is clearly action focused; he is advantage driven and benefit oriented; and he is able to build the teams necessary to drive his various ventures forward. Significantly, he chose to draw back from the large corporate-leader position, which is not where his main talents lie. He says, 'I have always seen myself as a designer first, rather than a businessman, although I've made things happen and enjoyed making them happen. … businesses are ways of putting my ideas and products in front of the public'.

George Davies

As with Terence Conran, we can ask: is he an **entirepreneur**? Transformation and design are certainly common themes for both men.

Davies was originally going to be a dentist, but he left university and returned to his native Liverpool, joining Littlewoods (a retail chain) in the early 1960s. He started his own school-uniform business in 1972 but it was not successful, and for a while he worked for Pippa Dee, a party plan company home-selling ladies' fashion. He joined the fading menswear retailer J. Hepworth & Son around 1980, when it had just acquired Kendall's (a ladies' fashion store). Davies also led the creation of the retail chain Next. Soon, Davies was responsible for a number of retail acquisitions involving more fashion brands, jewellery and leather goods. He also absorbed Grattan, a leading mail-order-catalogue business. When he later launched the more up-market Next Directory, some Grattan managers were said to be less than ecstatic.

It will always be questionable how many of these acquisitions were opportunistic and how many of them were part of a clear and coherent strategy. The real problem was that Next ended up with some expensive high-rent high street stores, and when inflation affected rent renewals adversely, Next experienced financial difficulties. Davies was accused of being too forceful a leader and failing to build a strong enough management team. He left and 'under new management', Next thrived. Davies would, however, reinvent himself as a leading clothing designer.

After a short spell 'writing his autobiography', Davies started Sporter, producing clothing merchandise for leading sports clubs, including Liverpool and Arsenal FC. He was invited to work with Asda, where he produced the George at Asda clothing range for men, women and children. When he walked away in 2000—after Wal-Mart bought Asda—annual turnover of the George label was £600 million. His real achievement had been to introduce clothing into mainstream supermarkets and make it a major selling item. Tesco and Sainsbury would follow Asda in this respect.

Immediately after resigning his association with Asda, Davies joined Marks & Spencer (M&S) in a distinctive and personal joint venture to develop the Per Una fashion range which, as a semi-independent label and range was, first, unusual, and second, a forerunner of later M&S branding developments. Davies controlled all the designs and supply chain; M&S, in effect, rented space to him in an increasing number of stores and took an agreed share of the revenue and profits. Turnover after three years was hitting £250 million a year—Davies left M&S in 2008 after senior personnel changes, but the range continues to thrive without him. In 2009 he started GIVe, a group of 25 High Street stores offering high quality but afford-able Italian-inspired ladies' clothing that he designed. The success did not match George at Asda or Per Una, and in 2011 both Sporter and GIVe were closed.

In the 20 years after he left Next, Davies was personally responsible for design-ing clothes with an accumulated retail turnover of over £50 billion.

James Dyson

James Dyson is a designer who was always been fascinated by engineering. He is best known as the creator of the bagless vacuum cleaner, which required over 5,000 prototypes before he was satisfied. Rival manufacturers have been forced to react and develop their own variants—from seemingly nowhere, he was able to seize market leadership of an established industry. He established his own manufac-turing facilities in the UK but later moved production to the Far East. He employs a large team of design and development engineers in the UK and is a champion for UK engineering. His later products are very innovative but none have yet made the same impact as his cleaner.

Henry Ford

Henry Ford built 'the first motor car for the multitude'—not the first car, by any means. His cars were modest but to perfectly adequate specifications, and with rela-tively low-cost production systems (borrowing assembly line techniques used to make other products, such as sewing machines and hand guns), they were able to be priced at an affordable level. People gained newfound independence with Ford's cars, and so much of what we take for granted today became possible for the first time.

George Eastman

George Eastman did not invent photography—instead, he was a hobby photogra-pher who wanted to make photography practical and affordable for more people. He invented small box cameras and, more critically, roll film, utilising the recently invented celluloid. In turn, Eastman's roll film encouraged serial inventor Thomas Edison to build the first motion-picture cameras and projectors, thus creating the movie industry. Transformational? Again, we think so.

The Eastman Kodak Company (commonly known as Kodak) survived and prospered for many years, until another transformational technology—digital photography—began impacting the company's fortunes in recent years. Ironically in some ways, the first electronic camera was actually built by Kodak, but it was electronics companies like Canon that have come to dominate the industry.

Walt Disney

The film industry also owes a great deal to Walt Disney, who, among his many other contributions, pioneered animation for the movies. Disney also had a transformative impact on the entertainment industry through the theme parks he began before he died, although a number of his close colleagues, including his brother, were sceptical of his proposals. After all, at that time, the section of Florida that would become the Walt Disney World Resort was undeveloped swampland. The lack of money and other resources to pursue his vision was a challenge—not a constraint—to Disney.

Juan Trippe

Juan Trippe was able to harness the potential of early airplanes and create Pan American World Airways (commonly known as Pan Am), which was the first truly international airline. Affordable, comfortable, fast and safe travel around the world is something we now take for granted.

Herb Kelleher

In a similar vein to Juan Trippe, and much later, Herb Kelleher had a similarly transformative impact as the key founder of Southwest Air in the US. The no-frills, low-price business model for Southwest has been widely copied by others, including Ryanair and EasyJet, and has made cheap air travel available to a mass market.

Richard Branson

Air travel is also one of the businesses we link with the Virgin brand and Richard Branson. Branson's entrepreneurial approach to business has had a transformational impact on several other industries (and established competitors within them), including music, media, rail travel and, most recently, financial services.

1.2 Entirepreneurs whose services changed the world

George Soros

George Soros became very wealthy—and very generous, giving away some $8 billion to worldwide good causes—because he could predict financial futures. He displays an element of visionary insight but also a real attention to detail, along with an ability to spot investment opportunities and the willingness to make the investments while realising and accepting the risks and uncertainty involved. We often associate Soros with hedge funds. He came from a wealthy Hungarian family, became a naturalised American, and is now famous as 'the man who broke the Bank of England' during the 1992 currency crisis.

Soros came to the UK as an economics student in the 1940s, but settled in the US in 1956, where he became a trader and analyst. He developed insight and expertise in stock and currency market movements, and in 1970 he established his own hedge fund. His beliefs on market movements were not in accord with the existing conventional wisdom adopted by many other economists. He believed that as markets move from one 'state' to another they overshoot before restabilising, and that there is a link between the degree of turbulence and the extent of the overshoot. Predicting the timing and the extent of the overshoot can provide real opportunities for a speculator. Computers were, of course, also providing new opportunities for building trading algorithms that respond immediately to tracked movements in the market, thus enabling speculators to make (and lose!) serious money by being speedily responsive (the actual amount affected by the hedge positions they take). Success basically requires more wins than losses, as nobody is likely to win every time. Critics, and those affected, will understandably be tempted to blame speculators for causing the overshoots as they try to manipulate events for personal gain.

In the early 1990s one of Soros' senior colleagues was convinced the UK pound was weak, but the government, locked into the European Exchange Rate Mechanism (ERM) that Margaret Thatcher had eventually joined under pressure and against her better judgement, was reluctant to either float the currency or raise interest rates. Soros opted to sell short by more than $10 billion in pounds. When the pound was devalued on 'Black Wednesday' in September 1992, Soros earned a cool $1.1 billion. Overall, the UK Treasury lost far more than this.

Around this time Soros was charged with insider trading in France (charges he denied). The alleged events took place in 1988; after being dropped, the case was reopened much later and Soros was ultimately convicted in 2006. His penalty was minimal because of the delay. His own hedge fund would not become the largest in the world; that honour goes to Ray Dalio, who has been described as the 'Steve Jobs of investing'.

Hedge funds, and the new investment opportunities they create, have had a transformational impact on financial markets and services and have been instrumental in the emergence of investment banking and investment bankers—who are seen on the one hand as positive revenue generators and on the other hand as overpaid and greedy predators, earning huge bonuses without really producing anything. Governments have always been keen to promote and protect their financial services, but perceptions changed markedly after the global banking collapse, which was correctly predicted by Soros in May 2008.

Paul Soros

The late Paul Soros, George's elder brother, was another **entirepreneur**, albeit a quite different one. He too migrated to America, and while on a business trip to Chile in 1956, saw an opportunity to create a low-cost iron ore loading system. His design allowed for ships to be loaded while moored out at sea against a large floating buoy, thus replacing the need for expensive long, fixed piers. His ideas were refined and adopted for various bulk commodities all round the world. He won several awards for engineering excellence, and he too became a very wealthy philanthropist.

Jeff Bezos and Amazon

Jeff Bezos has succeeded in 'changing the rules of competition' in an industry, but it is arguable that his vision really only materialised once he took the plunge and pursued what he believed was an emerging opportunity. Amazon.com, the 'Earth's largest bookstore', pioneered bookselling via the Internet and, in the process, changed consumer buying habits and forced the existing major booksellers to also offer electronic sales and postal deliveries. Paradoxically, this happened in an environment where—and in parallel—'good bookstores [at least those that survived] have become the community centres of the late twentieth century' by providing comfortable seats, staying open late and incorporating good coffee bars. Of course, Amazon now sells a wide range of products—not just books—and there is an argument that it only really became financially successful when it launched the Kindle e-reader.

Bezos, the son of a Cuban immigrant, had once dreamt of being an astronaut and consequently went on to graduate with a degree in electrical engineering and computer science from Princeton. After Princeton he became a successful investment banker on Wall Street—he was, in fact, the youngest Senior Vice-President ever at D. E. Shaw & Co., which he joined from Bankers Trust. Intrigued by the speed of growth of the Internet in the early 1990s, which he saw as a real opportunity, he decided to 'seize the moment'. He had experienced his trigger and he left the bank with the straightforward intention of starting an e-commerce business. He founded Amazon.com in 1994.

At this stage he had no specific product or service in mind, so he began by drawing up a list of possible activities. He narrowed down his first list of 20 to two—music and books—before choosing books. In both cases, the range of titles available was far in excess of the number any physical store could realistically stock. In 1994 there were 1.5 million English language books in print, and another 1.5 million in other languages. Yet the largest bookstore carried 'only' 175,000 titles. Moreover, Bezos appreciated that the distribution was fragmented. He believed there was scope to offer books at discounted prices and wafer-thin margins to seize sales from existing retailers, whilst also boosting the overall size of the market. The secret of Bezos' success would lie in his ability to establish an effective supply chain and, over time, build an all-embracing website listing most of the books in print. Warehouses have been strategically located and Amazon makes sure it can deliver either from stock or from publishers within days of receiving an order electronically.

His second fundamental decision, then, was location. He chose Seattle for his base, as he felt there would be a good supply of capable tech people and it was an attractive city to live in; he even recruited some ex-Microsoft employees. The criterion for his warehouses was rather different: Bezos would have to charge the relevant sales tax to residents of any state where Amazon.com had a physical presence, but others would be exempt. From the outset Amazon would price competitively and undercut retail stores.

He rented a house and started in the garage, using the coffee shop in the nearby Barnes and Noble bookstore to interview potential staff. After raising several million dollars from venture capitalists and private investors he knew through his networks, he moved into a 400-square-foot office and began trading on the Internet in July 1995. Bezos is adamant that he warned his investors of the inherent risks in his ambitious venture. Sales were immediate and income started flowing in—but more money was raised and investment into the business grew in order to create a multi-product global service. It was several years before Amazon was profitable; its backers needed to take the long view. For those that did, and shared Bezos' vision, the ultimate pay off has been substantial.

Music, computer games, toys and pharmaceuticals are just some of the products Amazon now supplies in addition to books. Bezos has also formed alliances with numerous other businesses that can sell books as an adjunct to their own goods—for a sales revenue percentage, their sites are hyperlinked to the Amazon site. And, for a slice of the revenue, Amazon allows other retailers to sell books, both new and second-hand, through its site. Bezos, himself, remains infectiously enthusiastic and firmly in control.

In 2000, and perhaps returning to his early dream, Bezos founded Blue Origin, a human spaceflight start-up company that aims 'to help enable anybody to go into space' and embraces the concept of 'space hotels, amusement parks and colonies for two million or three million people orbiting the Earth'. The company was kept secret for a few years until it purchased a sizable area of land in west Texas for a launch and test facility. In 2013, Bezos was reportedly discussing business opportunities and strategies with Richard Branson, who is also developing personal space flight opportunities for wealthy individuals. Might a more concrete vision emerge, as happened with Amazon?

M-Pesa

M is for mobile; pesa is Swahili for money. This is a story of entirepreneurship in action without there necessarily being an identifiable **entirepreneur**. The story can be usefully set in the context of Amazon, where people buy goods online using their credit and debit cards, and eBay, where PayPal is the default funding mechanism. These options are simply not available to large numbers of people in many parts of the developing world—and yet for both personal and (micro)business purposes they need to be able to buy goods and services from people from whom they are geographically separated. M-Pesa has had a transformative impact in this regard, and in the process it has enhanced the potential of microfinance to do good, which is something we discuss in a later story on Mohammed Yunus. M-Pesa 'revolutionised the use of mobile phones as a store of value and most importantly as a vehicle to bring virtually all the unbanked population [in certain countries] into a sophisticated payment system'.

Microfinance can provide loans to people who work for themselves, thus earning a typically meagre living. It is vital in helping them with their cash flow; without it they would not be in a position to trade. M-Pesa also impacts trading capability.

How does it work? Very basically, assume Person 1 in Location A needs to buy something from Person 2 in Location B. The two are not close enough for a cash transaction and the banking services they would need are not available to them. M-Pesa allows Person 1 to go into a local store or something similar that acts as an M-Pesa agent, and hand over cash in return for a code number that shows up as a money credit on his mobile phone once it has been loaded on to it. He then texts the code number to Person 2 who is able to use it to collect cash from an agent located close to where he is. Software embedded in the SIM card allows proper security. The online system the agents use records the transactions as well as issuing the code numbers. M-Pesa can thus help people in remote locations do business: once something has been paid for, or payment has been guaranteed, it can be despatched to the buyer. To access and use the system, people only need legitimate identification, such as their passport. The agents receive a commission for their role, and there are thousands signed up as accredited agents in the various relevant countries.

The system needs championing by a relevant mobile phone network in each country; the leaders were Safaricom in Kenya and Vodacom in Tanzania. One popular version of M-Pesa's history suggests Safaricom launched the service in 2007, following work that had originated with a student software development project—although the brief for the original project was more focused on the repayment of micro-loans. The idea that developed seemed to emerge when it was noticed that customers were buying mobile phone minutes and then transferring them as a form of currency, in lieu of actual money. Conceptually, this is similar to the way gift cards are now used. By 2012 there were reported to be 17 million M-Pesa accounts in Kenya. The value of the relevant transactions amounted to some 30 per cent of Kenya's GDP. IBM played a role in developing the software. Banks were taken by surprise and called the security of M-Pesa into question, but when audited it was found to be a robust and workable system.

Parallel systems were developed for Tanzania, Afghanistan, South Africa and India. A mobile phone network was always involved, and sometimes local banks.

There has been a counterclaim that the intellectual property belongs to Britain. British companies carried out the real development work, and early funding was provided by the British government. The student project in question came much earlier than 2007 and the development work subsequently took place under contract before Safaricom (itself part-owned by Vodafone) championed its launch. Credit should thus be given to identifiable Safaricom executives for seeing the potential and committing to the development, although there must be some debate on how they were viewing the potential. There was clearly a very considerable emergent element to the strategy before the real opportunity and potential was realised. Meanwhile, others have claimed they were the real architect and that the student project was not founded on an original piece of work. And some African politicians have not been slow in claiming involvement.

In the end, does it really matter anymore? The transformational impact is surely the key issue, with millions of people in the developing world able to benefit and do business more easily.

Stephanie 'Steve' Shirley

Dame Stephanie Shirley arrived in the UK in 1939, when she was five years old, as a Jewish child refugee from Germany. She started a software company employing mainly women in 1962, which she ran until 1993. After retiring she became a well-known hands-on philanthropist.

She studied part-time for a maths degree whilst working for the post office in London and then for International Computers Ltd. (ICL), an early computer company. She came to the conclusion that it was difficult for women to break through into 'top jobs', especially if they had dependants. Whilst she may not have been the first person to make this observation, her actions and determination make her an **entirepreneur** who influenced thinking and attitudes.

She decided to start her own business writing software; she did this before computers really took off. She said, 'If I had been a bit earlier or a bit later I wouldn't have made it.' This point might be debatable, but regardless, she was in many ways ahead of her time and certainly a challenger of conventional wisdom. She also opted to be known as 'Steve' and not Stephanie. People, she believed, could write software at home; they didn't need an office environment. This was perfect for women with child or parental dependants, and she thus became a pioneer of flexible remote working. She also appreciated that her focus on recruiting female home-workers would make her an attractive employer to some very bright people. Something of a perfectionist herself, she was a great believer in good products, good services and customer satisfaction.

Her business thrived over many years; she was, however, forced by legislation (the Sex Discrimination Act 1975) to relax her views on male employees, although at the time men did make up 1 per cent of her workforce. Her company, F. I. Group, was valued at £150 million in 1993. She sold it to her employees at a generous price and since then she has focused on philanthropic work, giving away some £67 million so far. The business continued to thrive. It was renamed Xansa and sold to the French company, Steria, for £470 million in 2007.

Autism has been a key charitable cause for her—her own son died of epilepsy related to severe autism. Summarising her motivation for her life's work she said, 'I do it because of my personal history; I need to justify the fact that my life was saved.'

Gerard Pelisson and Paul Dubrule

Pelisson and Dubrule opened their first Novotel hotel in 1967 in Lille, France; their Accor Group is now the largest hotel chain in the world, with some 3,500 properties. It was even bigger before two motel chains in America were divested. Over a third of the hotels are in France; the remainder can be found in 90 other countries. It has been claimed that Accor 'pretty much invented budget hotels' offering 'standard en-suite rooms, sound insulation, affordable prices and early booking'. But the founders soon realised the value of a chain of 'reliable' hotels at various quality and price points, thus catering for a wide range of people, as well as for the different needs of the same customers. People take holidays as well as business trips; sometimes there is a preference for pampering, whilst at other times money-saving is a priority. Recent records show Accor averaged 70 per cent occupancy in its budget hotels with an average nightly room price of around 50 euros; for more up-market hotels the occupancy rate came down to 60 per cent but the price doubled. There are significant cost benefits from a centralised booking system (telephone and online) and from supply chain economies. Regular customers accumulate loyalty points that can be used across the chain, in its casinos and with its travel and business services arms. Basically there is 'something for everyone', giving Accor a huge market reach.

The lowest price-point properties are branded F1 (Formule 1); they are practical and economical but do not feature en-suite rooms (customers have to share bathrooms). There are then three levels of Ibis hotels. Ibis properties are comfortable and to a standard formula; they are typically in city centres and near airports. Ibis Budget hotels are similar to the F1 brand, but with a trimmed service level. Ibis Style offers enhanced comfort and brightly coloured décor. Novotel is the large mid-range chain, with all rooms basically the same but offering full-service facilities. Mercure hotels are at a similar level but are more individualised and distinctive. The two upscale brands are Pullman (modern designs with some standardisation) and MGallery (more individualised). Sofitel, with 'French style, [which is] sophisticated and elegant' is the most luxurious (and expensive) brand. There truly is 'something for everyone'.

Club Med

Founded in 1950 in France, Club Méditerranée (commonly called Club Med) became Europe's largest tour operator, with a clearly distinguished product.

Serge Trigano and his partner, Gérard Blitz, set up Club Med as an organisation 'without rules' in a world where most companies operate with fixed rules and structures.

Trigano devised the distinctive strategy. The original Club Med represented 'beautiful people playing all sorts of sports, white sand beaches, azure sky and sea, Polynesian thatched huts, free and flowing wine at meals, simple yet superb food' (*The Economist*, 12 July 1986). It was an 'organised melange of hedonism and back to nature'.

The organisation systematically spread around the world, opening over 100 holiday villages and over 60 holiday residences (hotel/sports complexes) for both summer and winter vacations. Organisers were present in a ratio of 1 to 5 with guests, for whom they provided sports tuition and organised evening entertainment. Traditionally all tuition, food and drinks with meals were paid for in advance as part of the holiday cost, and guests were provided with beads which they used to buy extra drinks and so on. Clothing was permanently casual.

Club Med charged prices above the average for package holidays, its clientele consisted mainly of above-average income earners, and the organisation enjoyed a reputation for delivering customer service and satisfaction. The company grew successfully for over 30 years with little change to the basic strategy. By the mid-1980s, however, occupancy rates had fallen, and profits declined and then stagnated. The original vision was looking dated as tastes changed in a rapidly expanding global market. Club Med introduced a variety of changes, but has never managed to restore the position it once held—reinvention has to come at the right time or entirepreneurship can disappear. In 2004, Accor took just short of a 30 per cent stake in Club Med. Accor found that the hoped-for synergies were not forthcoming, however, and sold its stake in Club Med in two tranches relatively quickly.

At the same time, though, we might consider the growth in popularity of all-inclusive resort holidays, something Club Med pioneered.

1.3 Three retail entirepreneurs

Ingvar Kamprad and IKEA

IKEA was started in Sweden by Ingvar Kamprad, who pioneered the idea of self-assembly furniture in handy packs and thus had a transformational effect on the furniture industry. Involving customers in the assembly process offers cost-saving and competitive pricing opportunities while also providing a sense of attachment and achievement. It has been copied widely. Now well into his 80s, Kamprad is still involved but not running the company himself. His vision of 'a better, more beautiful, everyday life for the many' led to 'a wide range of home furnishings, of good function and style, at low prices, for mass consumer markets'.

Kamprad originally began with a mail-order business in 1943; the first IKEA store opened in 1958. Every year IKEA prints over 110 million catalogues, which is by far the single largest print run of any comparable item anywhere in the world. By 2011, IKEA had some 332 shops in 38 countries. There are 18 stores in the UK and one in Ireland. IKEA's strategy has always involved offering good-quality merchandise at prices which undercut the competition. In the mid-1990s IKEA's annual turnover passed the $5 billion mark; after-tax profits were estimated to be 8 per cent of revenue. Sales have risen in every year of its existence, and by 2001 revenues had doubled to $10 billion. They were growing at 15 per cent per year and reached 23.5 billion euros in 2011. A private company, IKEA has always been reticent about the financial data it releases.

Growth has been carefully regulated. IKEA waited for seven years before opening a second branch; the first branch outside Sweden was in the early 1970s; the first US store opened in 1985, with typically one new store being added every year. This approach has allowed IKEA to establish local supply networks and ensured that it never became stretched financially—the expansion programme has always been funded from cash generated by the retail activities. IKEA does not have a large market share in any single country; instead, it has sought to establish a global brand and an intriguing reputation which draws customers from substantial distances away.

Moreover, as IKEA has only recently started to target Russia and China, growth prospects appear to remain healthy.

There is considerable attention to detail, especially with stock and store layout. IKEA stores focus on sales of self-assembly packs which customers take away themselves. IKEA will, however, deliver fully assembled pieces for a premium price. Many other furniture stores take orders for assembled items and then there is a 10 to 12-week wait. IKEA stores have a wide range of facilities, typically including restaurants and game and video rooms for children; these are normally on the top floor, which is where customers come in. People are then routed carefully through a series of display areas to the downstairs purchase points, which resemble a typical discount warehouse.

The furniture packs are commissioned from over 2,300 suppliers in some 70 countries, many of them low-labour-cost countries in the Far East and Eastern

Europe. IKEA has an equity stake in several of its suppliers and insists on tight stock control programmes to reduce costs through the whole supply chain. IKEA designs all its own products and aims to lead customer taste. There is just one range of products for the global market, but not every country and store stocks the full range. IKEA chooses not to have mini-ranges for specific countries and prides itself on its ability to respond to local fashion and opportunities by quickly adjusting the range in any one store. Sales per square foot invariably exceed industry averages.

IKEA's mission statement emphasises 'functionality, good design, low price and good quality'. The company uses the word 'prosumers' to imply that value is added by both IKEA and their customers in partnership. Employees are empowered to be innovative and helpful and challenged to 'dare to be different'. IKEA asserts that always offering prices substantially below those of its competitors places considerable pressure on its staff. IKEA also expects, and gets, some complaints about busy stores and slow checkout service—a price they claim that has to be paid for low prices. Even though IKEA prices could easily be increased, Kamprad has stuck with his original approach and mission: 'we do not need to do things in traditional ways'.

Kamprad himself, despite his enormous wealth (estimated at £15 billion), is parsimonious. He drives a 15-year-old Volvo and uses budget airlines, preferring EasyJet. In this respect he can be likened to the late Sam Walton of Wal-Mart, who opted to drive a pick-up truck. Kamprad denies, though, that there is any truth in a published story claiming that his parsimony stretches to him buying cans of Coca-Cola from local supermarkets to replenish hotel room mini-bars because he is reluctant to pay hotel prices for soft drinks.

Today the company operates as three distinct activities. The core retailing business is now a Dutch-registered charitable foundation. The profits of the operations are subjected to a top-slice of 3 per cent to fund a separate business which has responsibility for managing the brand and IKEA's franchisees. The third arm is a banking and finance business; IKEA, for example, owns a majority shareholding in Habitat in the UK, the company founded by Terence Conran.

Sam Walton and Wal-Mart

Sam Walton was a truly great retailer. His legacy: the Wal-Mart stores that provide huge ranges and choices of household goods. They are the largest retail chain in the world. Prices are kept low through scale economies and a first-class supply chain network. Despite their size, the stores seem friendly and Walton always employed people simply to answer customer queries and show them where particular goods are shelved. Walton sought to learn from other organisations; in this respect he was opportunistic, but reflective. He never claimed to be an original thinker and he networked widely to find his new ideas.

Born in 1918 and raised in relative poverty, Walton started earning money by selling newspapers when he was very young. In 1940 he began selling shirts in a J.C. Penney store. Afterwards, and in partnership with his brother, he took on a franchise for a Ben Franklin five and dime store in Arkansas. The two brothers bought additional outlets, abandoned counters in favour of self-service, established central buying and promotion and quickly became the most successful Ben Franklin franchisees in America. In 1962, the same year that Kmart began opening discount stores in larger cities, Walton began with discount stores in small towns. Walton's principle was simple: mark everything up by 30 per cent, regardless of the purchase cost. This proved to be a winning formula—he understood his target customers. He toured, observed, absorbed and learned to develop his 'buy it low, stack it high and sell it cheap' strategy. Walton's first Wal-Mart store opened in Arkansas in 1962; turnover grew to exceed the figures for McDonald's, Coca-Cola and Disney combined. Yet the wealthy Sam Walton earned a reputation as a mean tipper!

Growth was gradual in the early years; there were 30 Wal-Mart stores by 1970. Once Walton opened his own distribution warehouse (another idea he copied), growth exploded. In addition, Wal-Mart was the first major retailer to share sales data electronically with its leading suppliers. 'We got big by replacing inventory with information'. Sam Walton was always willing to try out new ideas, quickly abandoning those which did not work. He created a 'culture that in many ways represents a religion—in the devotion it has inspired amongst its associates and in the Jesuit-like demands it makes on its executives'. Growth and prosperity continued after the death of the founder. Walton's descendants are still involved, but Sam left a strong management team in place. Wal-Mart has expanded selectively into other countries; in 1999, it acquired Asda in the UK. That said, Wal-Mart has its critics for the ways through which it drives and keeps costs down.

Maxine Clarke and Build-A-Bear Workshop

Maxine Clarke spent her life after university in retailing, becoming CEO of the discount-shoe retailer Payless Shoe Source. In 1996, at age 47 and after four years at the top, she stepped down. She was, she said, remunerated very well financially, but not stimulated creatively. She needed a fresh challenge.

The following year she took the ten-year-old daughter of a close friend on a shopping expedition. The girl collected Beanie Babies soft toys but couldn't find a new one she liked. So she asked if they might make one together. She was suggesting a craft project, but Clarke heard something much bigger. She had spotted a potential opportunity. 'I had visions of revolutionising an industry I spent my entire professional life working in.'

She had come to realise that if retailing is fun, people buy more. She also realised how much children enjoy crafts and making things, and how attached they become to stuffed animals, especially teddy bears. She saw an opportunity to bring all these things together. She also believed that her key customers, children, would judge her less on financial performance and more on what the in-store experience meant to them. Potential investors would think differently, of course, so the business would need to be run efficiently.

Initially she identified businesses that offered something similar to what she was imagining, and she attempted, but failed, to buy one. Instead, she created and opened the first Build-A-Bear Workshop in St Louis, Missouri, providing a more hands-on experience for children. The idea was that children would build their own soft toy; for each one of them it would be a unique experience. They would be able to select a bear skin from a number of different ones available and then help operate the machine that stuffed it and gave it form and substance. They would also select a heart that would be popped inside, as well as a voice. They would also help to seal the finished toy and give it a name, which would be printed on a tag and attached. As the business grew, more and more animals were made available. At first, parents said it wouldn't work, but children soon asked where the workshop was and when could they go.

Clarke invested $750,000 of her own money to get the venture started—she believed in her idea. But she sought additional investment, as one store was not what she had in mind. She wanted to build a chain as quickly as would be feasible. After 15 years there were over 400 Build-A-Bear Workshops around the world, roughly 60 per cent in the US and 40 per cent overseas. There is a mix of company-owned and franchised stores. Over 700 million bears and other animals are 'alive' somewhere in the world. Investors were soon queuing to invest in her business—just as children and their parents were queuing to build their own bears. 'You must believe you can truly achieve what you set your mind to… . Most people don't … instead they allow a lack of resources or experience to hold them back.'

The business would not have succeeded without solid and reliable retail systems, which Maxine Clarke was already familiar with, and strong relationships with her suppliers, especially those who supply the skins. Success, she believed, is always in the detail: 'tending to the things that others may overlook helps you soar above competitors—but it is important not to get bogged down with stuff that doesn't matter'. The abilities to focus and prioritise are important.

1.4 Transformations in transportation

George Stephenson

George Stephenson contributed to the Industrial Revolution in a vital way. Goods needed to be moved around the country—coal from the mines to where it was required for steam engines; finished products to ports and cities. Canals had been dug; wagon-ways provided wooden rails over which heavy horse-drawn wagons could move. But it was the railways that would change everything, and passenger railways are what Stephenson is best remembered for.

One essential component was steam engines. Early engines were static, and provided pumping and winching facilities; the challenge was an engine that could use its own power to propel itself. George (and later Robert Stephenson, George's son and business partner) would design and build innovative steam locomotives as well as the first railway, which was used to move goods between Stockton and Darlington in north-east England. This happened in 1825, and was a profitable operation.

George Stephenson was unable to read or write until he was 18. His parents were illiterate; his mother died of tuberculosis when he was young, and his father was blinded in an industrial accident. George—who was born and raised just outside Newcastle upon Tyne, England—started out as a miner, opting to attend night school. He also proved to be a natural engineer and was allowed to work on and build machinery at the colliery where he worked. His first steam-powered locomotive was finished in 1814 (when he was 33 years old). He also strengthened and improved the relatively new cast iron rails that were becoming popular, by using cushioning. He designed a locomotive with several wheels set to spread the weight, created the first flanged wheel adhesion locomotive and built the first railway passenger carriage. This single carriage was used—along with the freight wagons—on the Stockton and Darlington Railway. First used to transport dignitaries, the opportunity this railway offered soon became apparent.

Stephenson was also a visionary who appreciated that a railway was far more than a locomotive. Rails, bridges, viaducts, tunnels, embankments, rail heads, stations and platforms were all required as well.

In the 1820s Stephenson was commissioned to build a railway between Manchester, a leading textile town, and Liverpool, its nearest major port. The fundamental challenge: the land between the two included substantial peat bogs. A Bill requesting permission was put to Parliament, but Stephenson's ability to explain how he would deal with the physical challenges was unconvincing and the Bill failed. Stephenson was not to be deterred, however, and eventually permission was granted and the railway was built. Construction took just short of five years and the railway, which opened in 1830, incorporated numerous bridges and viaducts. Huge quantities of rubble provided a solid and robust 'floating platform' for the rails passing through the bogs. Another key to the success of this railway was the new 'Rocket' steam locomotive, which was largely designed by Robert. This locomotive incorporated a better-engineered means for transferring steam in order to create much greater power—and, in turn, speed. 'No human had ever built anything that would move faster.' In today's terms, of course, its ability to average some 30 miles per hour would seem slow! Robert's design provided the blueprint for all subsequent steam locomotives, which over the years became more powerful and much faster than the Rocket. Design and aesthetics also grew in significance, but the first step had been essential. Stephenson's chosen gauge became the industry norm for railways—his great rival (and friend) Isambard Kingdom Brunel, who built the Great Western Railway, used a different gauge.

Industrialisation was now possible on a much greater scale as goods could be moved around faster and more efficiently; the great cities no longer needed to be ports for economic development to make sense. And as passenger trains developed, the opportunities for people to travel were transformed. In the context of Stephenson's story it is interesting to consider the contemporary debate about the High Speed Two (HS2), a proposed high-speed railway that would connect London with several major English cities. Proponents talk about the prospects for revolutionising passenger transport (again); opponents claim the cost cannot realistically be recouped.

Malcolm McLean

Malcolm McLean is a name few would recognise, but when he died in 2001, the US Secretary of Transportation wrote, 'He revolutionised the maritime industry … result … much safer and less expensive transport of goods, faster delivery and better service. … we owe much to a man of vision.' *Forbes* magazine described him as 'one of the few men who changed the world'.

Malcolm McLean, in effect, gave the world containerisation; but he did not invent container transport. Who knows who did originally, but there was certainly evidence of a forerunner of what we have today on the UK Victorian railways, using flat-bed rail trucks.

McLean was born in 1914 in North Carolina. In the 1930s, working with his brother and sister, he started a trucking business which grew to be one of the largest in the US. Cigarettes were one product he transported in bulk. He claims he had an idea for moving lorry trailers by sea as early as 1937, but chose not to follow it through. During World War II, trucks were moved up and down the Atlantic coast by sea, and building on this afterwards, he realised it wasn't necessary to ship the whole truck; it was really the load on the trailer that was crucial. He worked on his idea and designed a metal container for dry goods which were normally transported 'loose' in a ship's hold.

He bought a shipping company in 1955 and converted one of his ships, the Ideal-X, so it could carry these containers. The first voyage was in 1956, when 58 sealed containers were stacked and shipped between New Jersey and Houston, Texas. Things developed from there as haulage companies, manufacturers with goods to move, customers, port operators and shipping lines all contributed ideas and innovations. The upshot was that transportation costs fell dramatically; in metal containers mixed freight could be moved for 16 cents a ton, down from $5.80 dollars a ton loose. Loading and unloading costs were slashed; mechanisation replaced people and reduced labour costs; damage and pilferage were reduced. The time in port came down and the time at sea increased. Large container ports using overhead cranes were developed, with many in new locations. Larger and larger ships were designed and built. (Many modern ships can now hold upwards of 4,000 containers.[1]) International transportation was transformed alongside systems for managing container ports and tracking the movement of goods. As systems become more and more complex, the ability to manage the details is essential. By 1996—40 years after the first voyage of the Ideal-X—around 90 per cent of shipping was moved in containers.

McLean renamed his shipping company Sea-Land Service in 1960 and grew it into an international business. After just ten years he had 36 ships, 27,000 trailer-type containers and Sea-Land connected 30 ports around the world. In 1969 he sold the business to cigarette giant R. J. Reynolds for $530 million, of which he received $160 million. Sea-Land is now part of Maersk.

McLean moved into real-estate development but also bought another shipping company, United States Lines, which he grew into the largest of its time. But he was building ever-larger ships which were fuel-inefficient, and the business was hit hard when there were oil shortages and consequential fuel price increases. The business went bankrupt, but by this point his legacy was in place.

Edward Stobart

One of the **entirepreneurs** who was able to benefit from containerisation was Edward Stobart. It is almost impossible to drive on Britain's motorway network and not be aware of the green-and-red Stobart trucks, which are invariably clean and always have a smartly dressed driver. The success of the business is very largely down to Edward Stobart, who died in 2011 at the age of 54. It is not implausible that his heart condition was at least in part affected by his years of hard and dedicated work building this business.

Edward's father, Eddie Stobart, started a transport business delivering fertiliser in Cumbria in the 1950s. Edward left school with little academic attainment; he was described as shy and retiring, affected by a serious stammer. But he showed early entrepreneurial potential, buying old railway sleepers which he would chop into firewood. He started working for his father and grew to love the business. He started running the trucking side when he was 19 and took over full control in 1976. In the next 25 years he transformed the business from eight trucks and 21 employees to 1,000 trucks, 2,000 staff members and 27 sites. It had become Britain's best-known haulage business, but not the largest. Today the Stobart Group includes warehousing, port operations, rail freight, rail and civil engineering and plant hire as well as haulage. And it owns and operates Southend Airport to house its air freight interests. The group is led by Edward's brother William, who, working with a business partner, bought Edward out in 2004.

From the outset Edward became immersed in the business. He drove a truck himself and worked long hours, 'leading from the front'. His staff were committed to him, in part because of his enthusiasm. He did have a reputation for always saying 'yes' when offered work and only then planning how it could be absorbed into an already busy business. He built up the fleet so they had growing capacity and he made sure the trucks were looked after and cleaned regularly. It was almost as if he was waiting for a big opportunity and making sure he was ready when it came along. The increasing switch to road from rail transport and the deregulation of the haulage industry were opportunities upon which he capitalised, even though the industry was very competitive with only limited barriers to entry. It has been argued that he was better organised than many of his rivals and always knew he needed to plan to have a return load and not run an empty lorry. His costs were contained and because he was willing to operate with tight margins, his prices were competitive.

Looking for opportunities to be different, he encouraged the growth of a fan club such that 'Stobart' became a brand in its own right, highly unusual for this industry. All the distinctive trucks had a girl's name painted on the front and 'Stobart spotting' replaced trainspotting for many enthusiasts. Today there is a range of merchandise, with sales helped by a regular television 'docusoap' programme. Others have commented he was the inspiration for them starting their own transport businesses; another young entrepreneur's model-and-collectable business started with a Stobart truck.

Edward claimed to have been thinking of selling the business and doing something else when he saw the opportunity to grow with warehousing and strategically located depots around the country. This was the spur to explosive growth—but it required serious investment. The company's first loss was recorded in 2001—had recent growth been too rapid and costly? Although the business was sold to his brother, Edward continued with other, less noteworthy business activities, and when he died he left personal debts. Nevertheless he had built a substantial business by looking at road haulage in a different way and seeing new opportunities for differentiation.

Fred Smith and FedEx

Federal Express (FedEx) provides an excellent example of an organisation (and an **entirepreneur**) opening up an unrealised market opportunity and beginning a new industry. 'The greatest business opportunities arise when you spot things your customer didn't have a clue they needed until you offered it to them' (Smith).

The idea behind FedEx is simple: provide a speedy and reliable national and international 'overnight' courier service for letters and parcels based upon air cargo. FedEx rightly claims to have invented the concept of overnight delivery, creating a whole new market where previously there was none. The company had a peripheral but significant role in the film *Castaway*, which featured Tom Hanks as a FedEx manager who survived the crash of a FedEx airplane only to spend several years marooned on a desert island. He held on to one of the packages from the plane and finally succeeded in delivering it.

FedEx is, however, unusual in a number of ways. Before it could even begin, FedEx needed a nationwide (North American) distribution system with a fleet of planes and trucks—a huge investment in planning and resources. The business was the idea of Fred Smith, whose father had founded and built a successful bus company. When Fred was a student at Yale in the 1960s he wrote a paper outlining his idea for a freight-only airline which delivered and collected parcels to and from a series of hubs. Traditionally parcels were shipped on scheduled passenger airlines as normal mail, whilst Smith proposed flying at night when the skies were relatively quiet. His paper was graded as a C; his ideas were seen as rather impractical. After graduating, Smith served as a pilot in Vietnam before he bought a controlling interest in Arkansas Aviation Sales, a company which carried out modifications and overhauls. Determined to implement his idea for a courier service he invested a $10 million family inheritance and raised a further $72 million from various sources based on a number of independent but positive feasibility studies.

FedEx took to the skies in 1973, offering a service in and out of 25 East Coast cities with 14 jet aircraft. The demand was there, as he had forecast. Unfortunately the rise in the OPEC oil price made FedEx uneconomical almost as soon as it started. Two years of losses and family squabbles—Smith was accused of 'squandering the family fortune'—were followed by profits, and Smith's belief, courage and persistence were rewarded.

FedEx opened a hub in Paris in 1999 and opted for a standard price across Europe. In 2006 it acquired UK-based competitor ANC, which it rebranded as FedEx UK. In 2004 FedEx acquired Kinko's, an American High Street franchise that provides a range of office services. This allows customers to more readily access FedEx services.

FedEx is successful because it delivers on time and speedily, and because it has a sophisticated tracking system—SuperTracker, which it introduced in 1986—for when something does go astray. It uses as a slogan 'The World on Time'. There are now some 700 FedEx aircraft flying over one million miles every two days. The central hub remains in Memphis, Tennessee but the flights are international. Six million packages from 220 countries are handled every night. FedEx's courier vans cover another two million miles every day collecting and delivering these parcels. To ensure FedEx can maintain its service it flies empty aircraft which track close to the pick-up airports every night and are brought into service if needed.

FedEx's success has, of course, spawned competition. But with learning and emergence, Smith's company has stayed at the forefront of the industry it invented.

Sam Shoen and U-Haul

Immediately after World War II Sam Shoen and his wife, Anna Mary, realised from personal experience that people often needed to move goods around the country on one-way trips. Shoen had earlier been thrown out of medical school for providing examination answers to fellow students, and he served in the Navy during the war. His naval nickname was 'Slick' and he was now moving home to the West Coast.

Whilst trailers could readily be hired already, at least in cities and large towns, typically they had to be returned to the point of origin, which could be expensive. By focusing on one-way rentals, U-Haul effectively spread the cost of owning a trailer amongst many users. Shoen's business model was built around local agents, normally owners of gas stations, who stored and rented the trailers, and a partnership commission-based remuneration linked to usage. Shoen built (or at least renovated) many of the trailers he used and retained ownership of them all. He was willing to accept small investments in individual trailers, paying the investors an agreed share of the earnings, which were easily tracked. All the trailers were painted orange to reinforce the U-Haul identity.

Success was not instantaneous, as the early lack of money in the business meant Shoen originally relied on cheap second-hand equipment which was sometimes unreliable. But with perseverance and hard work—he typically worked some 16 hours a day—he built U-Haul into a billion-dollar business, introducing trucks in addition to trailers. There are now some 16,000 agents in the US and Canada; like Hoover, U-Haul has become more of a generic term than a single company brand.

Shoen lost his first wife at a relatively young age but remarried more than once and fathered 12 children. Internal family feuds and litigation have been linked to ownership of the business, and when Shoen's car crashed into a tree in 1999 (he was 83 years old) it was recorded as suicide.

It is interesting to compare U-Haul with FedEx. U-Haul was started 'on a shoestring' and grew effectually: there was a vision, but more opportunism than there was detailed planning. FedEx required a complete infrastructure to be in place from day one, so there was serious planning to support the vision. But both businesses have had a transformational impact.

The Pony Express

The Pony Express is the story of a failed attempt at entirepreneurship ... although things might have been very different. It was a mail service along a route from St Joseph, Missouri, through the plains of the Midwest of America and across the Rocky Mountains to Sacramento, California—a distance of 1,900 miles. When the idea was formed, California was effectively cut off from the more developed Eastern states, but was expanding rapidly because of the Gold Rush. The Pony Express would use riders and fast ponies to carry mail from one relay station to the next. In all, there were over 160 stations; the miles between them varied, based on the distance a pony could travel at a gallop before tiring, which naturally changed with the terrain.

Horses were swapped at relay stations and rested; the riders would change ponies and carry on, covering some eight to ten relays in a single day. Mail was packed in secure pouches; including water, each pony was required to carry 75 kilograms. The riders carried guns, and little else. They had to be well-armed as the territory was generally lawless and their packs could be valuable. In any one day there would be some 80 riders on the route, and it took ten days for mail to complete the journey. The ponies were small and fast; the riders young, fit and lightweight. The most famous was perhaps William 'Buffalo Bill' Cody, who joined at age 15.

The Pony Express was founded by three businessmen who were already in partnership with a successful wagon-freighting business. William Russell started as a trader but expanded into freight. His main contribution was securing contracts to carry mail, but he was also instrumental in raising federal and other funding to allow their idea to happen. Alexander Majors had an overland freight background and he masterminded the logistics; William Waddell, another trader by background, was credited with managing the day-to-day operations and adminis- tration. They worked well together and complemented each other. The first Pony Express journey was in April 1860; the last was in October 1861. Although there is a legendary element because of the sheer ambition and daring involved, the Pony Express was not a successful business proposition. In 18 months it had gross earn- ings of $90,000 and posted trading losses of $200,000.

It was undoubtedly visionary, and logistically it worked very well. As a propo- sition, it was well conceived and executed. But the opportunity would only be short-lived. When the telegraph opened across the whole of America in 1861, it allowed instant messaging. Demand for the Pony Express fell away; its competition had come from an indirect source that the founders had failed to appreciate. Their vision had been for a better way of moving mail, whilst others had been looking for a better way of communicating. The impact of the telegraph can be compared to that of the Internet and email some 140 years later.

1.5 Organisational transformers

Jack Welch

Jack Welch was CEO of diversified US conglomerate General Electric (GE) from 1981 to 2002, when he retired. Previously a GE divisional head, he is credited with transforming GE's fortunes and making it one of the most successful, admired and powerful companies in the world. *Fortune* magazine christened him 'Manager of the Century' for his achievement in 'turning a slumbering dinosaur into a lean and dynamic company with a paradigm of a new management style'. Separately he has been described as a rebel, a self-made man and a business genius. Normally categorised as a leader, he was a complete and inspirational **entirepreneur**.

He had a vision for running a conglomerate of this size and diversity—amongst other things, GE was involved in heavy and light engineering (from aircraft engines to domestic lighting) and broadcasting (GE owned NBC)—in an era when more focused companies generally performed better. He found a good balance between centralisation and decentralisation. Welch was a liberator who inspired others to realise their responsibility as well as their talents, but he was always in control.

'If we are to get the reflexes and speed we need, we've got to simplify and delegate more—simply trust more. We have to undo a 100-year-old concept and convince our managers that their role is not to control people and stay on top of things, but rather to guide, energise and excite. But with all this must come the conceptual tools, which will mean continuous education of every individual at every level of the company.'

His approach was based on giving managers demanding targets (and support to achieve them) and the challenge of learning good practices and new ideas from other parts of the organisation (again in an enabled framework). Innovation was the desired outcome. He championed an organisational university, something others have copied. He is quoted as saying, 'We build great people, who then build great products and services.' Customer service was always high on his agenda: under Welch, GE created Six Sigma quality management, which is used extensively by other organisations.

Manager performance was monitored and reviewed continuously. Outstanding performance was rewarded with bonuses and promotion; sustained underachievement inevitably resulted in dismissal. Welch was nicknamed 'Neutron Jack' for his willingness to shed businesses, plants and people he felt were no longer required.

Strategically he targeted businesses which could be number one or number two in their industry segment. He knew his businesses were all cyclical in different ways, and he sought to find and retain balance across the portfolio. But every business had to be profitable. He also built GE Capital, a venture fund, into effectively America's fourth largest bank. He made sure that when he retired there was a choice of three strong internal candidates to succeed him.

If you live in the UK and are familiar with the challenges of running the National Health Service (NHS), you might like to muse about what might have happened if Jack Welch had been in charge of the NHS rather than GE.

Lou Gerstner

Lou Gerstner was CEO of IBM from 1993 until his retirement in 2002. He had previously held executive posts at McKinsey & Company, American Express and RJR Nabisco. His achievement as an **entirepreneur** was turning around IBM's fortunes and saving the business from effective extinction. In simple terms, he refocused the company on IT services and away from computer hardware, and at the same time ensured it fully embraced the growing significance of the emerging Internet. He also sought to change a deeply embedded culture that he felt was no longer appropriate: IBM had come to dominate the computer mainframe market with leading technology and aggressive selling—the downside of which was a culture of competitiveness that had become internally, as well as externally, focused.

IBM had pioneered the growth of the mainframe computer industry and prospered as a result, but these machines were becoming increasingly obsolete as the computing power of smaller desktop machines grew. IBM had become a 'once-mighty behemoth' in desperate need of a fresh direction. The company was losing money and in crisis.

Gerstner would not abandon PCs, which IBM had also been successful with, but he recognised the weakness of IBM's strategic position. The real drivers of the PC industry were Intel (chips) and Microsoft (operating systems) and they were able and willing to sell to a range of competitors. IBM had developed its own operating system, OS/2, which was a technically superior product, but this had failed to dent the power and position of Microsoft Windows. It was a product that IBM had continued to defend and champion, but Gerstner was a newcomer and he felt no residual loyalty to OS/2. He was willing to ditch any further work on it.

Gerstner also did not hold back from slimming down the size of the business. Again, as a newcomer, he felt able to drive a redundancy programme. This was his first big step to achieve cost savings. He followed it with asset sales to raise cash. When he arrived, IBM's intended strategy was one of disposal and divestment to break up the company; he completely reversed this and insisted that IBM should remain centralised. He believed the company had core strengths in hardware, services and software, but that these needed to be integrated fully and refocused to provide customers with technical solutions by using the company's knowledgeable and experienced people differently. This would demand serious changes to IBM's culture, as previously the independent divisions had (happily) seen themselves as being in competition with each other. He achieved the integration (and synergy) by tying manager compensation packages to corporate and not divisional performance—and he monitored what was happening. 'People don't do what you expect, but what you inspect' (Gerstner).

Gerstner believed his real achievement was in transforming IBM's culture and behaviour. He realised that strategic ideas matter, but alone they are not enough: proposed changes have to be implemented. People must also sometimes change, even though they might be hostile to the proposals. Interestingly, he commented that in his opinion, 'IBM's problems, challenges, complexity and inbred and ingrown culture were unique and that his fixes are not automatically transferable.'

1.6 Behaviour and communications transformers

Tim Berners-Lee

Sir Tim Berners-Lee gave the world perhaps its most powerful means of communication so far: the World Wide Web, or WWW. A physicist, he was working as a computer scientist at CERN (the European particle physics laboratory in Switzerland) when he realised how hypertext (linking information so it could be shared) could be married with the (existing) Internet (itself a system of linked computer networks) to allow fellow scientists to share their work. Berners-Lee had worked first in telecoms after he graduated and then started writing software for printers. He became involved in computer networking and his first post at CERN was as a software consultant.

Scientists from around the world have links with CERN, and 25 years ago they were eager to exchange their data and share results and findings, as academics typically do, but were finding this difficult and frustrating on a speedy and routine basis. Berners-Lee understood this need, and he also appreciated the unrealised potential of connecting the data on all the scientists' computers. The data, however, existed in various forms, and the computers were not all the same model. His solution ultimately overcame these barriers.

Berners-Lee first wrote a paper about the linkage possibility in 1989. It was barely acknowledged, but he was allowed to carry on developing his ideas. He created his first server in 1990; in August 1991 the Web went live. Users were given online instructions for putting up their own Web pages, and were encouraged to link their pages with others without any approval or permission. Moreover, there was no charge for access: there was no patent to infringe and no royalty to be paid. This invention and gift to the world enabled many things that we now take for granted, including personal email, online search engines, social networking, online trading and online dating—although, of course, not all of us use this particular product. The World Wide Web has also made some entrepreneurs, Berners-Lee amongst them, extremely wealthy.

Berners-Lee's fundamental contribution was to link things that already existed. Hypertext already allowed any electronic document to be linked with another; joining this with the Internet allowed the transmission of these documents instantly around the world via networked computers. He thus satisfied a need he knew about. He found a solution to a problem. He identified a genuine opportunity and acted on it. The truly visionary element was in realising the value of engaging others in the development process. Berners-Lee, for example, did his pioneering work on a very powerful NeXT personal computer at CERN; others developed the browsers that allowed the Web to function on less powerful computers. He was thus able to harness the creative and innovative minds of an army of fellow computer scientists such that what happened was evolutionary, emergent and effectual. One thing led to another. It is doubtful that either Berners-Lee—or CERN—truly appreciated what would emerge and the degree to which it would change the world. Had they had this level of foresight we might wonder whether they would have intervened to constrain those particular opportunities that some see as abuses of the web, such as freely-available online pornography. Berners-Lee, who has associations with a number of universities around the world, has made further contributions in the last 20 years. He was a featured guest at the opening ceremony for the 2012 Olympic Games in London, when he tweeted the words 'This is for everyone' from a NeXT computer.

Mark Zuckerberg and Facebook

This is another story about entirepreneurship in action. Facebook has transformed social networking and the lives of millions around the world. Facebook was not the first social networking site, but is has become the most popular. Started in 2004, it surpassed 900 million users in 2012. Hugely influential, it shapes how both individuals and businesses behave online: many companies feel they have to have a Facebook presence. It has without doubt created a communications revolution, but as yet the business model isn't fully resolved. The person behind Facebook is Mark Zuckerberg, but it is an interesting question as to whether we should describe him as a true **entirepreneur**.

Zuckerberg was a computer student at Harvard who was assisted in the beginning of Facebook's creation by his three college roommates, but their involvement dissipated as the business grew and relocated from Boston to California. At the outset, 'Facebook'—first called 'Facemash' before it next became a website called 'theFacebook'—provided an online directory of Harvard students so others could identify and find out more about them. The information was already published in paper form as The Harvard Facebook, which was essentially a directory of profiles. The data was obtained as a dormitory stunt by hacking into Harvard's computer network, for which Zuckerberg was later charged with breaching security and violating individual privacy. The charges were eventually dropped—but not before Facemash was taken down. The number of hits whilst the initial site was live told Zuckerberg he was on to something. His next move was to resurrect the site but offer people the opportunity to post their own profiles—subsequently he provided the same service at other leading American universities. Initial funding came from one of his co-founders and roommates.

Zuckerberg was accused of stealing the idea for what became Facebook from two fellow students, twins Cameron and Tyler Winklevoss. He had certainly talked to them about social networks and had allegedly agreed (for a fee) to write the software for a site they had in mind. Some time down the line Zuckerberg agreed to an out-of-court settlement of $65 million, but the core argument has never been resolved. Zuckerberg was always adamant that the idea the Winklevoss brothers had was not the same as the site he developed.

Zuckerberg—who is portrayed as something of a driven individual in the movie about Facebook, *The Social Network*, and who might readily be described as a computer geek—has shown himself to be someone who is able to attract and utilise the support of key individuals. The site came to the attention of entrepreneur

Sean Parker, who had earlier started Plaxo (essentially an address book and social network for business people) as well as Napster, the business that enabled illegal music downloads and later had to be shut down. Parker saw serious potential in Facebook and sought out Zuckerberg. He helped him secure venture funding and also persuaded him to relocate the business to California. Parker retains a small stake in Facebook, but he was forced out of direct involvement by later investors who were concerned with issues in his private life. He would later become a paper billionaire when Facebook was floated.

A second key player was Peter Thiel, introduced to Zuckerberg by Parker. Thiel had made his fortune as a co-founder of PayPal (which was bought by eBay) and become an investor in Facebook. A third and very key player in the story is Sheryl Sandberg, who was recruited from Google to be Chief Operating Officer at Facebook. It has been her role to build the organisation—recruiting other key people—and procure the necessary advertising revenue.

In just the same way that advertising is fundamental to businesses such as Google, it is a necessary source of income for Facebook. But evidence shows the click-through rate for banner advertising on social network sites like Facebook is lower than for search engines, probably because people are using the sites for quite different reasons. Herein lies a key dilemma. The information people post on Facebook constitutes a database without equal, and advertisers would like as much access as possible so they can target their advertising. Whilst users might anticipate advertising messages, they will not expect their personal details to be shared freely if they have sought to place restrictions on their page.

Facebook's challenge is to increase the amount of advertising revenue it has so far attracted. Not withstanding this, a stock market launch took place in 2012 to raise around $16 billion for a slice of the equity. This constituted the largest ever flotation for an Internet company, and it valued Facebook in excess of $100 billion—which some thought was too high.

Jack Dorsey, Evan Williams and Twitter

Jack Dorsey and Evan Williams are the two people whose names are most commonly linked to the development of Twitter, which has become the first-choice communications and social networking vehicle for many people. With Facebook, users have their own pages, onto which they paste information, photos and blogs and offer access to people they select. These pages do not have to be free and open-access. Twitter is rather different. 'Tweets' that users post are limited to 140 characters; any registered Twitter user can read anyone else's tweets and know theirs can potentially be read by very large numbers of people—people who, for whatever reason, have chosen to follow them. Their short posts can be a means of communicating information but they can also be a question—when they get responses, Twitter has become a search engine for them.

Launched in 2006, some 100 million people were using Twitter by September 2011; this number had doubled by December 2012. Some people send very few tweets whilst others tweet routinely all day long. The average—for what that might mean—is around 2.5 tweets per user per day. The most popular (those with the most registered followers) are celebrities: Justin Bieber (36 million followers) and Lady Gaga (35 million followers) are able to promote their music through tweets. Interestingly, though, President Barack Obama has 27 million followers and can thus use Twitter to try and influence public opinion.

Tweets can allow the news to build in layers, as short posts keep adding to the story. The media use tweets to both disperse and collect stories. Whilst this can be, and often is, very positive, there is a potential downside. It has been claimed that Twitter was the main vehicle used to rally people and supporters to riot in London some while back. That said, many tweets have no apparent or obvious point. They are fundamentally an opinion or a fact without any serious meaning. But shared ideas can be a spur to some people; after all, where do we get the basis for many of the ideas we have?

Jack Dorsey spent part of his teenage years writing routing and despatching software for taxis and truckers. He continued this work and developed related web businesses; it was from this that he had the idea for a short-message communications system.

Evan Williams is a serial software entrepreneur and a capable computer-code writer. He often sold the businesses he started, including one to Google, and moved on to the next challenge. He drifted into blog software and is credited with inventing the terms 'blogger' and 'blogging'. From this, his interest moved to podcasting and he co-founded a company called Odeo.

Dorsey approached Odeo with his new idea and, working with various people from Odeo, Twitter was developed as a free social networking and micro-blogging service. Financial backing and personal support from Williams was instrumental. Twitter was later spun out as a separate company and Williams was CEO between 2008 and 2010 before he moved on to the next challenge.

When Twitter was floated in New York in 2013, the business was valued at $25 billion. Williams held 12 per cent of the shares and Dorsey 5 per cent.

It has to be debatable whether Zuckerberg, Dorsey or Williams had any inkling of what they might be starting when they set out to develop their ideas. There is clearly a strong element of emergence, and perhaps a philosophy of 'if you build it, they will come'. But nevertheless, they saw something others didn't. And they knew how to build it. And they did build it. And it worked. And people liked it. As a consequence, they changed the behaviour of a generation and transformed personal communications.

1.7 Community entirepreneurship

Our stories generally focus on individuals and sometimes small teams, but it is possible for a community to be or become entirepreneurial, such that a cluster of entrepreneurial businesses develop. In such a community, a vision for new possibilities somehow takes hold and gives direction. The process and outcomes might seem somewhat unexpected and serendipitous, but people soon seem to 'get it'. Both entrepreneurs and enablers appreciate what is happening and want to be part of it.

Silicon Valley

Silicon Valley is a prime example of this, with a vision related to the potential of emerging computer-related technologies and the synergistic power of a community of both interlinked and competing businesses. Enablers such as Frederick Terman from Stanford University encouraged and facilitated new ventures; Terman introduced Bill Hewlett and Dave Packard (they were both his students). He subsequently built the Stanford Research Park, which provided the foundation for Silicon Valley as other new businesses opted to locate to this part of California. Fairchild Semiconductor and, later, Intel were started by ex-employees of Bell Laboratories in New Jersey who were attracted to the West Coast. The transistor had earlier been invented at Bell. Sometime later, of course, Steve Jobs co-founded Apple with Steve Wozniak in Silicon Valley.

One thing basically led to another: support mechanisms included venture capitalists who wanted to be close to the emerging businesses, and both formal and informal networks. Encouraged by Stanford's initiative, more and more land was made available for start-up businesses and a physical infrastructure was soon evident. There was a culture of sharing with, and learning from, other businesses. An opportunity paradigm took hold, built around, first, a belief in the potential of semiconductors and, later, personal computers. Inevitably there were some setbacks and failures, but Silicon Valley's rapid progress became an inspiration for other countries to try and replicate the phenomenon. Silicon Glen around Cambridge in the UK is an example, but Silicon Valley remains unique in the way that all the key variables came together to establish a community that is truly entirepreneurial.

The knife-makers of Laguiole

The community of knife-makers in Laguiole, France is also entirepreneurial, but this is a quite different story. Here, an innovative design for a farmer's knife led to the development of a local industry with several independent assemblers, based on tradition, hand-crafting and high quality. The design of the Laguiole knife was never patented, but the distinctive bee symbol which is used as decoration on every genuine knife has come to symbolise 'France's most celebrated knife'. Less expensive copies are produced in various Asian countries.

Laguiole is a small mountain village in south-western France. In the 1820s shepherds and cattle herders from the village often crossed into Spain to find work in winter; they brought back, as souvenirs, Navaja switch-blade knives. Local French cutlers blended aspects of these Navaja knives with features from existing French fixed-blade 'dagger' knives and created a superior model.

The basis of the knife always was, and still is, a single blade made from non-rusting carbon steel (stainless is now offered as an alternative). Carefully placed notches prevent the handler's index finger from slipping on the blade, which is housed in a distinctively shaped cut-away handle, and which can be made from various woods, horn or even ivory tusks. Spring stops protect the blade when closing the knife. The knives, when closed, are around ten centimetres long. Whilst the knife might have been referred to as a farmer's knife, it was used domestically as well as for work tasks. Typically, men would cut their meat and bread with one.

Additional features are available. The most popular are an awl (or punch) which shepherds originally used to pierce the skin of a bloated sheep in order to release surplus gas, and a corkscrew, which was introduced in the 1880s. A small cross was also normally embedded into the handle; removed and held, this allowed the shepherds to feel more comfortable when they were away from the village church and wanted to pray.

Laguiole's forge services several independent knife assemblers and their workshops, many of which are co-located. Producing a single-blade knife involves over one-hundred discrete steps; this number doubles if there are two extra features. Every knife is made with a 'one man, one knife' philosophy. Some workshops also manufacture individual corkscrews and steak knives.

1.8 Social transformers

Anita Roddick and The Body Shop

The Body Shop, which sources and retails (mainly through franchises) natural lotions and cosmetics, has been a highly successful business with a price-to-earnings ratio that stayed well above the retail sector average throughout the 1980s before declining as a result of expansion, competition and acquisition. Until 1999, mainly through a series of acquisitions, The Body Shop manufactured at least half of the products it sold. In many respects, its success has been linked to the brand and the values with which it is associated. The Body Shop has always been idiosyncratic, unusual, high-profile and controversial in some circles. When the first shop opened some undertakers were allegedly horrified at the name.

The Body Shop was started in England in 1976 by the late Anita Roddick and her husband, Gordon, who used their savings of £12,000 to open the first shop, partially to help provide an income for Anita and her two daughters. 'It was never meant to be serious—it was just to pay bills and the mortgage.' Shortly after the business was started, Gordon took a sabbatical leave to fulfil a lifelong dream and rode a horse from Buenos Aires to New York. Stores were subsequently opened in over 40 countries, and The Body Shop was floated on the UK Stock Exchange in 1984. Well-renowned for its environmental and ethical stance and strategies, The Body Shop made an impact around the world. 'If you think you are too small to have an impact, try going to bed with a mosquito' (Roddick).

As the business began to grow, Anita was increasingly influenced by her personal commitments to the environment, education and social change. Simply, her talent for business was channelled into a cause. She said, 'I am, in my skin, an activist. I am trying to free guys in prison in America and stop sweatshops. When I went into business, I didn't think you had to leave yourself and your beliefs at the door.' The business and its financial success has been a vehicle to achieve other, more important, objectives. The Body Shop's declared 'Reason for Being' dedicated the business to the 'pursuit of social and environmental change'. Roddick wanted to do something which was 'economically sustainable, [and] meeting the needs of the present without compromising the future'. Her ideas were the outcome of her world travels. She had visited many third-world countries, 'living native', and had seen how women used natural products efficaciously and effectively. She noticed how women in Tahiti rubbed their bodies with cocoa butter to produce soft, satin-like skin despite a hot climate. She realised women in Morocco used mud to give their hair a silky sheen. She also saw Mexicans successfully treat burns with aloes, the slimy juice from cactus leaves. From these observations and experiences she conceptualised—and realised—her opportunity. She would use natural products from around the world to produce a range of new products. People in third-world villages were asked to supply her with the natural ingredients she needed; a form of trade, not aid. The Body Shop has always been very strong on environmental issues, offering only biodegradable products and refillable containers. There is no testing on animals, although there have been accusations to the contrary.

The Body Shop has always aroused enthusiasm, commitment and loyalty amongst those involved with it. The sales staff are generally knowledgeable, and when Roddick was in charge she encouraged them not to be forceful or sell aggressively, and to offer advice only if requested.

The Body Shop was initially able to effectively integrate manufacturing and retailing and was efficient and operationally strong. Fresh supplies were typically delivered to its stores with a 24-hour lead time. These strategies, policies and beliefs generated substantial growth and profits in the 1980s, but global scale and success brings added complexity and global competition. 'As the business grew it lost some of its entrepreneurial spirit'—something which is not unusual. Leading UK retailers such as Boots, Marks & Spencer and Sainsbury's introduced natural products in their own label ranges; a further threat was posed by the US company Bath & Body Works, whose early trial stores were a joint venture with Next. Bath & Body Works became renowned as a fast-moving organisation, quick to innovate new ideas, and aggressive at advertising and promotion. In 1998, with shares trading at under 100 pence, Anita joined Gordon as a Co-Chairman, and a new Chief Executive was recruited from outside the company. In 1999, The Body Shop withdrew from manufacturing and established a strong supply network instead, after which neither Anita nor Gordon had any executive responsibilities in the business with which they remained irrevocably linked. (Anita was, however, retained as a creative consultant.) In 2006, the company was sold to French cosmetics group L'Oréal for £650 million. Anita Roddick died in September 2007.

Mohammed Yunus

The name of Mohammed Yunus is most closely associated with microfinance; indeed, he won a Nobel Prize for his achievements in this field. The Grameen Bank that he started is effectively a bank of self-help in the private sector. It needs to be profitable in order to survive, but it exists to help people achieve something for themselves.

Mohammed Yunus was educated in both his home country of Bangladesh and America; in 1974 he was an economics professor at the University of Chittagong. He met a woman who made bamboo footstools in a small local village. Her bamboo suppliers allowed her credit as long as she sold the finished stools to them—at a price comfortably below the price they would be able to sell them at. In other words, and not atypically in some developing countries, the balance of power lay with the distributors and not the manufacturers, who are in some way or other restricted in their ability to access markets and get a fair price for their products. Concerned that what he saw was unfair practice, Yunus 'did the sums' and worked out that a loan of just $27 would allow her to buy the bamboo without credit and thus sell the finished stools at a higher price. He also believed—and he has been proved right—that people able to borrow these small amounts will be keen to pay them back as then their earnings are even higher.

Yunus first approached a traditional bank, which agreed to work with him as long as he was able to provide a degree of security for a loan which effectively he would be loaning on. This was affordable to him individually, so he agreed—but time and experience showed that the necessary administration, which was in part handed over to him, delayed everything. So, and with some Central Bank support, he ended up starting what amounted to his own local bank. This was known as the Grameen Bank Project, and it led to other similar banks in various villages. The Grameen Bank grew out of the project and was up-and-running by 1983. Initially the state owned 60 per cent, but it was not very long before the clients were recognised as the major shareholders, with 75 per cent of the ownership. Donations from benefactors were accepted, but an offered loan from the World Bank of $200 million was rejected because of the imposed conditions.

Success has bred success and new supporters have come on board. The bank has grown in size and made hundreds of thousands of small loans—a loan would generally be between $70 and $130. Business activities supported include mat making, fishing nets, napkins, sweet meats, garments, pottery, farming and trading, food stalls, rickshaw drivers and people with push carts who move stuff around in markets and similar places. The Grameen Bank concept has spread to Pakistan, India, Nepal, China and the Philippines. It covers 60 per cent of Bangladesh with its multiple local and independent branches.

Traditional bank loans to small- and micro-business owners in Bangladesh, when they were available, would require repayment in a single sum after some agreed period of time, and women would be largely excluded from the facility. The Grameen Bank offers the opportunity for lots of small, regular repayments—even daily payments. Loans will be expected to be paid off in a year, although more can be advanced afterwards. There is a great emphasis on trust; collateral is neither demanded nor expected. The focus is on women, who comprise the majority of clients. Yunus dedicated considerable time to going out to the villages to explain everything to would-be customers and win over their trust. Rarely are loans made for any significant amount—but, then again, larger amounts are not needed to underpin an economy such as this. It is an entrepreneurial approach to support enterprising people—it gets around the bureaucracy that not only slowed things down but also made microfinancing too expensive for some people to contemplate.

David Bussau

Like Mohammed Yunus, David Bussau has transformed lives. Whilst he is also involved in microfinance for the developing world, his story is rather different. Bussau became a millionaire from a series of business interests and then focused his not-inconsiderable talents on helping poor people.

David Bussau spent the first 16 years of his life (1940–1956) in an orphanage in New Zealand, and the next 19 years making his fortune as an entrepreneurial businessman. When he left the orphanage with 'no family, no close friends and no money' he managed to start a hot-dog stand. Within six months he had six other people leasing stands from him. With his profits David bought (and later sold) a small bakery and then a biscuit factory and a pancake restaurant. He never had any formal business education; he was simply able to grow businesses.

In his mid-20s, after marrying, he sold off his ventures and moved to Australia. His wife was ill at the time, and they believed that for her particular condition the medical facilities in Australia were superior to those in New Zealand. He got a job in construction. Perhaps inevitably, he was soon to become a partner in the business he joined—before he bought the business outright and used it as a base to set up a whole series of construction firms. He was a millionaire before he was 35.

On Christmas Day in 1974, Darwin (in the Northern Territory) was devastated by a cyclone. A committed Christian, Bussau set off with 20 of his employees to help—short-term—with rescue and rebuilding activities. This experience changed his philosophy of life. A year later, David sold a number of his businesses, leaving managers in charge of the others, and moved with his wife and family to Darwin to continue helping with the rebuilding programme. In 1976 the whole family moved to Bali, to help there in the aftermath of an earthquake. There he organised the construction of a dam, bridge, clinic and an irrigation system. He earned nothing from this; in reality, he invested in these projects. Travelling around Bali he sensed potential entrepreneurs who were being held back by a lack of money at affordable rates of interest. He started making small, short-term loans to very poor people. Some would buy tools which they would use to boost their family income. Others would buy basic ingredients and bake them into saleable products.

He returned to Australia, but was persuaded to go back to Bali in 1980. With the help of others, he set up a church-based revolving credit scheme to provide short-term loans. Local banks were not interested in loaning small amounts such as the $50 AUD that microbusinesses required to start up, because their processing costs made the rates of interest prohibitive. Bussau's idea was for small loans, paid back very quickly so the money can be re-lent to others. A first loan could, of course, be followed by subsequent, and usually larger, loans as the businesses began to grow. The interest charged covered the operating costs and nothing more. Project officials also provided advice to the small businesses whilst ever they had a loan. Now under the umbrella organisation to which he was linked (Opportunity International), there are over 40 partner agencies in 19 other countries around the world. At any one time the number of active loans is between one and one-and-a-half million. Over 80 per cent of these are to women and the repayment rate is 95 per cent. Opportunity International's assets are in the order of $550 million with a loan portfolio of $400 million. Although Christianity is at the heart of the programme, two-thirds of the loans have been made to non-Christians. In 2002 micro-insurance was added to the portfolio.

In recent years Bussau has concentrated on persuading other Christian business leaders in developing countries to 'use the gifts and skills God has given them to help the poor'. In 2008 he was recognised as the 'Senior Australian of the Year', and his story is an excellent example of someone following the Christian preaching of John Wesley: make as much as you can; save as much as you can; give away as much as you can.

We retain the Christian theme in the next two stories of influential social transformers from the Victorian era—**entirepreneurs** whose legacies are still important today.

Florence Nightingale

Florence Nightingale was born in 1820, the daughter of well-off and well-connected parents. Her parents and society had expectations for the way she would grow up and spend her adult life, but Florence was determined to be different. As a child she was 'exceptionally intelligent', and at the age of 17 she began to believe she was called to the service of God in some way or another. However, the next five years of her life comprised foreign travel. She returned to England in 1842 to find a country in the grip of an economic depression, where poverty, starvation and disease were manifest and widespread. She upset her family and friends by opting out of the social life she was expected to enjoy, turning down offers of marriage, and ultimately deciding that her vocation lay in hospital work and in helping sick people. In the 1840s 'the only qualification required for nursing the sick was to be a woman'. Nursing was not perceived to be a worthy occupation for Florence. No skills or training were required, and the female nurses were 'frequently drunk and an occasional prostitute with the male patients'. Her parents were horrified and opposed her choice. Nevertheless, Florence was determined and persistent. Whilst caring for sick members of her family and their friends, she started studying both medicine and administration.

In 1851 she was able to visit Kaiserswerth, a dedicated training centre for nurses in Germany, and in 1853 she finally persuaded her parents to support her application for the honorary post of Superintendent at the Institute for the Care of Sick Gentlewomen in Distressed Circumstances. She used this opportunity to transform nursing practices. One year later she helped nurse cholera patients at the Middlesex Hospital during a major epidemic. Florence's vision for a new form of nursing care to support doctors was becoming clearer. She became determined to make nursing a respectable profession for women who were skilled, trained and professional. She believed this would provide a foundation for higher standards of hygiene in hospitals; at this time hygiene was inadequate except for the hospitals where nuns provided nursing care. But, of course, the nuns were again not trained in any formalised way.

Drawing on family connections, she obtained permission to form a team of nurses who would travel to Crimea and care for the war casualties. In first obtaining the permission, and then when she was out there, she exploited the fact that this was the first overseas war where journalists were providing newspapers back home with regular reports on progress and conditions. Finding it difficult to recruit the volunteers she wanted, Florence ended up with 24 nuns in a group of 38, and at Scutari she found a field hospital 'where a soldier was more likely to die than if he were fighting on the battlefield'. She was also resented by senior army staff and had to overcome a series of obstacles. Tackling issues of diet, supplies, sewers and drainage, and the actual physical handling of the casualties, she was still able to demonstrate a real difference in just six months. Through her persistence, she succeeded in transforming the perception people had of nurses and nursing care. Suddenly Florence Nightingale had become a national heroine.

After the Crimean War she initially withdrew from public life and devoted herself to taking her campaign to senior politicians and the Royal Family. Afterwards, she was again active in the establishment of new civilian hospitals and training schools for civilian nurses. In essence, her work and inspiration provided the foundation for the modern nursing profession.

William and Catherine Booth

William Booth was a contemporary of Florence Nightingale. Born the son of a Nottingham builder in 1829, he moved to London after the death of his father and found work as a pawnbroker's assistant. He had already converted to Christianity and he became a revivalist Methodist preacher, arguing that church ministers should pursue a strong social role as well as their pastoral one. (He was later to practice what he preached.) Not atypically, he saw women as 'the weaker sex', but married a strong, self-willed woman, Catherine Mumford, in 1955. Outraging many Christians, Catherine herself began preaching in 1860. Soon supported by an originally sceptical husband, she was 'outstanding and inspirational'.

As a preacher in Nottingham, Booth attracted socially deprived converts to Christianity at his open-air meetings, but those who were particularly dirty and smelly were not always welcomed in chapel by other Methodists. In 1865, working together, William and Catherine opened a Christian mission in Whitechapel, a district in the squalid East End of London, to help feed and house the poor. Their trigger had been the poverty and social deprivation they had witnessed. At this time they had seven of their eight children; their eldest son, Bramwell, soon joined them in the mission work, as did Booth's second key assistant, George Scott Railton, a Christian businessman from Middlesbrough who read of the mission and came to London specifically to work alongside Booth. Booth had now built a strong central team. When the mission was reorganised along military command lines in 1878, with the preachers called officers and William Booth the General, the Salvation Army was formed.

Influenced by Catherine, the Salvation Army gave equal preaching and welfare responsibilities to women. The services were informal and 'joyous music' played a significant role. Again not unexpectedly, there was hostility from the established Church of England. Army members were imprisoned for open-air preaching and Booth was declared the 'Anti-Christ' for his support of women preachers. But the Army prospered—more and more people joined and opened citadels throughout the country. Booth started his own newspaper, *The War Cry*, and wrote a book about social conditions in England, offering his personal suggestions for overcoming poverty.

Booth's entrepreneurial characteristics were clearly demonstrated when he became determined to improve the working conditions for women at the local

East End Bryant & May match factory. Pay was low, but more significantly the women's health was being damaged by Bryant & May's preference for using yellow phosphorus for the match heads. Toxic fumes caused skin discolouration, followed by discharging pores and ultimately death from necrosis of the bone. Other European countries had begun to use harmless red phosphorus as an alternative, but the campaigning Booth was told this would prove uneconomical. Consequently, in 1891, the Salvation Army opened its own match factory in competition. Workers were paid double the Bryant & May rate, and, using red phosphorus, Booth was soon producing and selling six million boxes a year. Members of Parliament and journalists were encouraged to visit the 'model factory and compare the conditions with other sweat shops'. In 1901 Bryant & May also switched to red phosphorus.

The Salvation Army became established abroad, and Booth himself travelled widely throughout the UK, America and Australia. He died in 1912 at the age of 83, 20 years after his wife. Railton died very shortly afterwards and consequently Bramwell Booth succeeded his father as General. The growth and significance of the Salvation Army has clearly continued. Indeed, when the widow of Ray Kroc (McDonald's) died, she left a legacy of $1.5 billion to the Salvation Army, largely to build community centres.

Harish Hande and SELCO

SELCO is short for the Solar Energy Light Company, which is a declared 'for profit social enterprise' based in Bangalore, India. Its activities are concentrated in the poor rural areas away from, but relatively close to, the wealth-creating software businesses in that part of India.

SELCO was established to help improve the living conditions of poor rural households, many of which are made up of local farmers growing a few crops or producing milk they can sell to yield some income. Annual incomes of around $1,000 are typical. The company provides solar 'interventions' for lighting and heating water and also provides low-smoke cooking stoves. When solar panels appear on houses in the developed world they are normally placed flat to the tiled roof to attract the sun's rays. But these rural farmers are more likely to have thatched-roof houses, so the panels are raised above the roof and mounted on a post which protrudes through the roof itself. They look rather like television aerials. They are not a replacement for electricity, which is available in some places but from a system that is likely to crash at any time, especially if there is peak demand. Instead, kerosene burners are more popular.

Dr Harish Hande was a PhD student in America—an engineer—when he imagined what SELCO could become. The conceptual model was part of his thesis. In 1994 he returned to India and persuaded Tata BP Solar to let him have a single solar panel on credit, which he could then sell to and install for a wealthy small farmer. Once he had a customer, a sale and was paid for the installation, he carried on in the same vein to prove the concept. The problem was that his target market would not be able to pay in full for the solar installations.

Hande got to know Neville Williams, founder of a non-profit solar energy business in the US, and he agreed to co-found SELCO with a modest personal investment. This got the business off the ground in 1995, and in 1997 they received a loan of $130,000 from the United States Agency for International Development (USAid). Later, some $1.5 million equity capital was provided by five social investors.

Hande's revenue model was based on the premise that a customer would be expected to pay between 15 and 25 per cent of the installation cost, ideally at the higher end of this range. A basic installation would cost $450, which usually amounted to about a month's income. The intention was that the rest be paid in monthly instalments at an agreed affordable level. It has been said that the prevailing borrowing philosophy amongst local farmers was that '300 rupees a month is expensive; 10 rupees a day is affordable'. Loans and repayments was not something they were necessarily used to—in large part because nobody was willing to lend them money.

Hande set out on a charm-offensive with local banks and suggested they see loans to fund the down payments as a form of well-intended microfinancing—even though it was really directed at improving lives rather than supporting a business. But he succeeded, and millions have been lent. The default percentage is under 10 per cent. The banks were not being commercially negligent: the local people would actually be able to save on their energy costs with solar power and so be in a position to pay the interest on the loans as well as SELCO. Over 125,000 systems have been installed at a cost of over $50 million. The investment in SELCO and the local bank finance has circulated well.

It was 2000 before SELCO broke even, but the ambitious Hande was drawn to establish a franchised dealer network in the state. This did not turn out to be a sound strategic move and proved expensive for SELCO, which lost money. The problem was that the global cost of solar panels was increasing and the opportunity for franchisees was lower than forecast. SELCO managed to get emergency funding from the International Finance Corporation, part of the World Bank, and this kept the business going. The loan is still being serviced. SELCO now employs some 170 people who work through 25 service centres, each with a dedicated rural area.

One important spin-off from stories like this is that they show what can be done and thus encourage others to replicate their achievements, albeit in different ways. In the 2013 Google Global Impact Awards, for example, a UK-based charity, SolarAid, was awarded £500,000 to distribute 144,000 solar-powered lights to rural villages across Tanzania in order to replace the use of kerosene lamps. Successful interventions of this nature can transform the lives of socially and economically disadvantaged people and can, therefore, amount to entirepreneurship in action.

Michael Young

When Lord Michael Young died in 2001 an obituary in the *Guardian* described him as an 'educator, author, consumer advocate, policy maker, political activist, rebel, innovator and entrepreneur who seeded social ideas and institutions'. We would describe him as an **entirepreneur**, but an unusual one. He was a great believer in change and progress but he wanted to be sure they met people's needs. He was also an enabler who instigated change and who, once something was properly established, moved on to a fresh challenge. His many achievements include: The Consumers' Association and *Which?* Magazine, The National Consumer Council, the Open University, The University of the Third Age, the School for Social Entrepreneurs and the Economic and Social Research Council (ESRC). In this story we focus on his transformative impact on UK education.

Michael Young was born in Manchester in 1915. His father was an Australian violinist and his mother an Irish painter and actor. He was first brought up in Melbourne but came back to England at age eight when his parents' marriage crumbled. His own childhood was insecure and he attended several schools before his Australian grandfather paid for him to attend the progressive Dartington Hall in Devon. Here he learnt fruit farming; it was assumed he might return to Tasmania and farm. He loved the school and felt at home there. Afterwards he graduated and qualified as a barrister at Gray's Inn in London. He was overlooked for World War II as he was an asthma sufferer, but he did work as a manager in a munitions factory. By 1944 he had become Director of Research for the Labour Party and had worked extensively on the post-war manifesto. He was a key draftsman of what became the Welfare State. Although he has said some senior Labour politicians did not expect to win the 1945 election and could therefore think 'outside the box'—not anticipating having to actually implement the policies—he personally forecast the outcome.

He left this role in 1950 and studied for a PhD in sociology at the London School of Economics and Political Science; he became a prolific researcher and author who came to believe he could continue to achieve more by staying outside government and raising money to set up new institutions.

Asked how he achieved what he did accomplish, he summarised it as follows (we paraphrase his words):

> Spot a problem, imagine a solution, give it a working title, write to everyone you can think of who might be interested and seek their views, write a paper summarising your opinions and theirs, form a steering committee, set up a charitable trust, keep talking about it to others, launch it to the press, apply for funding, stick with it as long as you need to and then move on once it is established.

Simple, really. He always encouraged others 'to go for it', saying that 'there will always be resistance to new ideas. The only way to overcome this is guile and persistence… . Don't dismiss all your good ideas if they don't initially seem like good ideas to your friends and others.' Ideas flowed throughout his life.

A number of names, including leading politicians, have been associated with the founding of the Open University (OU) in 1969. The OU provided part-time distance learning degree-level education via open media, especially broadcast television in the early days, and thus brought part-time education opportunities to a new, larger and more socially inclusive market. It catered to 'people who had slipped through the rungs of the conventional education system'. Prime Minister Harold Wilson was a visible and important champion. But five years before it got underway Michael Young wrote a paper proposing it and also started an early version, The National Extension College in Cambridge. He had put the foundation—the building blocks—in place. The vision he had proposed for education was way ahead of conventional thinking. The real success, however, came down to fresh ideas on resourcing and delivery. Students had access to excellent dedicated and tailor-made teaching materials in book and multimedia formats, written by staff who were expert in both their subject and in written communications. Students were also exposed to many other university academics who agreed to work part-time for the Open University on weekends and at summer schools. Local tutors provided coaching to small groups and one-to-one at times that were convenient for the students. It was not long before some assignments were carried out online.

When the brand new, state-of-the-art Open University Business School opened in 2001, the year Michael Young died, it was named after him. Before the OU, around 10 per cent of the population received degree-level education. This number has since more than quadrupled. The OU, of course, is not the explanation for this growth in access—the number of universities and degree courses have both grown significantly—but one might wonder about the extent to which Michael Young's early intervention was catalytic, opening a floodgate to rapid innovation and progress.

Ebenezer Howard

Sir Ebenezer Howard, the driver of the Garden City movement in the UK, is not really a well-known figure, and yet his legacy and influence has affected urban planning around the world.

Howard was born in 1850, the son of a shopkeeper in London. His family was able to send him away to school in the country, but afterwards he returned to London and worked in an office as a shorthand writer. When he was 21 he emigrated to America and tried his hand at farming, but this wasn't a successful venture for him. He returned to office work in Chicago, which was being rebuilt after the great fire of 1871. He witnessed regeneration with a genuine intent to incorporate green areas in the form of gardens and parks.

Back in the UK, where he returned to work in the Houses of Parliament, he saw Victorian poverty. The migration of people from the countryside to towns, in part driven by the Industrial Revolution, had led to urban sprawls with congestion, poor living conditions, little open space, disease and poverty. He knew how Parliament saw the problems and issues, as his job was to record debates. In his mind, they did not have the answers. He was inspired to a different vision by an American book proposing the design for a utopian city. He set about writing his own book, suggesting a broad design for a new town that was able to blend in harmony the best of the countryside with the best of urban living, without the inherent drawbacks that each had. Key buildings like a hospital would be central and easily accessible; main transport routes would be on the periphery; people would have access to green spaces. He used his own resources to publish the book and then, generally without payment, he travelled and spoke anywhere in the country where people would listen to him.

Industrialists such as the Cadbury family, William Lever and Titus Salt had already built model towns for their workforces, each on a limited scale. Howard was proposing a much bigger initiative. Social benefactors offered him support and he was able to raise the money to start building a new Garden City. This began in 1903 and it became Letchworth Garden City (or Letchworth). It was acknowledged as a success, but Howard was convinced that one single new Garden City would not be enough to prove his concept. He set out to raise the support and build another. This would become Welwyn Garden City, which was built in the 1920s. Howard himself saw most of the work completed; he died in 1928. He was knighted the year before he died. His place in history was secure.

He had earlier created the Garden Cities Association, which eventually became the Town and Country Planning Association. It is generally accepted that it was Howard's ideas that influenced the design of later new towns such as Stevenage and Milton Keynes. His ideas also influenced urban planners around the world. He was neither an architect nor a planner, but he was a man with a vision, a determination to act on his ideas and an ability to secure support and resources. Critically, he was able to persuade others to follow him and his ideas.

In early 2014 the press carried reports that two new Garden Cities were being considered as an alternative for dealing with the housing shortage in the UK.

1.9 Sports entirepreneurs

Sir Alex Ferguson

Sir Alex Ferguson is the most successful 'manager' in English football. He retired, aged 71, in 2013 after being in charge at Manchester United for 27 years. Whilst it is typical for the person in charge of the team (not the football club's CEO) to be called the 'manager' (and more characteristically to be known as 'the boss') some are much more than managers in any conventional sense. Ferguson certainly was, to the point that his style and approach have been studied by Harvard Business School. Some managers, certainly in other European countries, might have achieved more in the short term, but his longevity and consistency single him out. He rebuilt and steered his club through waves of change in professional football—'he was able to change as the game changed'. He commented, 'I believe that you control change by accepting it.'

When Ferguson arrived at Manchester United in 1986 the club had not won the league title for 19 years; Ferguson himself had enjoyed some success in management in Scotland, following a modest playing career. Manchester United had lost much of its team in 1958 in the well-known Munich air crash and since then had enjoyed some great successes but without true consistency. When he started, Ferguson set out to study, ask questions and listen; he wanted to understand the culture and values of the club before he set out to change things. Ferguson's win rate was 60 per cent over 1,500 matches—with another 22 per cent of matches ending in draws. He lost fewer than one in five matches over many years, and under him United won 38 trophies, including, in 1999, the Premier League, FA Cup and UEFA Champions League, or 'The Treble'.

Ferguson built a football club rather than a football team. Determined to learn, improve and master the professional game, he successfully built (and dismantled) several winning teams, each one around a series of key influential players that he brought in. He was regarded as inspirational and sometimes able to realise promise that others had failed to bring out in players, some of them difficult characters to manage. With his purchases he was an opportunist—in addition to talent, he was also able to sense when certain gifted players were ready to move for a fresh challenge. But he also presided over the building of a new stadium with a capacity of 76,000, which he was able to fill match after match. He also made Manchester United into a global brand and saw it bought by American businessmen of the Glazer family. Fans and players are fiercely loyal; Ferguson's background in the Glasgow shipyards has made 'group solidarity and macho leadership' instinctive to him. He has attracted criticism for challenging authority and losing his temper, however; the media made a great deal of him once throwing a hairdryer at David Beckham (and hitting him with it). Basically he was strong but respected.

He was a master tactician, helped by a strong and hand-picked team. His approach was to delegate training sessions to his coaching team but to always watch and observe everything from the touchline. A lover of attractive football, he was arguably inspired by Real Madrid's approach in the 1960s. He was intelligent, passionate and strong. 'His ability to think on several levels at once, and across 10 to 12 problems simultaneously, is rare.' Clearly he had command of both the 'big picture' and the details. He rotated his squad, mixing experienced players with new blood. He was willing to sell players who were at the top of their game if it was, in his mind, right for the team. He sold David Beckham when he was still maturing and traded Cristiano Ronaldo, whom he bought as a youngster, for £80 million to Real Madrid. He was a consummate networker—'always on the phone'—keen to find out what was happening in the game and who might be available.

He was very strong on motivation, believing some players lack real commitment. He knew all his players well and treated each as an individual. He built a reputation for teams who never gave up. Many matches were won in the last few minutes, sometimes with extra-time goals. It was rare that one of his teams would fade at the end of a tiring season; generally it was exactly the opposite. They could be relied on to finish strongly. The phrase 'Fergie time' was coined for his alleged ability to persuade officials to add on extra minutes at the end if United was losing.

He became regarded as 'unsackable' for his consistent success, and this worked in his favour. It allowed him to take a long-term perspective in a game where immediate results seem to count for so much and managers are frequently blamed and sacked when results are poor. At the same time, his personal loyalty to the club and its owners never seemed to be in question. The relationship seemed to be one of mutual respect and trust. It is interesting that in recent years the four leading clubs in the English Premier League have been United, Arsenal, Chelsea and Manchester City. Arsenal has stable management; Chelsea and Manchester City, both with big-spending benefactor owners, have hired and fired managers almost routinely.

Writing about professional sport in the *Independent* newspaper and citing Sir Clive Woodward, who coached England Rugby Union to its only World Cup win, Brian Ashton says, 'New managers, if that's what they should be called, should have some entrepreneurial spirit. ... This entrepreneur shows leadership by selecting the correct staff; he perceives opportunities that others may not see, or at least before others do; he is prepared to take risks in pursuit of eventual success; he shows himself to be innovative in his grasp of any new technologies that might be available, increasing efficiency and productivity as a consequence; he acts as a catalyst for change.' Ashton might have been describing Ferguson—he was certainly describing the **entirepreneur**.

Kerry Packer

Kerry Packer was a successful media magnate who created World Series Cricket in the 1970s and thus transformed the game—introducing floodlit games, bringing in new money, and later heralding the popular twenty over cricket that fans love but others criticise. 'He took a game run by amateurs, played by part-time professionals, and watched for the most part by a coterie of aficionados and turned it into an entertainment experience' (Bob Stewart, Victoria University). Cricket simply became a richer and better-supported game—but it required serious change. The interesting aspect of this story is how Packer went about it.

Packer inherited his family's press holdings and television network in Australia. His station already transmitted some golf, but cricket was monopolised by the national network—Australia's equivalent of the BBC. The relatively new one-day limited over games were growing in popularity and he saw them as an attractive and lucrative opportunity. In 1975 he offered a much higher price for the television rights, but his bid was turned down by the Australian Cricket Board. He was incensed but unwilling to give up. In 1977 Australia toured England for an Ashes test series and some one-day internationals. He bid for the rights to televise these games in Australia and was awarded the contract by the English cricket authorities.

This proved successful, so he decided to create his own tournaments in various countries and sign up as professionals many well-known players from around the world, some of them nearing the end of their careers. The money was very tempting for several players, who automatically fell out of favour with their national teams for siding with Packer. He was able to sell 50,000 tickets for a limited-overs day and night match in Sydney. But what was particularly controversial was his team that toured South Africa. At the time, South Africa was banned from competing abroad as a nation because of apartheid; international teams simply did not go there. He just went ahead and took an international cricket team, which South Africa welcomed. The games attracted huge crowds because of the novelty element in a country starved of international sport. The whole tour was very high profile with massive media coverage. They may not have liked him, but the cricket authorities now simply had to deal with Packer.

Packer died at the age of 68 in 2005. He was 'the richest and one of the most influential men in Australia'. He might well have been described as 'larger than life'. He played polo aggressively and enjoyed a drink; he also gambled. It was reported (and confirmed) that in one night in London he lost £15 million playing roulette. 'He could charm the birds out of the trees, but he could be a brute' (Malcolm Turnbull, politician, quoted in the *Sydney Morning Herald*). Packer appears to be a person who succeeded by finding a winning formula, but perhaps one where the ends were seen by some, and perhaps even the majority, to justify the means.

Russell Coutts, Ben Ainslie and the America's Cup

This is a story about how entirepreneurial individuals can inspire a team to be entirepreneurial.

The America's Cup series of yacht races, between the current holder and a pre-selected challenger, lasts over several weeks and requires considerable preparation and dedication. When Team New Zealand won in 1995 it was only the second time a team from outside America had won in 144 years, the first being Australia in 1985. Moreover, in the 1995 America's Cup, including the elimination races to select the final challenger as well as the final itself, New Zealand won 41 and lost just one—an incredible margin of victory. The team had 'continually expanded its ability to create its destiny'. There had been a driving vision throughout the preparation and the race series: 'to build, modify and sail the fastest boat on any given day'. This vision had brought together the (technical) designers with the users (the sailors), and created synergy where often there is conflict. Their respective perspectives are, quite simply, different. Team New Zealand was successful in defending the trophy in 2000, but then events took an unexpected turn.

There are normally 17 sailors on board an America's Cup boat. The Skipper has overall responsibility and is the leader whilst the team is at sea. He relies on his Tactician (who makes critical decisions about changing course as the race unfolds) and Navigator (who looks after the sophisticated electronic tracking instrumentation). A Helmsman steers the boat and a Strategist monitors the slightest changes of wind speed and direction. Decisions to alter course or rigging are often made very quickly and they need implementing instantaneously. There are then 11 sailors with specific roles mainly related to the deployment of the huge sails. The 17th man is really something of a spectator and is often a team sponsor.

In 1995 and 2000 Team New Zealand had an inspirational but non-sailing leader in the form of Sir Peter Blake, who was an experienced sailor, but not the skipper of the actual crew. Nor was he an experienced boat designer. Blake convinced everyone that winning was possible, and set out to make sure that happened. Blake had built his reputation as a round-the-world challenge sailor and has been described as a 'meticulous planner and gifted leader who inspired loyalty'. The skipper was Russell Coutts. Coutts, 33 years old in 1995, was an Olympic gold medallist for sailing (in 1984) and a previous winner of many leading races. He was 'obsessive about detail and technically very skilled'. Blake and Coutts became a formidable partnership who provided leadership onshore and at sea. Together they took and practiced an entire perspective.

Blake held meetings between the designers and sailors at regular intervals during the build-up period and encouraged people to be creative in their search for different and unusual answers to problems and issues. Team New Zealand did not stop searching for improvements, even when they were winning every race! They built on their successes to reinforce their advantage. During the pre-race trials, Team New Zealand sailed two identical boats, rather than two different designs in competition. Their choice of design had been made by simulation. Because the two boats began as identical, any successful modifications to the design of one could be copied by the team sailing the other. As a result, considerable emphasis was placed on improving sailing skills as well. Here we can see considerable focus and attention to operational details.

The team was carefully selected to ensure they were people who would 'own' what they were taking on. They needed to have individual sailing skills and experience, but they had to be able to interact well with others. They also had to demonstrate they were able to handle disappointment and quickly put it behind them. Outstanding individuals who might be reluctant team players, however good they were personally, were rejected by Blake, who built his team around the tasks.

Could this successful combination defend the America's Cup for a second time in 2003 and make it three in a row? After the victory in 2000, both Russell Coutts and Tactician Brad Butterworth 'defected' to Alinghi, a team bankrolled by Swiss billionaire and yachting fanatic Ernesto Bertarelli, who would sail as the Navigator. A disagreement and fall-out with the non-sailing Directors of Team New Zealand was given as the reason by Coutts. The final Alinghi team for 2003 would include seven New Zealanders and just two Swiss sailors. Its successful challenge was devastating for New Zealanders as really it was the core of the previous winning New Zealand teams that won the America's Cup for a third time in a row—but this time for Switzerland, a country without a coastline! Blake, unfortunately, was unable to contribute to either team. In December 2001 he was shot on board his boat by people described as pirates whilst sailing up the Brazilian Amazon.

Alinghi would go on to defend the Cup successfully in Europe. Coutts left Alinghi in 2004, and was replaced by Butterworth. In 2007 Alinghi again defeated Team New Zealand (but only by the narrowest of margins in the final deciding race). Coutts was later recruited by the founder of the Oracle Corporation, entrepreneur and racing enthusiast Larry Ellison, to lead Oracle Team USA in a serious American bid for the 2010 America's Cup. They were successful, but again only by the narrow margin of 9 races to 8. (The winning team in the final is the first to nine wins.)

Oracle Team USA's final challenger in the 2013 series was again Team New Zealand. Coutts was once more in charge of the American team, but this time he seemed to be staring at defeat as Team New Zealand opened up a 6 to 1 lead. Sir Ben Ainslie, the British Olympic sailing multiple gold medal winner, was a member of the team but had yet to sail, when Coutts had appointed him as the new Tactician. Soon the losing margin was 8 to 1. Then, and inspired by Ainslie and his ability to read and respond to changing wind and weather conditions, this was turned around and Team USA triumphed by 9 races to 8; a remarkable change of fortunes.

Clearly then, certain individuals can make a very significant difference if they are the 'right person in the right place at the right time'.

1.10 Entertainment entirepreneurs

Gerald Durrell

Gerald Durrell is perhaps best known as a television presenter of serious programmes on zoology and animal conservation and for his 37 books, which mix fiction and non-fiction and were written for both the adult and children's markets. He has been described as a 'natural storyteller'. A dedicated conservationist, Durrell was able to fund his zoological work from his books and television work—both an enjoyable means to an end.

Durrell was born in 1925 (he died in 1995) and brought up in Corfu. His most successful book, *My Family and Other Animals*, recounts his childhood. He started working at Whipsnade Zoo but when he received a family inheritance (when he was 21) he was able to fund trips overseas to find and collect animals, most of which he sold to zoos. He also started writing. In 1959 he opened the Jersey Wildlife Preservation Trust (and associated zoo) and in time he found an effective balance between science, education and entertainment. He believed in the value of controlled breeding programmes in captivity for endangered species. His approach: provide a safe sanctuary, build a colony and then return some of the animals to the wild, but in a controlled environment. He spent much of his life in the field, building a team who could look after the work in Jersey. He tried to make his enclosures as natural as possible so the animals could be at least part-prepared for what they would face in the wild. He wanted to focus on those animals in greatest danger of extinction, which are often not necessarily the most attractive to zoo visitors, but also realised it was important to also have animals that would attract visitors. David Attenborough credits him with having a natural skill in 'handling animals and divining ways to make them happy'.

He was a pioneer, and many leading zoos, including London and San Diego, have later followed his lead. He had a fresh vision for animal conservation that became regarded as far-seeing but was, at the time, controversial. Attenborough summarises him as a 'renegade who was right'. He challenged conventional wisdom, 'but now everything he did seems so logical and obvious… . We easily forget how radical and revolutionary everything seemed at the time.'

In more recent times Attenborough, making use of modern photographic capability and his own natural style of broadcasting, has built on Durrell's pioneering work and has also had a transformational impact on the way we view wild animals, birds and the natural environment.

Guy Laliberté and Cirque du Soleil

The 'big top' travelling circuses of the type pioneered by showmen such as the legendary P.T. Barnum—and which featured animals, typically lions, tigers and elephants, alongside acrobats and the ubiquitous clowns—still exist, but they cannot command the audiences they once did. And there are fewer of them. The main ones today include the Ringling Bros. and Barnum & Bailey and the Russian and Chinese State circuses. Competition for the 'entertainment spend' has increased.

Spectacular specialist acts featuring animals became popular in Las Vegas many years ago, although when a white tiger mauled one of the partners in Siegfried & Roy in 2003, serious questions were raised about them. There were, of course, already many animal lovers who were critics of shows such as these. Meanwhile, the circus industry had been reinvented without needing animals.

Dubbed 'the New American Circus', Cirque du Soleil was started in Montreal, Quebec, Canada, in 1984, the invention of a small group of street performers led by partners Guy Laliberté and Daniel Gauthier. By the end of the century they had entertained some 30 million people with a range of innovative and daring production shows. The shows combine circus acts with performing arts and typically feature jugglers, trampolinists, trapeze artists and clowns who work together rather than have individual feature spots. The shows are operatic as well as acrobatic; they are choreographed; they stretch the talents of the performers; they are visually impressive; and they all have a clear theme or story.

The shows are different and innovative—and relatively highly priced. Originally the focus was on a traditional moveable 'big top', but quite soon Cirque du Soleil moved into dedicated resident theatres and also introduced some shows that worked in existing venues such as the Royal Albert Hall in London, which they visit regularly. Las Vegas was an obvious early target; Walt Disney World Resort is another home. When this story was written there were eight long-running shows on offer in different Las Vegas hotels and new residences were being prepared in Moscow and Dubai.

Fundamentally, Cirque du Soleil has eliminated animals and markedly cut down on the sales of food and other merchandise whilst the show itself is live—something quite different from the traditional circus and most American sporting events. There is less emphasis on thrills and danger—something circuses used to try and create competitive advantage—and a more creative use of different venues. What really sets it apart from the original circus model is its seamless element, where music, opera, dance and acrobatics are combined into a holistic show.

P.T. Barnum

Guy Laliberté successfully transformed and resurrected the circus. In his time, P.T Barnum had been similarly transformational. Born in Connecticut in 1810, he was destined to be America's second millionaire.

In his youth he sold lottery tickets and ran a newspaper. He would later produce New York's first illustrated newspaper and build a circulation of 500,000 regular customers. He became an incredible networker, befriending the rich and famous around the world. He knew Abraham Lincoln very well, Mark Twain was a close friend, and he went hunting with General Custer. At heart, though, he was an entertainer who succeeded by taking unknowns and making them into international stars. Examples of these stars were Tom Thumb, a tiny boy whom Barnum taught to sing and dance, Joice Heth, a black slave who was allegedly 160 years old and Jenny Lind, the Swedish soprano. One might question whether contemporary programmes such as *Britain's Got Talent*, which is by no means the first of its kind, recognise Barnum was on to something that can be made appealing to the public. In this context it is perhaps worth commenting that Barnum's name is often associated with the phrase 'there's a sucker born every minute', although it appears highly doubtful that he ever actually said this.

As well as the circus, he is also credited with inventing both beauty and beautiful baby contests and was also a significant property developer. An astute dealer, he would acquire a piece of land, divide it into plots and secure planning permission. (His regular donations of common land to city councils seemed to help here.) He would then sell non-adjacent plots and help the purchasers finance the buildings they put up. He would hang on to the other plots until the buildings were complete and then release them at inflated prices.

★

New businesses (and other initiatives) will continue to emerge and evolve as those involved adapt to events and find new opportunities—and as long as the business is run properly and profitably. But in many ways it is an ability and willingness to 'think outside the box'—to envision something meaningful and different, to realise what is required to deliver on this promise, to gather supporters for the vision and the challenge, and to make it happen—that help us understand why some people accomplish what they do. Having read our stories, reflect on people you know and other stories that we might have told. How significant are the people we describe as **entirepreneurs** in the uncertainty of today's 'New Normal' world?

Later in the book you will also be asked to think about whether you too are an **entirepreneur** or an **entirepreneur-in-waiting**. This question could be just as relevant if you are a (potential) change-maker in an established organisation, regardless of size and sector, as if you are thinking of starting a new business.

PART TWO

The entirepreneur and the 'New Normal'

> If a man will begin with certainties, he shall end in doubts. But if he will be content to begin with doubts, he shall end in certainties.
>
> *Francis Bacon,* The Advancement of Learning

In Part Two we look first at the challenges for organisations of the 'New Normal' (Chapter 2). We then examine and critique what is held to be conventional wisdom, but is no longer an adequate explanation of what is required if organisations are to cope with—and exploit—the challenges and opportunities of today's turbulent world (Chapter 3). Chapters 4 and 5, which discuss what organisations and people have to do and achieve if they are to survive and thrive in the modern world, provide a foundation for Part Three, where we identify and explain the attributes of the **entirepreneur***.*

Introduction

The term 'New Normal' has been popularised in the last five years to describe economies around the world after the 2008–2012 global recession. When people started using the term more extensively, the intention was to highlight that even though economies would recover, they would not return to being as they had been prior to the recession. 'Life would not be the same as before', so to speak. There have, of course, always been economic recessions and recoveries, but this latest, prolonged, recession was not 'normal' in the sense that it was similar to previous recessions, especially those within living memory.

Given the world has changed and there is a 'New Normal' of uncertainty, turbulence and change, it seems reasonable and logical to question the extent to which the business lessons from the past remain relevant for today's challenges. One key challenge is that people we conventionally describe as entrepreneurs, leaders and managers find it increasingly hard to predict which issues will next have to be faced. We are not dismissing the value of past work on entrepreneurship, leadership and management, but rather questioning how much of what we might call 'conventional wisdom' is still truly fit for our purpose.

It is our conclusion that **entirepreneurs** who are able to blend 'big-picture' vision with operational detail while also commanding the change agenda (finding and seizing new opportunities) are highly relevant for the new challenges. Moreover, it is important we understand and champion such people.

In the early years of the twenty-first century, growth was often seen as desirable and high on the agenda for many businesses, and in industries such as IT and communications, companies grew rapidly. New company founders and management teams of established, successful organisations enjoyed the rewards of success. In the case of bankers in particular, these rewards later came to be seen as excesses that needed to be curbed in the future. Entrepreneurship, thinking fast, seizing opportunities and taking (measured) risks was prominent. Governments were seen by some commentators to have allowed business leaders and bankers too much freedom, which eventually exacerbated the length and depth of the economic recession when it happened.

In the recession, companies needed to adapt quickly in order to survive, and fight hard to remain profitable. Cost reductions were high on the agenda for many in order to protect their profits when sales and revenues fell.

Opinion seems to be that the 'New Normal' after the recession will be a period when many established economies are likely to grow more slowly than in the past boom years. There are exceptions to this, of course, as some of the newer economies (and businesses) in the developing world have prospered better than those in established 'Western' countries. One story we might have included in Chapter 1 is that of Jack Ma and Alibaba, a business which has grown rapidly in recent years and provides an online route to markets around the world for small- and medium-sized Chinese companies. But, in turn, slower growth does not necessarily equate to greater stability. Profits will not be achieved easily when competition remains strong. At the same time, it is understandable that governments are likely to want to have some control over businesses, with a hope that the (inevitable) next recession will not be as severe as the last one. The general view is that in today's dynamic, uncertain and competitive post-recession world companies need to find new strategic ideas, focus hard on strategy execution and implementation and continue to adapt quickly and innovate constantly. In other words, they will demonstrate both directional and operational excellence. The belief that people will always be willing to pay for value and quality holds, but requires that decision makers appreciate what this implies.

Whilst economies might grow more slowly, the pace of change in industries like IT and communications is likely to remain high; in recent times it has been extraordinarily high. What is seen as normal behaviour today will continue to become very quickly out of date.

In addition, *Fast Company* magazine (May 2003) had earlier stressed the importance of 'honesty, integrity and authenticity' for businesses generally, and these values seemed highly appropriate in the 'New Normal' world. The need to create and deliver real value for all stakeholders matters. Robust performance is essential; there is little room for 'smoke and mirrors'.

> [When I started Virgin some 40 years ago] ... I felt then, and still do today, that business—every business—has enormous potential to be a place for good in the world. Companies can realise this potential by looking for ways to do things differently.
>
> *Richard Branson,* The Virgin Way

The 'New Normal' is going to present serious challenges for businesses and those who run them. We believe people who are entirepreneurial will be well placed to deal with these challenges.

2

THE 'NEW NORMAL' WORLD OF BUSINESS

Dealing with the pressures of change to keep an organisation strong and possibly even growing has never been easy. Products and services must improve and change in line with competition—and sometimes they need to be abandoned and replaced. People must adapt and change. Some people are more flexible than others, and the culture in which they work can help or hinder. This book takes a person-centred approach to the challenges of change in today's world, but in this section we look first at the operating context and the strategic opportunities and challenges it brings for people and organisations.

Introduction

Today's organisations might know where they have come from and how the business is performing, but their people cannot see into the future with any certainty. They are not blessed with an accurate map. Other people have not been there before to tell them what to expect.

If we use the metaphor of a flowing river, then the 'New Normal' river is running high and fast. It is turbulent and unpredictable; at some points it is carving out a new path. Those who seek to travel down this river must deal with the force of the flow, accepting that they don't know when the river might settle down again and start behaving more predictably. Any maps they have will be of only partial value; the course may have changed. Just as the original explorers did, when they meet unexpected challenges, they have to adapt and cope in order to keep going. The river might not be easily navigable—it may not be navigable at all if there are serious obstructions.

To deal with the challenges of the 'New Normal', organisations need **entirepreneurs**.

The 1982 book *In Search of Excellence* by Tom Peters and Robert Waterman identified the behaviours that helped successful organisations become successful. Some people who read the book took away the message that this was what all organisations should do, and the book was soon criticised when some of the businesses cited as 'winners' became less successful. They were no longer coping in an increasingly uncertain world. The theme of sustainability was picked up by Jim Collins in two very successful books: *Built to Last* (1997) and *Good to Great* (2001). Meanwhile Tom Peters wrote two other books—*Thrive on Chaos* (1989) and *Re-imagine* (2003)—where he argued businesses cannot be built to last. This he calls a 'myth of perpetuity', saying, 'Once they cease to add value they will vanish.'

The message we take from this surely has to be that sustainability will be unlikely without flexibility, change and adaptiveness, and that we have to accept that not every organisation will be able to achieve this: some will disappear and be replaced by others that are entrepreneurial and called 'outliers' in Rita McGrath's book, *The End of Competitive Advantage* (2013). On the other hand, those that can adapt their 'big picture' and change the things they do will be more sustainable. To achieve this they will need people who are comfortable with the entirety of the challenge.

'New Normal' organisations

In the past it has generally been accepted that survival is an important requirement for any and every organisation. Whilst this may seem a 'no-brainer' statement, the actual challenge of survival cannot be taken lightly. The statistics quoted may vary, but it is unquestionably the case that the failure rate for new micro and small businesses remains high in their early years. In addition, of those that do survive the early years, only a small percentage are likely to grow in a meaningful way and create a serious number of new jobs. Spotting which ones will make it is tricky.

Governments are aware of the problems and successive governments experiment with different programmes to try and address them. These initiatives all seem to work up to a point, but a policy which makes a dramatic difference remains elusive. One challenge for any government is whether to focus their intervention on the business environment—perhaps reducing red tape; perhaps offering tax incentives for new job creation—or on supporting or training individual people. Evidence of true impact is hard to gather; a challenge that isn't made easier in the uncertainty of the 'New Normal'.

It remains debatable how many of these programmes and initiatives take a person-centred approach and focus on the actual individuals involved, attempting to select those who are most worthy of support, as distinct from assessing the businesses and activities that people are proposing.

Survival during the early years, coupled with good results and growth, is no guarantee of long-term survival. Established organisations get taken over or sometimes go out of business. Brands that were once prominent on retail shelves disappear. Their life may have been relatively long or relatively short, but only a few stay popular for year after year, and those that do remain popular change, sometimes out of all recognition. Often, though, they reach a point where they cease to be relevant for their customers, suppliers and/or funders. In a changing and competitive world, better options become available for some or all of these stakeholders. These businesses will disappear and be replaced by others that are more 'fit for purpose'.

To survive, organisations need to be innovative and entrepreneurial—after all, entrepreneurially minded competitors are likely to be targeting them because they are successful.

The organisations that survive and thrive will be clear about what they are doing—a clear direction in the form of a 'big picture' that makes sense for customers, suppliers, employees and funders such that they commit to it. Organisations can strengthen this commitment by exhibiting clear and relevant values and by paying attention to the detail. Customer value is created and added through activities and operations—they need to 'get things right' and to keep doing so.

In the past it has not been unusual to see growth as a desirable objective. Financiers are certainly concerned with growth prospects; government initiatives have attempted to identify and target businesses with high growth prospects. It is, however, worth questioning whether the main focus of our attention should be on growth or survival and sustainability in a turbulent world—accepting that neither is readily achieved.

Whichever, the challenge for organisations (and their people) is the need to be able to align with the changing world of the 'New Normal', and to stay aligned by adapting—which in turn means flexibility and change. Staying aligned requires the ability to spot opportunities; adapting implies these opportunities are acted upon. Opportunity spotting and opportunity taking are behaviours we conventionally attribute to the entrepreneur: yet when we discuss people in organisations, we are more likely to focus on the management hierarchy. The 'New Normal' world presents attractive prospects to entrepreneurially minded people, many of whom will welcome and relish the challenge. But to others the 'New Normal' world will appear threatening because of its very unpredictability.

So to what extent are our organisations and our people 'fit for purpose'? Inevitably the answer to this question is not definitive.

Our stories in Part One cover several hundred years and show that transformational people who have changed the way we think and behave are not a new phenomenon, and yet they are not necessarily a common phenomenon. We have looked at people who took what already existed and improved it by making it more attractive and meaningful for people; at the same time we have looked at people who appeared to start with a blank canvas and create something 'people always wanted'.

Fortunately, we have people who possess the attributes of an **entirepreneur** and who are keen to start new businesses—but do we make it relatively easy or difficult for them to do so? The more difficult it is, the more would-be entrepreneurs with genuine potential will remain 'hidden in the woodwork'.

We have people willing and able to champion innovation and change in more established businesses. Do we always welcome them and provide them with the necessary resources and encouragement? In other words, do they have the opportunity to be creative and innovative in a supportive framework, or are they the lone thinker who doesn't fit the culture of an organisation?

Current strategic thinking

This section looks briefly at relevant aspects of contemporary strategic thinking in the context of the 'New Normal'. This thinking embraces both directional issues and more detailed operational activities. As we have said, the challenge is to have control over both, and it is people who are able to embrace and control both that are best placed to deal with the pressures—and the opportunities—of the 'New Normal'. But how many organisations can truly substantiate that they are 'doing the right things right', that this is not accidental but deliberate, that everything is under control, and that they are clear on when and how things need to change?

Speed and flexibility

One core contextual theme appears to be that when change is needed, speed is essential. In a volatile and uncertain world, the ability to react quickly (and generally with incomplete information) to opportunities, as well as to threats, whether they offer short-term or longer-term prospects and implications, is important. Procrastination will simply open the door to others. The opportunities in question might be ones that become apparent in a changing world, ones to which the organisation reacts, or they might be ones the organisation creates in an attempt to destabilise further the already uncertain world. In other words, they are looking to spring surprises on other competitors. These may be their existing competitors as they seek to strengthen their position and market share, but they may be new competitors if they are seeking to enter an industry or sector for the first time.

It is a mistake for any company to believe that because they can name their main competitors today, these same names will be their rivals in the future. In our stories earlier we mentioned Richard Branson, who has always liked to spring surprises on large, established organisations that he feels have become a little sleepy and complacent. A few years before Virgin launched its trans-Atlantic flights, would British Airways (BA) have foreseen serious rivalry from someone they would perceive to be an 'upstart' distinct from an established American or European airline? That said, could BA have been expected to predict such a brazenly entrepreneurial intervention? Whilst the threat must always be there as a possibility, identifying a potential source is quite another matter. Entrepreneurial outliers like Branson do not win every time—perhaps the best they can hope for is more wins than losses—but overall show bigger wins than losses. Branson also launched Virgin Cola as a rival product to Coca-Cola and Pepsi, but this failed to materialise into a sustained challenge. He simply failed to build enough market share.

Competing

Organisations, then, need to be able to both defend and attack simultaneously. These are different approaches and, like sports teams, they require different strengths and frames of mind. Attacking football teams are often seen as more attractive than those that defend robustly and grind out results by keeping a clean sheet and relying on quick counter-attacks. But both can be winners. The really successful teams seem to be able to manage both robust defence and strengths in attack. The sporting analogy is useful in another way: the most influential players are not the ones who know where the ball is at any time, but rather the ones who can see where it will be passed to, or where it needs to be passed to. They are thinking and seeing ahead and acting on these opportunities.

Established businesses have to defend against entrepreneurial challenges, but from time to time they need to attack and spring surprises themselves; typically it is the same people who will be involved, and they need to be flexible and adaptive. Different strategies make different demands on people, and yet organisations are likely to be pursuing more than one at the same time. They may, for example, be integrating a new acquisition at the same time as developing new products; one of these might be in the same industry and the other in a new, different industry.

For a long time Michael Porter's work has informed strategic thinking. He argued that the first key challenge is to examine the industry in which a business competes, to study the forces that prescribe the nature of that industry, looking to clarify the extent to which it is relatively attractive or unattractive. The second key challenge is to discern opportunities to open up a competitive advantage. Whilst he put forward a case for potentially sustainable generic positions—which other authors critiqued—he did draw attention to the key drivers of competition, namely cost and difference. He also emphasised that deciding what not to do is just as important, if not more important, than choosing what to do. This is, again, discernment.

The 'New Normal' demands that organisations change if they are to be sustainable; they may have to alter what they do quite radically. No competitive position is perpetually defendable. Organisations should always be seeking to leverage their resources—their people and their embedded knowledge, their capabilities and their technologies—to both drive costs below those of rivals and open up new opportunities to be different. Both of these have innovation implicit. Stretching ambitions and a lack of complacency are essential. Sometimes the changes will be gradual and emergent—the organisation will adapt and morph in changing circumstances. Occasionally, though, the change will be transformational and internal upheaval will be evident. Not unexpectedly, many people will be more comfortable with gradual change.

Innovation and change

But innovation and change are not something that can be switched on and off. They need to become natural, instinctive, embedded behaviours, regardless of the industry. Ideally there will be a facilitating structure and a culture of expectation and encouragement. Stories of how organisations like 3M have succeeded by offering and encouraging employees to spend up to one day every week developing new initiatives which can be shared—and how Jack Welch facilitated idea-sharing across all business areas in General Electric—are often told in the literature and offered as exemplars of good practice. These are organisations that have successfully embedded flexibility and change, and yet it would not appear that this is common practice everywhere. With Internet companies like Google that have a similar approach and culture, it seems appropriate and natural, but in more established industries, where technology and customer demand does not move quite as quickly, it might seem more of an alien concept. Not taking this change-oriented perspective opens the door for the unexpected challenger: the outlier.

The innovation framework in an organisation, assuming it exists, should embrace both top-down and bottom-up initiatives. Programmes and staff employed for research and development and for new product development imply a top-down strategic approach; this approach is generally common practice. A culture that encourages, finds space for, and rewards more individual efforts is less common-place, but where it has been practiced seriously it has often brought positive out-comes. This is where we would anticipate entrepreneurial people feeling at home and valued. Simply, it seems necessary in the 'New Normal' world to encourage innovatory improvements in any and every area of the business, whilst simultane-ously looking to enhance core activities with new products and enhancements and also exploring possibilities for venturing into unknown territories. Different people will be able to contribute in different ways—after all, these options imply different directions of thought—but all their ideas and creativity should be harnessed.

If we return to our story of Sir Alex Ferguson, we see evidence of an **entire-preneur** who was always looking for opportunities to strengthen and improve his players and his team's results. He was keen to acquire and bring on new talent, and he was not afraid to sell popular players if he felt they were no longer appropriate for the current side. During his years in charge there were several United teams—it was only with this degree of change that Manchester United was able to enjoy a sustained period of success. With many clubs, it is more normal for a period of real success to be followed by a period of relative disappointment and rebuilding—to be rebuilding a team whilst still consolidating and succeeding at the top level is a real challenge, but it is one that more and more organisations will have to face if they are to survive. Without the changes it is unlikely Ferguson would have stayed as long as he did.

Developing this story and linking back to the point on speed, flexibility and tim-ing, Ferguson's personally chosen successor, David Moyes, was dismissed before the end of his first season as manager of Manchester United. This is not unusual in foot-ball if results are disappointing, but it raises the issue of how long one might expect a CEO to stay in post in any organisation. If a newly appointed CEO believes their time might be limited, they may either be reluctant to change things until their posi-tion is properly confirmed or they may instigate rapid change so that they appear dynamic. Neither approach may be the most appropriate action to take.

Dealing with the challenges of the 'New Normal' is not easy, and will not become easy. There is no 'one best way' but there are some common themes. Those organisations—and those people—who are able to embrace the strategic challenges will become more important and more valuable. They will be able to deal with ambiguity and uncertainty; they will be able to drive change and to change themselves; they will appreciate that they have to find the answers through experimentation, trial and error.

In part because of the speed at which things can change—linked to our ability to move information rapidly—any competitive advantages are often relatively short-lived in the 'New Normal'. Products need constant refreshment. Even though a command of modern technology might suggest the importance of 'left-brain' (logical) thinking, 'right-brain' (creative) thinking is hugely significant. It is a paradox, for example, that IT is providing access to extensive information, but thus requiring more time to absorb the information and make sense of it. Some might argue that there is too much information! Whatever information might be available, including new knowledge generated through R&D, possessing it is only part of the story: what really matters is the sense that people make of it, the opportunities they spot and the subsequent actions they take. Expressed very simply, strategy is about what you see and what you do.

The ability to see the proverbial wood for the trees and spot new opportunities is something that **entirepreneurs** can do. And, of course, they do something about it.

Later, in Chapters 4 and 5, we examine success, failure and the 'New Normal' challenges for both small, growing businesses and for more established organisations, but before this we offer a critique of conventional wisdom. We explore further our question: to what extent are we fit for purpose in the face of the demands of the 'New Normal'? We conclude that conventional wisdom fails to provide adequate answers to the challenge of the 'New Normal'.

3

CONVENTIONAL WISDOM

A commentary and critique

A great deal has been written about entrepreneurs and entrepreneurship, leaders and leadership, and managers and management. The points are often valid—they are certainly not wrong—and they provide valuable insights. Our concern is that by treating the roles and contributions as separate themes, which we typically do, our thinking becomes narrower than it needs to be. We have concluded that in the 'New Normal' world, attention needs to be focused on the entire person and their total contribution rather than whether they fit particular roles or can improve as a leader or manager. Here we outline and review some key aspects of the conventional wisdom.

Introducing conventional wisdom

We have written this book to disrupt the conventional way we think of people as entrepreneurs, leaders or managers and categorise them as one or the other—accepting, of course, that people can change roles and that the distinctions are blurred. Entrepreneurs (in many people's minds) start new businesses and run their own small businesses, but this view is too simplistic. Conventionally, we see the manager as someone who plans, organises and controls activities and the work of the people who carry out these activities, whilst leaders inspire and influence what others do and how they behave. These convenient summaries can be applied in any context, not just business.

Managers might well become leaders; entrepreneurs (or owner–managers) might develop into managers or more realistically leaders. In fact, if they fail to do this, the growth of the business may be compromised, as we discuss in Chapter 5.

Moreover, managers lead and leaders manage all the time as part of their roles and contribution.

Conventional wisdom on organisations sees successful people rising through the managerial hierarchy; they progress from one level of management to another.

The word 'management' is deliberate, as the term 'manager' typically defines most jobs below those of 'directors'. They are (or they become) leaders as well as managers, and leadership becomes more significant as they become more senior and ultimately directors.

There is an underlying premise that both organisational performance and individual progress is helped by order and structure. To progress up the structure, knowledge, expertise (skills) and experience are all required.

In large organisations in various sectors, public as well as private, it would be quite normal to see a corporate structure with a CEO (Chief Executive Officer) and several layers of 'managers': senior managers, middle managers and junior managers. The most senior managers (and/or directors) would be seen as the 'corporate leaders'. The assumptions are that these corporate leaders lead the other managers and to some degree dictate what they do, and that ambitious people look to work their way up the management hierarchy. Innovative, enterprising people who 'think differently' and are keen to drive changes may be welcomed or suppressed, depending on the nature of the organisation.

Sir Gerry Robinson, the retired businessman who investigated the UK National Health Service (NHS) in a number of television programmes, commented that 'there are too many managers and not enough management' in the NHS.

Separately, *Financial Times* columnist Lucy Kellaway argues there are now some five million managers in the UK—although in a number of cases this, she says, amounts to little more than a job title. She asks, 'Have people got distracted by roles, titles and administration?'

It is certainly easy to find commentators who argue that so-called professional managers have become focused on analysis, systems and procedures and are somewhat distant from customers and operations. It is not unusual to find very knowledgeable people, including many who are qualified to MBA level, in managerial positions; indeed, the MBA has become a valuable asset in manager development and progression. MBA degrees have genuine value. Often, though, an MBA will treat the various subjects being covered as separate disciplines, seeking to integrate them with a strategy module. In our experience it would be relatively unusual for an MBA to start with an entirety perspective. In effect, 'business schools are functional whilst businesses are cross-functional'.

In the public sector it would also not be at all unusual to describe what happens as a bureaucracy, and assume that many people are selected for promotion because they conform. This argument has certainly been made to explain progression to the top levels in the Chinese government. Here, the ability to deliver results and meet agreed objectives without controversy and disruption is valued. It might be a safe and reliable approach if a situation of stability exists or can be created and sustained. Critics would though, and perhaps not unexpectedly, contend that too little changes in China and that people are not using their initiative to change things that (in their view) obviously need changing.

A similar but different story might be told of Japan. One of the reasons for Japan's rapid rise as a post-war industrial nation came down to working practices.

It was traditional to involve workers in decision making—consulting them and allowing them the opportunity to offer thoughts and opinions. Once decisions were made, much as with the military, there was the assumption people would not question decisions or authority and would get on and execute what needed to be done. When Japan needed to change as a result of economic pressures in the 1990s, such 'reflexive obedience' was a barrier; it led to a reluctance to challenge management decisions, let alone initiate change.

Followers, progression and expertise

When people start work in an established organisation it is possible that they will be employed in a designated managerial role, but many others will start as 'followers': people who are not truly and directly responsible for the work of others. In a sense they are on the bottom rung of a ladder—they may stay there, and they may be content to stay there. Their ambitions may be very limited. They may prefer to just do as they are told by others. Such people do not want to make decisions for themselves, take on a great deal of responsibility or change things. They can still be valuable contributors as followers, of course. At the same time, they may be overlooked for promotion for a whole variety of other reasons: they are idle but perhaps 'doing enough'; they don't fit well within the organisation; they lack focus; their talents and capabilities are limited.

But others will have ambitions to progress. They will chase promotion to a position in the hierarchy which carries the word 'manager', and continue to seek further promotions. They may, of course, leave and join another organisation for a more senior position.

Whilst they might be described and named as a manager, this does not automatically mean that individuals are not exercising leadership in the way they do what they do and how they deal with people. They may well provide leadership but not actually be called a leader, a word we rarely find in job titles. Some would argue that as managers progress up the hierarchy then leadership becomes more prominent, but this is a very simplistic approach. Most managers lead; many leaders manage. The balance between them is affected by an individual's personal style and attributes rather than the level they are in the organisation.

To complicate matters further, some people who are called 'manager' don't truly manage. They administer—the distinction being the extent to which they are responsible and held accountable for what other people do and how they do it. This is not unusual in small businesses where the owner-manager wants to make all the key decisions but still needs to give some employees a manager title to increase their credibility with suppliers and customers.

Leading is not 'more of the same' at a higher level than a manager. Leading is about giving direction, inspiring others and *influencing* what others do. It does not require taking direct responsibility for line-managing others. The contribution, then, is less operational than that of the manager. Some people can do this and lead very well, even though they might not be particularly effective in a managerial role. And, of course, some excellent and high-performing managers are not natural leaders.

Sometimes certain 'managers' will always seek permission before carrying out a decision. Indeed, there are organisations where this practice, which might be described as delegating upwards, is encouraged or even required. Managers with leader attributes are, however, more likely to try and influence their line manager's decisions!

There are various styles of leading and managing which will have some bearing on an individual's success and progression. The more enterprising ones will be keen to stamp their individuality on the work they do. They may well be creative and innovative people who believe they can improve the way things are done—and they will want to try out their ideas and 'prove they were right'. Their keenness to change things may or may not be welcomed.

At this point it is worth commenting that as people progress in organisations they are likely to be offered management development programmes and, later, leadership development. With many managers there is likely to be a marked emphasis on techniques and skills. It would, though, be rare to find an entrepreneurship development programme, albeit that this is exactly what is required to support some executives in dealing with the challenge of instigating and implementing change.

Flow

Mihaly Csikszentmihalyi talks about a state of 'flow' where people are happy and productive in a work environment because of two things: they are challenged and stretched, but at the same time they believe they can cope because they have the necessary skills and competencies. Challenge without capability implies anxiety; competency without challenge allows people to see work as relaxing, which implies underachievement against potential.

The Peter Principle

Flow implies people have found an appropriate level and means of contributing. The so-called Peter Principle (named after its creator) contends that people are promoted to a level where they become incompetent. They (sometimes) aspire to progress, and they move upwards in the organisational hierarchy, but eventually their effectiveness weakens. Good school teachers don't always make good Heads of Subject; good Assistant Heads are not automatically Head Teachers in the making, for example. One problem is that it can be uncomfortable for a person to accept this and move back to the level where they are truly competent and effective.

The Peter Principle is persuasive but perhaps too simplistic. The problem is not just about level; it is also about contribution within an organisation. The issue is that some specialists or 'experts' (whose personal knowledge and specialist expertise might be both significant and valuable) should never become managers—or sometimes owner-managers if they start their own business—in the first place.

As we said, managers have a key role in planning, organising and monitoring the work of others. They need to delegate but also keep a firm, watchful eye. They are no longer mostly responsible for their own work and contribution.

Expertise

Particularly in larger organisations, many people are recruited because they have specialist knowledge and expertise, perhaps reinforced with academic qualifications that influence how they are utilised.

These so-called 'specialists' might be categorised into four broad groups:

1. those dealing with customers (sales and marketing);
2. those involved in operations, including engineers and people in procurement and logistics;
3. those with expertise in finance and information technology;
4. 'people people' engaged in HR activities.

Any individual's preference might be to continue to specialise and become more of an expert—using their expertise to provide leadership, perhaps even technological leadership—but their expected progression and promotion route might still demand they take on more of a managerial role and more responsibility for the work of others. Others will be attracted by the opportunity to switch from one specialism to another and, in doing so, become more of a generalist. There is no clear-cut answer as to whether a specialist or a generalist is the best candidate for a CEO role.

Whilst an individual might be a genuine expert and enjoy mastery of their specialism, we believe (and argue in Part Three) that the CEO who is likely to be most effective in meeting the challenges of the 'New Normal' will offer mastery of a range of attributes that we have conventionally associated with entrepreneurs, leaders and managers.

In the UK and the US there are clearly various progression routes to the CEO role. Most popular is the finance route, although engineering and occasionally marketing are also clearly evident. Sometimes managers will have worked in various disciplines rather than concentrate on one specialism, but not always. People who specialise in human resources are rarely the ones who make CEO, and yet there is the assumption that, through managing the work of others, aspiring CEOs will be acquiring people skills. This may not be a valid assumption.

These arguments are not confined to the 'world of business'. The same arguments can be applied to universities and the individuals who aspire to be Vice Chancellors. The majority will have achieved mastery in an academic specialism and often have considerable research expertise.

We looked at the background of the Chief Executives in post at all the hospital trusts in one region of the UK. Not one was a medical consultant by background, although a small number had enjoyed a career in nursing. Predominantly they were public sector managers whose background would best be described as administration.

This might well lead to conflicting perspectives on medical priorities, but, of course, senior medical consultants may not aspire to become CEOs.

The challenge for an individual, then, is finding where one can make one's most valuable contribution. Organisations must be clear as to what type of person is best qualified to be CEO. We believe that finding a person with the attributes of the **entrepreneur** is becoming increasingly important. At the same time, not everybody with the ambition to start and/or lead an organisation is an **entrepreneur**.

Sir Clive Sinclair was always good at mathematics and he taught himself electronics. He wrote for, and subsequently edited, electronics magazines before becoming a product designer and entrepreneur. Miniature radios, pocket calculators and a series of small computers were followed by the much maligned Sinclair C5 electric car that was simply underpowered. He ran his own businesses for some years, but, 'overwhelmed by debt and unsold stock', sold his interests in computers to Alan Sugar's Amstrad. More recently he has been producing battery-powered bicycles and in 2011 he launched the X-1, a two-wheel, battery-powered cycle with a cover to protect the rider against the elements. Sinclair is now over 70 years old and wealthy from his inventions. But he will be remembered as an inventor; he was not an **entrepreneur**.

By contrast, Caroline Redman Lusher's background is music. Her degree is in popular music and after graduating she started as a solo singer but hated the lifestyle. She started teaching. In her 30s she started the Rock Choir. Now there are over 8,000 members in over 200 local choirs across the UK. People pay to be members; would-be choristers do not have to demonstrate they can sing in tune—it is about enthusiasm and inclusivity. The choirs all sing rock music that she has specially arranged, but they all have local choir leaders. Well over 90 per cent of the members are female. The choir is incredibly successful. CDs have been released (which have done well) and Lusher has booked (and sold out) Wembley Arena and other similar venues for her choirs singing together. She qualifies as an entrepreneur (this is a successful original idea that took off), a leader (she clearly inspires others and provides them with opportunities) and a manager (keeping this viable and growing at the same time is challenging). More realistically, she is an **entrepreneur**.

Entrepreneurs and entrepreneurship

Conventionally, entrepreneurs are associated with business start-ups. Many people would call anyone who starts a microbusiness or becomes self-employed an entrepreneur. We personally believe that many people who start microbusinesses might be enterprising, but that the word 'entrepreneur' should not be attributed to them automatically. In our view, entrepreneurs are people who make a difference by doing something different. In that respect many microbusinesses are not entrepreneurial.

In addition, entrepreneurial people can be found in all walks of life. Entrepreneurship is a way of behaving that has change at its heart. Entrepreneurial people are present in the public sector and the charitable sector (where they are often called social entrepreneurs) as well as in business. And they can certainly be found in larger organisations, although their desire to change things may not always be welcomed by everyone, even when they clearly need changing. Entrepreneurial people in corporate environments are often called 'intrapreneurs'.

They may target what can be improved upon—after all, most things can be done better—but sometimes the changes they enact are transformational. On some occasions an entrepreneurial person can see an opportunity in the chaos of the 'New Normal'; on other occasions they contribute to the uncertainty of the 'New Normal' by proactively disturbing the existing state of something.

Innovation and invention—supported by a creative mind—underpin entrepreneurship. But it does not follow that all inventors are entrepreneurs, as we saw with the example of Clive Sinclair. Something that is 'a great idea' may not be a real business opportunity, and the failure to realise this explains why a fair proportion of new products simply do not make it. In addition, the people with the ideas are not always the best people to see them through to fruition. Equally, they may not want to—they may be happiest working with ideas and not building businesses.

Opportunity is thus at the core of entrepreneurship. Opportunities have to be found and acted upon. Some authors have commented that one key distinguishing feature of an entrepreneur is that they will seize an opportunity they spot regardless of the resources they currently have at hand. They believe they can and will secure the resources and they want to get on with things. This helps explain their willingness to accept the risk involved when anything is being changed or something new is being introduced. There is always uncertainty, and it has to be dealt with.

Entrepreneurs and managers are seen to take a different approach to problems and opportunities, something that is often linked to the underpinning personality dimensions that affect life choices. Managers are often taught to analyse, plan and prepare; the credo of many MBA programmes. Entrepreneurs are more like explorers. They have a broad intent (opportunity) in mind which gives them direction and a spur to act, although they do some planning. They work out what resources they are likely to require—both at the outset and along the way—and how these might be obtained at various times. As their journey unfolds, they are faced with a series of choices; judgement and serendipity are involved in their decisions and the outcomes. In this way they deal with uncertainty and risk. They appreciate that uncertainty and risk are real and will need dealing with, but they do not try and eradicate them, as they appreciate this is unrealistic. Saras Sarasvathy uses the term 'effectuation' to describe the behaviour of entrepreneurs.

Many people have written books about entrepreneurship, and many academics have produced research to try and explain who they are. Such research (aggregated and summarised) indicates that entrepreneurs are often:

- firstborn males;
- sons of fathers who were self-employed or professionals;
- people who have served some kind of informal apprenticeship;
- individuals who have experienced a life event that has acted as a trigger;

- people for whom education is a low priority, sometimes because they are dyslexic;
- people who started out in business when they were young.

The majority of these apply to Edward Stobart. He was working in his father's business from a young age, but was always looking for opportunities to make money for himself.

There are many other examples of outstanding entrepreneurs for whom these criteria do not apply to the same extent: therefore, such conclusions about entrepreneurs should not be regarded as definitive cause-and-effect criteria.

Again aggregating various pieces of work, the following seven themes appear time and time again as characteristics that define the entrepreneur:

- Vision
- Need for achievement
- Need for autonomy (independence)
- Calculated risk-taking
- An opportunistic tendency
- An internal locus of control—a desire to be in control of what happens in one's life
- Creativity and innovation

We support the relevance of these themes and agree that it is easy to see how some of them help to explain an entrepreneurial person's temperament, but there are other critical talent attributes that are not really encapsulated in this conventional wisdom.

Nature–nurture

The nature–nurture debate has been associated more with entrepreneurs than with either leaders or managers, and it remains a relevant debate for the **entirepreneur**. Although some people would claim that 'anyone can be an entrepreneur', we do not subscribe to this view. The presence of particular talent attributes is important, as is a person's motivation and ability to harness their talents and deal with the consequences of the actions they choose to take, driven by the talent attributes. Certainly the experiences that are offered to people are also important, as are those that they find for themselves. What really matters, though, is the path people choose to take, and having the ability to learn from their experiences. Circumstances therefore do matter. To understand any individual we need to take some account of their knowledge and experiences and the expertise and capabilities they build as a consequence—but critically important too are their talent and temperament attributes. These affect both the experiential choices people make and their ability to learn from their experiences. We develop these arguments further in Chapter 6.

It is talent attributes (along with temperament) that we develop in Part Three to explain in greater detail just who the **entirepreneur** is. We will explain how attributes we have conventionally associated with the entrepreneur, the leader and the manager all come together to make up the entire person who is best suited for the demands and challenges of the 'New Normal'.

Leaders and leadership

CEOs—Chief Executive Officers

The CEO is the figurehead for the organisation who will be held ultimately responsible for what happens: he or she may or may not actually take all the key decisions that determine these outcomes. The fate of a CEO who fails is often symbolic. Some might resign; others might be dismissed by the Board of Directors.

It is conventional wisdom to see the CEO as the number-one strategist who provides direction such that people both inside and outside the organisation know where it is going and how it intends to get there, and inspires people in the pursuit of this vision. This requires him or her to understand and relate to the organisation's customers and their needs and expectations. He or she also works with, and through, other key stakeholders to enable the organisation to achieve its goals. He or she is the key link with the main funders for the business, and he or she is ultimately responsible for how people are managed and rewarded. The cohesion amongst the 'top team' and the extent to which they share and commit to the CEO's vision, is critical. The CEO is typically expected to be a good communicator: having a visible profile and a larger-than-life persona would often be seen as a positive thing. It is also conventional wisdom to link the CEO role with corporate leadership and to see the CEO as the 'ultimate leader' in the organisation. The argument in this book, though, is that there is more to an outstanding CEO than the attributes normally attributed to the conventional leader.

> If I had to say what are some of the fundamental attributes of leadership that matter to me, the following would be high on my list. First, the attitude of the organisation toward change is established by the tone set at the top. For me, that means a continued statement, restatement, communication, and validation of the company's mission and values, which includes reinforcing its culture. This is the CEO's first and most important job and a clear requirement of leadership. As leaders, we must not only determine the appropriate strategic course but also define how we, as individuals and as an organisation, will conduct ourselves. Second, and most obvious, leaders must ensure the development and execution of a clear, well-communicated, and appropriately measured operating plan. Third, effective leaders ensure that the right team, with the right values, is in place to execute the plan and can pivot appropriately when factors change. Fourth, effective leaders show an intellectual flexibility that recognises there are different ways to achieve goals and objectives within different environments. To me, it is important that environmental and market changes do not modify the company's, or

the executive's, basic values. And finally, I think a good leader is a problem solver. How an organisation deals with problems, failures, and missed opportunities clearly defines an important aspect of its culture.

Richard Bracken, CEO of the Hospital
Corporation of America (HCA)

Leaders

A corporate leader, then, needs a clear view on the desired ends being pursued and broad strategies for achieving them, but this 'vision' need not be their personal vision. They could have inherited it from previous leaders, but they still believe in it and are committed to finding (sometimes new) ways to achieve it. Effective leaders are, therefore, always required to be strategic and able to influence other people. Managers typically exercise power more directly.

Harry Truman, once President of the US, talked about leaders 'persuading people what they ought to do without them feeling they have been persuaded'. Put another way, leadership is getting people to do what you want them to do, while believing it is because they themselves that want to do it. They have come to believe and trust in the leader, who must then help them to achieve.

Influence can also work indirectly. Leaders who become high-profile individuals with extensive media coverage and visibility can, assuming they are liked or respected (or ideally both), become opinion leaders and influence the behaviour of people they are never likely to meet.

The word 'visionary' might be legitimately attributed to some leaders, but certainly not to all. Nelson Mandela was a visionary, but, of course, he was more than this. He was able to inspire and gather support from a whole—and previously divided—nation, and change things root and branch. He also earned the respect of people around the world for his style and achievements.

Mandela was released from prison in 1990 after serving a 27-year sentence for opposing apartheid. He soon became President of South Africa, but the country's black and white populations were not integrated. He believed that if the South African (white-dominated) Springboks could win the 1995 Rugby Union World Cup then that victory would go a long way towards uniting the country. He would be proved right. He personally inspired the team captain, Francois Pienaar, with a poem, 'Invictus', written by W. E. Henley in 1875. The last two lines are: 'I am the master of my fate / I am the captain of my soul'. Pienaar in turn motivated his team and led them to glory.

Warren Bennis argues that leaders who survive the challenges, tests and setbacks they will inevitably face typically develop certain traits. They become adaptive, which in a dynamic and uncertain world is hugely significant. Many leadership failures can be linked to a failure to adapt to changing circumstances. Such leaders are able to create shared meaning; they can motivate people behind a common goal, even in the face of adversity. Perhaps paradoxically, tolerance of and even the encouragement of dissent can be important—this again emphasises the significance of self-belief.

These leaders develop a set of principles about how people should be treated, something which defines them and their personal values. Again, this can be linked to an important trait of the entrepreneur: never ignore the importance of customers and employees. Finally, and related to this, they have integrity. There is a clear balance between ambition (both personal and organisational), competence and moral compass. This is one reason why they gain respect and, particularly, trust.

Our discussion here has really focused more on corporate leaders than leaders or leadership in general. We now need to widen the discussion and critique.

Leaders and followers

Conventional wisdom often looks at the contributions that individuals in leadership roles are expected to make, regardless of their level, in any organisation. We believe the attributes that are conventionally attributed to the leader are relevant for an understanding of the **entirepreneur**. It is, though, important to also consider the extent to which individuals can be effective leaders in different situations and contexts. This comes down to relationships.

Haslam et al. (2010; see bibliography) explain that 'leaders lead teams and managers manage teams'. Both use power and influence to encourage and persuade people to follow their (strategic) direction, requests and instructions. Some leaders are able to inspire others to follow their lead. Individual followers, whatever their level in the organisational hierarchy, have personal motives for what they do; the question is whether there is a sense of 'greater good' which encompasses both loyalty to their colleagues and the interests of customers and clients. The CEO might be expected to set in place certain relevant 'pull factors' to help engineer this—the issue is, do others want to really 'push' in the same direction? As we highlighted above, getting people to do things is not the same as getting them to *want* to do things. In the end, a leader is unlikely to have supportive followers unless he or she can demonstrate authenticity—they can claim a 'right' to be in the position they are, regardless of what delivers them that 'right'.

Haslam et al. further argue that leaders need to be seen as part of the team for which they are responsible. Relationships are critical; leaders cannot be perceived to be outside the team if they are to both generate and enjoy commitment and trust from followers. Telling a good story certainly helps, but leaders must also convince others they can deliver outcomes for a range of stakeholders. They have to be believable and seen to really care.

This in part helps explain why some leaders are successful in certain contexts but less successful in different contexts. Churchill was an outstanding and popular leader during wartime—indeed, on the basis of his leadership during World War II, one leading poll declared him to be the greatest leader of the twentieth century—but afterwards he lost a general election and his government was soon replaced. Others with excellent careers in the armed forces fail to replicate this success in different organisations. Leaders in a sporting context may experience similar problems. Fitting naturally into the social context of the organisation is critical and often requires individuals to change or modify their behaviour for a different con-text, where the attributes, motives and expectations of followers may be different. In summary, effective **entirepreneurs** (like effective leaders) have an understand-ing of, and an empathy with, the team they are leading and an appreciation of how they can be best influenced and persuaded.

Managers and managing

'Managers manage', and managing involves planning, organising and controlling activities and operations. Generally, this is work that will be carried out by subordinates to the manager in question—again, followers. It involves providing resources and, ideally, a good working environment. Managing is, then, naturally more operational and tactical than strategic and directional, but there are still important elements of discernment and choice. There is no single best way of doing it, so some managers are more organised than others—they plan more. Some are more hands-on than their colleagues; some are more willing to delegate; some are clear team players; and so on. The approach is personal and based in large part on that person's natural attributes.

The nature of the manager's work and responsibilities will change and increase as they progress upwards, and the role will often become more strategic and less tactical in nature. Hence there might be an expectation that the higher the level of the manager, the more leadership qualities will be required. In many ways the CEO is the most senior manager in an organisation and his or her role is—or at least should be—very largely strategic.

Realising what needs changing—and how it might be changed—requires the attributes we associate with the entrepreneur. As does taking on the challenge. Harnessing support and driving through the change in a partly hostile environment brings in conventional leader attributes.

There are inevitably some occasions when a person with strong operational and financial attributes that we conventionally associate with the manager will be sought to take overall control. Organisations in difficulty, that need stabilising and any financial losses stopped, need such a person to diagnose the problems and pro-pose a remedy, but other attributes are going to be valuable for building support and engineering change. Later, growth may need a person with different attributes.

Without managers and management there would be no organisations as people understand them. And without organisations, how would work be organised and controlled? Whilst leaders influence the hearts and minds of others, effective man-agers engineer situations where others can perform efficiently and effectively to deliver outputs and outcomes. Motivation is a key element.

Karren Brady, who has been CEO of both Birmingham and West Ham United football clubs has told the story of the ticket-office salesperson earning £15,000 a year and a footballer earning (at least) £15,000 a week. (Some top players will earn at least ten times this amount!) How do you motivate the former? After all, unless you sell tickets there won't be a crowd, and without support there won't be money to pay the footballer and keep a good team. At the same time, without a decent team people won't want to buy tickets anyway, so the club might not need the person in the ticket office.

It has been suggested that the trick to management is taking things that are complicated and specialised and turning them into something productive by making it possible for others to perform and deliver.

Good managers obtain (or are given) and provide resources to their team and then support them to do their jobs to the best of their ability. They may help develop their team, coaching and mentoring as appropriate. Good managers know their team and understand their strengths and capabilities; they recognise and reward good performance and confront underperformance. Sometimes they look to utilise the key strengths of individual subordinates; on other occasions they will encourage people to try and deal with key weaknesses. In turn they need clear direction from their own manager, whom, if they have leader qualities, they will seek to influence.

Summarising and aggregating various contributions on the subject, managers:

• appreciate what needs to be done;
• are responsible for the well-being of the people for whom they are responsible;
• plan and organise those people's jobs;
• acquire the resources needed for the tasks that need completing;
• maintain control of activity and performance;
• reward success and deal with failings;
• when necessary, deal with (external) key people.

For much of their time at work managers make and take decisions. They are often responding to problems and issues; such managers are largely reactive, whereas one might expect to see someone (who might be operating in a managerial role) we regard as a leader being more proactive—making sure he or she has time for the thinking required to get ahead and stay ahead in the competitive game.

Henry Mintzberg has written extensively about how managers' jobs are characterised by interruptions, constant activity and pressure and a series of tasks that each take just a few minutes. Mintzberg further argues that managers have a choice about whether they opt to manage through information, people or action—or a combination of these.

The most directly hands-on approach for managers is to manage through action and to be seen to be doing things themselves whilst involving others. The potential downside of this is constant pressure and an inability to secure thinking time.

Managing through people is a step back from this. Here the focus is on recruiting, motivating, delegating work and managing outputs—in part building value through harnessing the creativity and innovativeness of followers.

When managers manage through information they rely more on establishing objectives, agreeing budgets and delegating more responsibility to subordinates. The potential downsides of this third approach are, first, that managers might appear to be too hands-off; they sit in offices away from the point of action and assume others are doing whatever needs to be done. It is only later that they receive information that confirms whether this is indeed the case. Second, they become tempted to believe that past performance can be a good indicator of future success, when this may well not be the case.

Hence, some appropriately balanced mix of the three approaches is required and this will in part be determined by the circumstances and work demands as well as the capabilities of the people being managed.

COOs—Chief Operating Officers

Some (typically larger) organisations also include the post of Chief Operating Officer, or COO. A COO exists to manage organisational operations following the direction that has been set by the CEO and Board of Directors. He or she will be ultimately responsible for making sure 'things get done', and will be largely internally focused. In turn this will free up the CEO to have a more strategic and external role. It is very much the key 'Number Two' role. One might expect a COO to have solid leadership attributes as they are directly responsible for the contributions of a large number of other managers, but they will probably have been selected for their ability to handle detail.

There are, though, also opportunities for a COO with entrepreneur qualities to exercise these. Systems and operations are invariably capable of improvement, to both speed up things and also save costs. Some COOs will eventually become CEOs.

Tim Cook, for example, replaced Steve Jobs as CEO at Apple when Jobs retired through ill health in 2011 and shortly before he died. Cook had stood in for him in the past and demonstrated both strategic and operational capability. Cook has been described as the 'absolute master of the supply chain'; the man who could get products manufactured and delivered to customers with a decent profit margin when products are changed rapidly and demand for them is growing at a staggering rate. He had been recruited by Jobs specifically to do this within a year after Jobs returned to Apple in the 1990s, and Cook systematically withdrew Apple from manufacturing in the US and elsewhere and thus reduced both inventory and costs. Some creatives in Apple, whose credo is to 'think differently', might find this perspective relatively dull, and would have anticipated someone more visionary replacing Jobs, but it is a vitally important contribution. In fact, it was the lack of attention to detail that had led to the original demise of Apple.

> The CEO must keep the business on the right course... . This requires someone with the wisdom to recognise hazards and the fortitude to steer clear of danger... . It is often a lack of these qualities which prevent effective Number Two's being good Number One's.
>
> *Michael Woodford, ex-CEO of Olympus, who*
> *resigned after exposing financial irregularities*
> *amongst his senior colleagues*

Styles of leading and managing

X and Y styles

Douglas McGregor, whose work is discussed in more detail in Part Three, has distinguished between two natural styles of leading and managing based on perceptions of other people's motives and expectations. His Theory X is an authoritarian management style which assumes that the average person dislikes work and will avoid it if possible. The premise is that most people need to be coerced (with the threat of punishment) to work towards the leader's or the manager's goals. The average person actually prefers to be directed, which allows them to avoid any significant responsibility. It assumes people typically lack ambition, wanting security above all else.

It may seem extreme to some, but it is certainly not irrelevant: some 'followers' do prefer to be led and managed this way. They do work best when someone else is making all the important decisions. The question is: just how many people work best in an authoritarian environment? In any organisation some will respond to this style of management and others won't.

So, in contrast, the more popular Theory Y is a participative management style. Effort in work is seen as natural, much as it is in what people choose to do in their spare time. The arguments are: people can and will apply self-control and self-direction in the pursuit of organisational goals; they can be tasked and left alone to do the work; they do not need external control or the threat of punishment. Commitment to goals is a function of the rewards associated with their achievement. It is not unusual for people to accept—and often seek—responsibility. The capacity to use a high degree of imagination, ingenuity and creativity in solving organisational problems is widely, not narrowly, distributed in the population; and at work the intellectual potential of the average person is only partly utilised.

Managers and leaders who utilise an X style may achieve results: coercion can be persuasive. But hearts and minds are not won. To achieve a real commitment and belief in the change being proposed invariably requires a Y style. Y managers and leaders, therefore, are the ones likely to drive real and sustained change.

Anita Roddick (The Body Shop) took the argument further. She believed that businesses need to become communities; that it is common values that bind people together in pursuit of the purpose and vision.

We might express this sentiment differently: growth and sustainability matter, but so too do purpose and impact.

Leading, managing and personal styles

The essential characteristics that conventionally define the leader are related to strategising and influencing. But strategies are only truly valuable when they are implemented and yield results and returns. This implementation requires a tactical contribution, and it is not at all unusual to find some corporate leaders involved and hands-on to the point of making sure that things get done. But really this implies manager attributes coming into play, given that conventionally the manager is seen to be more focused on operations.

Reviewing our commentaries of entrepreneurs, leaders and managers above, it is clear that they all have both an external and an internal focus. Establishing direction; strategising; finding new opportunities; working with customers, suppliers and funders; and telling the story of the organisation's achievements are largely outside-facing. Operations and control at one level and championing the culture of the organisation at a different level are more internal in nature. Establishing and championing distinctive values is both internal and external. On balance—and there is an element of generalisation—there might be a conventional-wisdom expectation that leaders would be more external than internal, and managers more internal than external. The implication of this assumption would be that as people progress to more top management (corporate leadership) roles, their perspective might be expected to change. Of course, both direction and operations are critical if an organisation is to succeed.

It is, therefore, appropriate to examine in more detail the different personal styles of individual leaders and managers. We developed the framework in Table 3.1 from our reading and observations of people in a variety of contexts. It identifies seven different personal styles; each style represents an important contribution that is required. The contention is that an individual will have one dominant (and probably preferred) style that characterises them, but will invariably exhibit elements of

TABLE 3.1 Personal styles

	Style	Relevant behaviour	Contribution
1	The Aspirational Visionary	Provides clear direction (and inspires support)	Directional
2	Public Relations Style	Provides a high and visible external profile to ensure recognition for achievements	Tends towards directional
3	Opportunist	Sees and champions new opportunities	Directional
4	Reflective Style	'Sense maker' whose key contribution is to provide thoughts and routes forward. Embraces an analytical approach but can involve more intuitive insight	Both directional and operational
5	Operational (Tactical) Style	Hands-on involvement in activities, often continuing to stay involved in activities for which he/she was previously responsible	Operational
6	Financial Engineering Style	A champion of tight control systems who 'manages' through a thorough grasp of the details	Operational
7	The Human Resource Style	Provides support to others in a more open (and possibly more informal) internal environment where considerable empowerment is in evidence. Embraces encouraging innovation and intrapreneurship.	Operational, but by enabling change through people

more than one. The challenge for any CEO—and would-be CEO—is to appreciate their own natural style but to realise that someone else will need to make a balancing contribution to ensure everything that needs to be done gets done. This is what we associate with a management team. Anita Roddick, for example, was very strong on the visionary and public relations styles—she was a persuasive communicator both inside and outside The Body Shop—but her husband and business partner, Gordon, had a strong grasp of detail. She was directional; he was operational; together they were formidable.

We present the **entirepreneur** as someone who possesses many attributes and who can achieve directional and operational excellence and be effective both internally and externally. These people do exist, as we saw in Part One earlier, but being realistic they are relatively 'thin on the ground'. Being entrepreneurial should be aspirational for many people, and, as we have said, the holistic perspective is the key. At the same time we must not underestimate the ability and value of entirepreneurial teams that together contribute directional and operational excellence. The whole is more important than the individual parts.

It is important at this point to stress that there is no 'best' individual style profile. The natural style of the visible leader, though, will be a strong determinant of the culture of an organisation, what it feels like to be part of that organisation, and how it is seen by outsiders.

Steve Jobs would be seen as a visionary, as would Walt Disney.

> It is in Apple's DNA that technology alone is not enough. It is technology married with the liberal arts, married with the humanities that yields the results that make our hearts sing.
>
> *Steve Jobs, explaining his vision for Apple*
> *and its stream of innovative products*

Walt Disney was a creative visionary who saw the potential in theme parks and was determined to develop them—he saw them as a perfect vehicle for storytelling. His brother and co-director Roy was sceptical and he was able to persuade the Disney Board not to back Walt. But Walt was determined, and raised the money he needed on his own. He was proved right. There are, though, many reasons behind the success of Disney theme parks: attention to detail, slick operations and committed staff who deliver very high levels of customer satisfaction are amongst them.

Richard Branson is an ideal example of the high-profile entrepreneur and leader who 'is his company'; he is also an opportunist. (Lord) Alan Sugar is another example of someone who realised the value of image and publicity and set out to build a profile with *The Apprentice* on television. Steve Jobs was also strong in this role. Pacing the stage at product launch events, and invariably dressed in jeans and a black turtleneck sweater, Jobs 'had an unrivalled ability to create an air of excitement and suspense. … He was Apple's most effective marketing tool.'

Fred Smith, the man behind FedEx, dreamed up the idea of a global courier service for a university assignment and, again despite scepticism on the part of others, set out to make it happen. A visionary, he always knew success would come down to the details—his ability to plan the operational aspects was critical.

Michael O'Leary at Ryanair realised the potential in the Southwest Airlines business model and set out to improve it; again, he has major strengths in operations and this drives the relentless cost reductions. Ray Kroc (McDonald's) and Howard Schultz (Starbucks) both made sure their operations delivered consistent high quality in businesses which rely on dispersed franchises and often staff who are young, part-time and relatively transient.

Sir Arnold Weinstock, who built General Electric Company (GEC) in the UK into a leading electronics and defence company, was seen as a financial expert, and his leadership style was based on stringent financial controls. He was actually criticised for the size of the cash mountain he built up: critics from the banking system were concerned that he had no need to borrow from them! He was once described rather tellingly as 'the best manager Britain has produced'. Weinstock began his working life at the Admiralty but then switched to be an estate agent. After marrying he joined his in-laws' business, making radios.

He rose to the top and, with a series of acquisitions, built GEC. After he retired Weinstock was replaced by George Simpson, a Scottish accountant with experience in the motor-vehicle industry. Simpson was more of a risk-taker, and, encouraged by a Finance Director who favoured high-growth industries, the pair invested the inherited cash mountain in telecommunications. Within a few years GEC had all but disappeared with a series of strategic misjudgements. Thousands of jobs had been lost. Weinstock had the 'control mentality' and discipline we associate with accountants; Simpson, who actually was an accountant, acted more like an entrepreneur, but not a good one.

A brief summary of conventional wisdom—where next?

Conventional wisdom tells us that managers get things done: using power, they organise and control people and activities. Leaders influence people to do (and want to do) things. Entrepreneurs see the opportunities that, first, kick things off, and second, keep the momentum going with innovations.

But managers lead and leaders manage, and both can be intrapreneurial. Entrepreneurs who start new businesses will need to be or become managers and/ or leaders if the business is to grow and be sustainable.

Nevertheless we persist in separating the roles and labelling people as entrepreneurs or leaders or managers. Bookshops have plenty of texts on management, small business management, leadership and entrepreneurship. Significantly, the majority of titles reflect a process-driven approach whilst this book takes an alternative person-centred approach.

The pressures and demands of the 'New Normal' world require, we believe, that we adopt an 'entire perspective' and look at an individual's ability to combine the traditionally role-related contributions of the entrepreneur, the leader and the manager into a single entirety. This person we are calling an **entirepreneur**.

Entirepreneurs like Steve Jobs, Richard Branson and Jack Welch were successful not simply because they were outstanding entrepreneurs or great business leaders—although they were both of these—but because of how they behaved and what they did and accomplished. And this is not fully captured by what is conventionally described as 'entrepreneurship' or 'leadership'.

Drawing on points we have made in this chapter, **entirepreneurs** learn from people both inside and outside the organisation and organise resources outside traditional boundaries; in the 'New Normal' world these boundaries, like organisation structures, are increasingly fluid. Their perspective and their 'horizons' are often unconventional.

To understand such people, we believe that we must start by looking at their personal goals and attributes, and then further examine these in the context of their loyalty and commitment to organisational colleagues and the organisation's customers and other external stakeholders. Fitting the organisational context will matter, as will flexibility, which helps explain why some people are able to move readily from a senior position in one organisation or setting to another, whilst others find this difficult. Really it is personal motivation that largely determines whether individuals opt to work for a particular type of organisation or start their own business, and it is their motivation that affects how they behave and the extent to which they want to drive and change things.

Essentially in Part Three we will argue that *who* you are determines how you see the world. This perspective is affected by one's passion and self-assurance. *Why* you choose to do what you do is in turn affected by your motivation and values.

These temperament factors impact on *what* you do, and the actions you take, which can be separated into directional and operational actions. Directional and operational behaviours, then, are outputs from how people deal with their temperament and use their talents. In turn, these are influenced by a person's 'world' and their experiences (some of which they create for themselves) and also by their underlying personality dimensions. Learned capabilities and skills develop the expertise which underpins this.

How you relate to other people—and deliver through their support and contributions—is also critical.

The next two chapters, which complete Part Two, discuss issues involved in dealing with the 'New Normal' (Chapter 4) and growth and sustainability (Chapter 5). Basically in these chapters we are looking at the directional and operational challenges before exploring the personal attributes of the effective **entirepreneurs** who are well-placed to deal with these challenges in today's 'New Normal' world.

4

DEALING WITH THE 'NEW NORMAL'

A large percentage of start-ups are recorded as failing in the first few years. Some close down; others 'disappear' but actually survive with a new owner after being bought out. Established organisations are not protected from the forces of change and competition, and the same things happen to them. There is an important difference between (complete) failure and failing but coming through with resilience. To give themselves the best chance of succeeding, organisations must (continue to) 'do the right things right'. In this chapter we explore what this means—in a changing world it invariably implies change.

One of our motivations for writing this book is to help individuals and organisations become more successful, because business failure comes at a price. There is a financial and economic cost when businesses fail; people lose their jobs and communities are affected. At an individual level, people can even be traumatised and certainly many lose self-confidence and self-efficacy. In turn, this can have a detrimental effect on others, especially family members.

By being more aware of the issues raised—and looking for opportunities to improve and change—individuals and their organisations could well improve their performance and thus social and economic outcomes in the turbulent times of the 'New Normal'.

Meeting the 'New-Normal' challenge

There are no easy answers to sustainability and success, especially when the business environment is turbulent and uncertain. Governments can help to make it easier for companies to access loans by reducing red tape and offering other incentives and support, but this is not enough. Running any business in the 'New Normal' world carries a risk that those involved must be willing to accept and take.

One conventional view that we continue to support is that making—and learning from—mistakes is important.

Fortunes change periodically; success today is no guarantee of success tomorrow. At the same time, by making the right changes, poor performance can be turned around and improved. 'Keeping faith' is sometimes important when things are not happening as one would like, but, equally, it is possible to be too loyal to products and people such that the need to change is ignored. Being vigilant and looking for fresh opportunities is, therefore, essential. Knowledge and skills help, but there is still some reliance on instinct, intuition and luck. What happens relates to the people making the decisions and the choices they make. Building a strong team and looking to bring out the best from those involved therefore matters, as does paying attention to the details. This will always be easier if there is clarity of purpose and direction. Put simply, organisations, and the people who run them, are looking to find a successful strategy linked to a genuine opportunity, to execute it well and to change it at the appropriate time.

Succeeding

The basics of success

No business can hope to succeed if it fails to meet two basic tests. First, its products and services must be 'fit for purpose'. They must work—reliably—and do what they promise to do. Second, they must be affordable to the target customers. If there is competition, they should appear to offer better value than rival products and services. Price will often matter, but other things constitute value for the customer.

Really successful businesses, though, offer more than functionality and affordability. Design and aesthetics—how something looks and feels—can have an impact on buying decisions. One of the reasons for Apple's success is the design and look of its products; Stobart trucks stand out because of their distinctive colours and clean appearance. When ownership of a product or brand is meaningful to customers, the business concerned has something of genuine value. Ownership or involvement has become aspirational. Apple's products do not have to be the best technically, because for many they are the 'ones to have'. McDonald's burgers may not win in taste tests against some leading rivals, but it remains the preferred fast-food destination of choice for many people. Everyone recognises the golden arches and what the brand stands for. There is an emotional attachment to it. Many fans around the world who support Manchester United and wear their red shirts—but who may never attend a live United match—want to be associated with the recognition and success attributed to the club and the brand. The values associated with the brand provide significant reinforcement to this message; when such loyalty can be built up and maintained, the businesses concerned command loyalty. Many successful **entirepreneurs** have realised this but, again, realisation and appreciation do not mean something can be achieved easily.

Successful businesses

At the simplest level, successful businesses are doing the right things right. They are satisfying their various stakeholders, and they are doing it efficiently. Their existing strategies are sound and their execution strong, and they are finding new opportunities.

One simple strategic evaluation test is appropriateness, feasibility and desirability—this is relevant for both existing strategies and new proposals. Simply, *appropriateness* implies a potentially winning strategic position and a sound business model, which we explain in more detail below. A need exists and it is being met. There is a potential customer base and they have a compelling reason to buy the product or use the service. They are choosing it rather than an alternative offering. *Feasibility* means the strategy can be implemented by the organisation in question. It has, or it can obtain, the technical capability and the required resources, and it can produce the product or provide the service at a lower cost than the selling price that can be commanded. In addition, it has a route to market. *Desirability* requires a belief by the staff involved in the product or service and a genuine will to follow through and 'make it happen'.

From an outcome perspective, a business needs to perform effectively if it is to succeed, which implies:

- a good underlying 'idea', whether we see this as a product, a service or an opportunity;
- how well this idea is brought to market and the relevant key strategic choices that provide direction;
- the activities (operations) required to execute the strategic decisions;
- the team of people involved and how well they work together;
- the level of desire and the determination to succeed, particularly amongst the people 'doing the driving';
- how well the team deals with the uncertainties and competition they have to deal with.

Here we can see evidence of contributions we conventionally associate with the entrepreneur, the leader and the manager.

Evaluating success

One approach to evaluating success might be to test for the presence of the 'virtuous circle', which links satisfied customers with committed employees and financial success. It takes motivated employees to continuously achieve high levels of customer service and satisfaction. Customers' willingness to buy the product or service (as well as its price, which in turn is affected by efficient operations) dictates revenue and profits. At least some of the surplus should be reinvested to support the employees. This virtuous circle is attractive and relevant to our arguments because it carries the idea of entirety.

A cause-and-effect approach is to discuss and evaluate what we have opted to call 'the measuring pole':

- **P** is people: who they are, what they do, how they do it and how well they do it.
- **O** is opportunity: organisations must always be on the lookout for new opportunities.
- **L** is leadership: by this we mean the ability to envision a direction and strategise; to see what's possible and be clear about how to achieve it.
- **E** is execution: resourcing, organising and controlling—in essence, operationalising.

Again, if we relate this to conventional wisdom we will see evidence of the roles we normally associate with the entrepreneur (opportunity), the leader (vision and discernment) and the manager (execution). The people aspect is something shared by them all.

The business model

Strategic success is clearly related to the quality of the 'business model', which comprises:

- **What** the organisation does (its products and services).
- **Who** its target customers are.
- **Why** they have a compelling reason to buy this particular product or service, which relates to the key entrepreneur characteristic of advantage.
- **How** the product or service is procured, manufactured and delivered.
- **When** necessary changes are made in a dynamic and competitive environment.

An excellent example of a successful business model is that for low-cost (and no-frills) airlines such as Southwest Airlines (in America), EasyJet and, of course, European-market-leader Ryanair. This type of airline does not set out to offer the same level of service as the leading global long-haul carriers, and never implies that it does. Its prices are lower and what it offers can be very attractive to anyone who is satisfied with a basic value-for-money flight, whether for business or leisure.

Organisations, then, succeed because of what they do and achieve. But this success must in part be down to the person (or people) behind what the organisation does—the people who 'call the shots'. The most outstanding CEOs, like Michael O'Leary of Ryanair, are often **entirepreneurs**.

To reinforce this point it is worth pointing out that although we often talk about funding for business, businesses really receive investments. When this happens it is because the people behind the business are seen to be worth investing in. Investors are persuaded by their motivation, hunger, passion, determination and drive just as much as, if not more so, than they are by the idea being proposed. This is why we have taken a person-centred approach to explaining the **entirepreneur**.

Success is typically measured by performance, and we really should put performance into context before deciding how successful an organisation is. How well is it performing when set alongside its major competitors? How does it compare with the average performance in its industry? Is it achieving the outcomes and outputs that its key stakeholders expect? Performance is both absolute and relative.

Failing

A large percentage of new business start-ups disappear in the first few years of life. Some are acquired but many more close down. Something goes wrong. A number of UK- and US-based businesses—including Silverjet, Eos Airlines and MAXjet Airways— were set up by entrepreneurs determined to take the low-cost, no-frills airline model and adapt it for all business class flights to America. None have succeeded, although British Airways operates a small subsidiary that flies all business class from Paris to New York and Washington. The idea might have seemed like a good one, but there was no real opportunity. Demand for such a service was not sufficient.

Some new businesses that do survive reach a point—sometimes quite quickly, sometimes after several years—where they appear to metaphorically run out of steam. Maybe the product or service needs changing or replacing; maybe the owner has failed to develop, is over-stretched and unable to envision a new future. This is a critical time and situation for any business. Large businesses also sometimes make major errors of judgement which cause their performance to deteriorate— with varying degrees of consequence.

Some years ago, Coca-Cola launched 'New Coke'. The long-standing formula for the drink had been changed, apparently as a reaction to blind taste tests implying consumers preferred the taste of rival Pepsi Cola. Disgruntled customers campaigned aggressively and even poured the new drink down street drains for television cameras. Eventually the new product was withdrawn in favour of the original. After a few years, sales and profits—and clear market leadership—were restored to where they had been. It has been argued that despite the company's incredible success, Coca-Cola executives had underestimated the pull of the brand itself, which made Coca-Cola 'the drink' to have, whether or not it was outstandingly the best tasting. The CEO at the time, Roberto Goizueta, who had earlier launched the very successful Diet Coke, made it through, and he led the company until his death in 1997.

We earlier cited George Eastman, founder of Eastman Kodak Company, as an **entirepreneur**. The business he started has survived as a completely different organisation after film photography was largely abandoned and replaced by digital technology, but it is no longer the company it once was. Kodak became the leading name in film photography but, although the first electronic camera was built by an Eastman Kodak engineer, Steven Sasson, Kodak is no longer a leading name in digital photography. Electronics companies such as Canon, Nikon and Fuji are dominant.

When businesses fail there are many reasons and stories involved. Time and again there will have been a failing in one or more of three broad, but key, aspects: competitiveness (the business either never had or lost its attractiveness to the market); misjudgements about opportunities and poor decisions relating to activities;

or financial meltdown (the business could no longer cover its costs, either through poor investment or poor management of daily activity). We can see how these imply weaknesses or shortcomings in direction and operations, although it would be more conventional to summarise the issue as either weak leadership or poor management.

Sometimes, though, businesses fail because they are too ambitious. It is possible to be too visionary and too far ahead of prospective customers. People are simply not yet ready for what is being proposed. Simply making something available will not automatically generate demand, although this definitely happens on occasion (Apple's iPhone was an example of this). The risk of waiting, of course, is that another competitor might launch and be successful. Timing is therefore an important element. Get it right and there is a real opportunity; get it wrong and there really isn't an opportunity. Ironically, some time later the opportunity might well materialise. We can see evidence of this with notepad computers. The models that have taken the market by storm (including the Apple iPad) were not the first ones available. The timing was right when there were additional applications that increased the all-round attraction and usefulness of the machines relative to their cost. Some commentators would see the earlier attempts as worthy failures as, in a way, they created opportunities for others later on. In the turbulence of the 'New Normal' we wonder whether timing might become more challenging.

Luck

Finally, it is important to briefly mention luck. Being in the right place at the right time (to perhaps talk to someone of influence or spot an opportunity) is sometimes purely opportunistic, but on other occasions there is an element of smart luck. Simply, organisations—or more realistically, people—have put themselves in a position to capitalise on an opportunity, should it arise. They really make their own luck.

There is also hard luck, which happens when some external event threatens a business. This might or might not have been foreseeable. Returning to our sporting metaphors, television sometimes confirms that referees or umpires make 'wrong decisions' that affect the outcome of a match. Those affected adversely maybe did nothing wrong; in fact, they were perhaps doing the right things and doing them well, but circumstances and events changed the rules dramatically and unexpectedly. Effectual and emergent events can work both positively and negatively.

The story of the 'Dambusters' in May 1943 features both entirepreneurship and luck. In a legendary bombing raid, a squadron of Lancaster bombers succeeded in destroying two of the three dams that controlled the water supply to the Ruhr Valley industrial area in Germany—although the loss of life amongst the airmen was high. The No. 617 Squadron was formed for the raid, with the men largely hand-picked by its leader, Wing Commander Guy Gibson—who also led their training in low-level flying. They were required to fly the complete mission at low level and drop the specially designed circular bouncing bombs from a specific height and distance. The very low height required for releasing the bomb was to prevent it fragmenting before bouncing across the water in the way that a skimmed pebble does. Gibson helped design the spotlight system they used to make this precision bombing possible—he got the idea from theatre spotlights. The bomb itself was created by Barnes Wallis, an inspirational engineer whose inventions had a major impact on the war. They only had two months' time for planning, preparation and successful execution. On the night of the raid the first bombs did not breach the first dam, in part because of enemy fire. After his own bomb missed, Gibson flew alongside several other bombers when they were making their runs in order to draw the flak away from them. In this respect he was 'making things up as he went along'; this had not been planned.

The luck element? The need was urgent and the raid required a full moon to allow the low-level flying. The window of opportunity was therefore just a few days, and fortunately the weather was clear and dry. It may not have been—some later raids by the No. 617 Squadron were relative failures, thwarted by adverse weather conditions, most notably fog. In addition, one young German anti-aircraft gunner later confessed he forgot to unlock the firing mechanism on his gun when he had a southbound 'Dambuster' plane in his sights; the bomb from this plane is believed to have hit its target. The same gunner was good enough to shoot down a Lancaster on its return journey.

Gibson did not survive the war; he was shot down in action in 1944. Somewhat tellingly perhaps, Wallis later described Gibson as a man 'born for war but born to fall in war'.

It might be concluded that some failures are unfortunate, some are more worthy than others (it was a 'brave attempt'), and many come down to errors of judgement and mistakes made by people. Captain Robert Falcon Scott is portrayed as a heroic figure, even though he was beaten by Roald Amundsen in his quest to be first to reach the South Pole. Along with others in his team, Scott lost his life in the attempt. Amundsen's success has been attributed to a clear direction for his expedition as well as more rigorous preparation and attention to detail than was the case with Scott.

When failure happens it is likely that those involved lost sight of the big picture, or failed to innovate and find new opportunities, or were weak on the detailed execution of their ideas and plans. In other words, at least one of the key strands of entirepreneurship was missing.

It is important to appreciate why organisations tend to succeed and fail, just as it is important to understand how to do things (techniques), but there is no 'magic formula' or right answer. It is not a question of 'do this and you will succeed'. What happens comes down to people—how they make sense of things in the 'New Normal', their ability to spot opportunities, their willingness to act, and their capabilities to make things happen. It is for this reason we take a person-centred approach to the **entirepreneur**.

Finally, two critical thoughts: anything can cease to be an opportunity in the dynamics of the 'New Normal', however successful it is today; and everything an organisation does is capable of improvement.

5

GROWTH AND SUSTAINABILITY

All around the world people continually start new businesses. This must continue. Some of them are a 'necessity' to provide an income for people without jobs, but others have growth potential—if the potential is seized. Only a small proportion of these start-ups will actually grow into something substantial and have a marked impact on people's lives. Those that do are different. Their products and services are different. The would-be entrepreneur who starts the business is different. They also succeed in meeting the growth-cycle challenge.

New businesses

Generally, many people think of would-be entrepreneurs as people who start new businesses. Those who do this may or may not turn out to be true entrepreneurs, who, as we have argued, are people who *build* businesses that grow into something significant.

One key proviso, however: entrepreneurial people don't just build businesses. They can be present and active wherever there are organisations building something of sustainable value. They are important contributors in schools, hospitals, charities, churches and other public services.

Many new businesses that do survive stay small and don't grow in any significant way. They are still important both economically and socially. The lack of growth might be because there is no real growth potential based on there being nothing really innovative or distinctive in what they are doing. They can employ themselves and maybe a few others, but often they are competing on price and relying on high levels of customer service because their customers could readily buy something very similar from someone else. This may not be sustainable in the long run. But a failure to grow might also be because of the way they run their business.

Think about it for a moment. If you were planning (and maybe you have planned) to start a new business, chances are you would begin developing your ideas around something you know you can do—which, ideally, would be something you can do easily and well but that others find difficult, and something for which there is a demand and customers. Once the business is started around your skills and capabilities, it is quite likely that you are the expert, or perhaps the 'technician', in that business. Everything revolves around you, and you might well allow it to continue that way (which can be a mistake or, at the very least, a limiting factor). If that business is to grow you have to build a team of people to whom you can delegate specified tasks. You have to give them direction and you have to specify what the tasks are and set goals. You have to lead and influence this team; you have to organise and control the work they do and monitor progress. This is where you would find out the extent to which you possess attributes we would typically associate with a leader and a manager as well as a technician (or, in this context, an expert). Eventually, the assumption is that you will need to move further and further away from the activity front line and orchestrate the work and possibly leave others to get on with it whilst you move on to to develop new initiatives.

There are, then, likely to be significant organisational weaknesses if the founding 'entrepreneur' fails to develop, as he or she will remain absorbed in the operational issues, doing everything rather than establishing systems and procedures others can implement. Equally, though, it is sometimes the case that the founder does move on and step back from the operational issues, but in the process loses the entrepreneurial drive that started everything off. There is no search for new opportunities; the focus is on maintaining what is working today. But as we know, in the 'New Normal', what is working today may not be appropriate tomorrow.

We saw earlier that the ultimate personal development path in an existing organisation might be:

Employment (as a follower) > series of promotions > appointment as CEO

Here we are describing a somewhat similar path:

Self-employment > growing a business > running a larger business > development into a corporate CEO

Growing businesses

It is important to factor in that when a new business succeeds and grows there are likely to have been three transformations:

- First, an idea for a new product or service has been developed into a winning opportunity, where customers have been found and satisfied.
- Second, a raw or would-be entrepreneur has become a competent practitioner and has proved to be entirepreneurial.
- Third, an activity that started with a hot desk or in a garage or spare bedroom has evolved into a proper organisation with employees.

The informal approach that often characterises new start-ups will have given way to more formality and professionalism, but not to the extent that creativity and innovation has been stifled. The New Zealand business community uses the expression 'Number 8 wire' to describe the make-do-and-mend approach adopted by the small business owner to deal with unexpected problems and issues: they find a way to fix it. The phrase comes from farmers in New Zealand, who often live in isolated rural areas and use 8-gauge wire as a solution to many of their problems. In one respect it is an approach in which they can and do take great pride, but 'just fixing it' is not the approach required by a successful business, which is often required instead to adopt a more formal and systematic style. Changing the culture and approach can be a tricky challenge as organisations grow.

From this it should be apparent why any potential investors are generally more likely to commit when they declare they like the product and they also believe in the person. The challenges of innovation, change, sustainability and growth are real for every organisation. The most recent economic recession reinforced how important it is to have products and services that people select and prioritise and that are affordable for them. When selling is tough and supply exceeds demand in an industry, the strongest competitors are the survivors. Who are they? Typically they are the ones who have differentiated products and services that change when they need to in order to 'stay ahead of the game', and who are productive: their costs are not wildly (if at all) higher than those of their rivals. And for some there are also additional and visible social and environmental concerns that put them in a favourable light with certain influencers and stakeholders.

Entirepreneurs and growing businesses

Entirepreneurs, then, make sure the organisation has a clear vision and direction for what can make it successful into the future. They set about making sure this promise is delivered by building a team of capable people and influencing what they do, always accepting that others will be doing much of the actual work.

This team will organise, keep things going and keep things 'on the rails', making sure that the resources needed are available, that operations are planned and run efficiently, that products and services meet deadlines and hit quality targets, that customers are satisfied, and that costs are controlled.

This implies a long-term vision that gives a clear sense of purpose, a direction that people understand, and a set of integrating values that encourage a shared commitment. All the time there is also a need to be looking for new opportunities to improve things and keep the business innovative and competitive, and in the context of uncertainty in the 'New Normal' world. People need to be flexible: activities and operations will change, sometimes reactively, sometimes proactively and sometimes very quickly.

It is wrong to assume that people always start out as entrepreneurs who spot and act upon an opportunity and then develop manager and leader attributes. There is no sequential process per se. **Entirepreneurs** typically have multiple directional and operational attributes from the outset, although these all can, and invariably will, be strengthened over time and with experience. Critically, **entirepreneurs** know which attributes to engage and draw upon at any time, depending on where the focus of their energy and activity needs to be.

People who are not **entirepreneurs** may well be dissatisfied or frustrated that they are failing to achieve their aspirations—although it would not be unusual for them to be relatively vague in the way they articulate these aspirations. Moreover, too few of them will be able to explain their vision and strategy with any real clarity. Some of them will be in this position because they have failed to move on from what Michael Gerber describes as 'doing it, doing it, doing it' which was their main role when the business started. The business will not be progressing through the 'cycle of growth'.

The cycle of growth

Figure 5.1 builds on the theme of the three transformations mentioned above. The diagram is based on the idea that there is constant movement clockwise around the circle, but that there is always the likelihood of iteration—rather than there being only one direct route around—and that at any point there is the possibility to drop out of the circle.

The diagram reflects how a business takes root when someone has an idea. Usually, there is an injection of creativity: at the extreme this will be a vision of

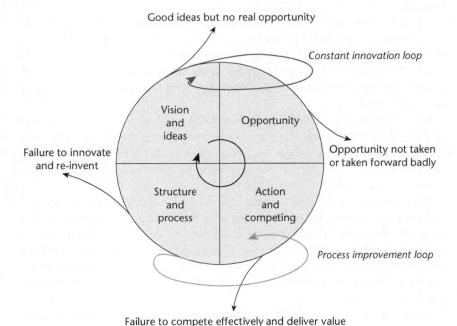

FIGURE 5.1   The growth–cycle challenge

how something might be made markedly different in a way that people value. This becomes an opportunity once the potential is confirmed with research, investigation and further thought—the person with the idea should be receiving positive material feedback. Some ideas are never opportunities—they are perhaps very creative, but really they are little more than good ideas. There is no real business opportunity.

When there is a genuine opportunity it needs to be taken forward and acted upon. At least some time for further reflection can be valuable at this point—jumping straight in without any detailed thinking can be a mistake. Of course there is the risk that planning can stifle action, and action will be required. Resources—financial, people, operational—will need to be secured as necessary. Customers need to be found and orders secured. They then need to be satisfied. The chances are high that even at this early stage things will not go fully to plan. Those involved must learn and adapt, as the strategy will be emerging all the time. As people learn, there is always an opportunity for refinement, innovation and improvement. There should be a search for improved productivity opportunities as well as opportunities to add fresh value for customers. The potential risk in some businesses is that the founder will probably still be doing much of the work, taking most of the decisions during at least the early part of this phase, and not finding enough time to reflect and learn. Opportunities to improve may well be lost.

Any potential opportunity is lost if it is not taken or its execution is flawed. The failure to learn, a common characteristic of many small businesses, can be a serious drawback.

It is also at this point that the founder can get locked into the present. He or she is fully hands-on, and probably enjoying the buzz and the challenge. Problems crop up all the time; dealing with them satisfactorily can be personally rewarding. The issue is the business has become caught up in the cut-and-thrust of daily competition and the key decision makers can lose sight of the big picture as they focus on day-to-day details.

When this happens, there is a real danger that the business will become—and remain—more reactive than proactive. Others are driving the agenda. The likelihood of this will increase if there is a failure to reflect and learn as the opportunity truly materialises. The downside outcome is the business loses its competitiveness; it ceases to be relevant.

What needs to happen is that a proper structure is put in place and people have clear roles and responsibilities. The business has become a proper organisation. It is critical that this more formalised organisation does not become overly bureaucratic and lose sight of the need for fresh ideas, innovation and sometimes reinvention to perpetuate the cycle. Those in charge need to both influence and organise others, exercising empathy and appreciating the contribution of people at both the individual and team levels.

Moreover, what we understand as 'structure' is not rigid thought: ideas and options on structure change. Recent years have seen networks and partnerships with an emphasis on collaboration and sharing provide growth opportunities for many organisations. Indeed, in technology-driven industries it is not at all unusual to see organisations with particular expertise in one component element of a product collaborate with a number of others, all with different areas of expertise. There are instances where companies that compete with each other in certain product areas collaborate on the development of other initiatives.

As some businesses grow there is a tendency for increased diversification, especially if there is merger activity. This brings fresh challenges and pressures. As we saw with our stories of entirepreneurship, it is important to maintain control as the strategy and scope become more complex.

An effective **entirepreneur** will, of course, grow and develop as the organisation develops. He or she will understand the significance of all the quadrants and the need for positive momentum. That doesn't mean he will automatically be comfortable and competent in every contribution. You might like to think about where you naturally fit in our diagram. Thinking about the following four activities and ranking them in order of preference will give you an indication. Which of these would you enjoy the most? Least?

1. Creating and making something from cast-aside household items, ideally something you have conceptualised rather than following someone else's pattern.
2. Reading a book that makes you think, or simply sitting or going for a walk and taking time to reflect on decisions you have to make.
3. Playing a sport of choice actively and competitively.
4. Taking control of something, perhaps organising, building and managing a team of volunteers involved in something useful for the community—something that requires you to take charge and make sure the desired outcomes are achieved.

We might loosely reconcile these four alternatives with the four quadrants of the figure, starting with number one in the top left and moving round in a clockwise direction. It is often a critical issue that numbers one and three are more popular than numbers two and four. But taking at least some time to reflect rather than jump straight in, and also being willing to step aside from intense hands-on engagement will always be critical issues.

Sustainability

> The challenge: institutionalising success and still keeping an edge of craziness and wildness.
>
> *Anita Roddick*

Businesses do not necessarily have to grow bigger in order to survive and thrive, but they do have to grow in terms of their capabilities. It is rare that changing nothing or 'staying as you are' is a realistic option. Sustainability, therefore, demands an approach and perspective that embraces continuous change, but not necessarily change for the sake of change—rather, change as appropriate. Sometimes this is the pursuit of a fresh growth opportunity; on other occasions it can be change to help the organisation recover from a setback. Change stops being a managed process as such but instead it becomes a way of life in and for the 'New Normal' organisation. It is important to recognise that every employee is potentially the source of a good idea that the organisation might take forward. Drawing out and recognising their thoughts and ideas should become natural and culturally embedded in the organisation.

The **entirepreneur's** approach to controlling things has a strong ethos of creation. Protection (of present products and ways of doing things) can be really important whilst ever they remain relevant for customers, but preserving existing strengths should not be allowed to stifle progress. It has long been understood that many successful organisations have a portfolio of products or services. Some are established and successful; they generate serious revenues. They are clearly important, but without periodic improvement and refreshment, they may soon lose their edge. New products are required to replace products that are no longer as successful as they once were. Some of these will, at any time, be in the development stage, whilst others will have been launched but are still establishing themselves. New product development (driven by innovation), establishing new products in the market (with a strong emphasis on marketing) and nurturing established products (with a strong operational and quality orientation) imply different mindsets, but they are all important and must be blended together. The question we must address is whether many organisations actually want to be entirepreneurial. There is a comfort zone in continuing with the known and trusted—especially if it is working ... for the moment, at least.

Let us not forget that Steve Jobs began as the co-founder of Apple, but systematically became culprit (blamed for poor performance), outcast (sacked from the company he started), returning prodigal son (brought back when the company was in even deeper trouble) and ultimate saviour. But one thing he did do was inspire a stream of radically new products, never losing sight of the need to keep refreshing each one as rivals started to challenge Apple's position. The products were of high and generally reliable quality; design was always at the forefront. Whilst it may not have been Jobs' personal forte, he learned the significance of operations and a sound supply chain, and recruited people to make sure Apple delivered on its promises. This is how Apple became dominant and inspirational. Put simply, Jobs' imagination for what was possible—and encouraging others to make it possible—drove Apple to greatness. Only time will tell how truly sustainable Apple will be without his larger-than-life presence. Regardless, he built one of the most outstanding companies and iconic brands the world has known. And he was an **entirepreneur**.

PART THREE
The person dimension

Introduction

Thus far we have provided real-life examples of what it is to be an **entirepreneur**. We have given our reflections on today's 'New Normal' and how it calls for a person who is entrepreneur, leader and manager and more—all rolled into one. In Part 3, we consider what defines **entirepreneurs** as people, and what makes them special. We term this the 'person dimension'. We do not concern ourselves with the processes and procedures of business; there are many books already available that cover these topics. Instead, we describe the key personal attributes of the **entirepreneur** and provide you with the opportunity to measure your own attribute strengths.

We appreciate that **entirepreneurs** are thinly spread among the general population and that not everyone can reach the top of an organisation. But this does not mean that we should not seek a better match between those who have the ability to be **entirepreneurs** and those who serve in that role. Since most people are not aware of where their strengths lie, it is not surprising that mismatches do occur. We hope that this more analytical part of the book will help you to think through where your own strengths lie and thereby identify your career potential.

We group the attributes required of the **entirepreneur** under four headings, using the symbols of a pack of cards.

- ◆ Talent
- ♥ Temperament
- ♣ Technique
- ♠ Discernment

There is a perhaps surprising correlation between the symbols and the attribute groups they represent.

- ◆ The Diamond is rare and precious, like *talent*.
- ♥ The Heart is the seat of the emotions and determines our *temperament*.

Technique and discernment have a more tenuous link with their symbols, but there is still a connection.

- ♣ The Club is made from a tree with bulbous roots and was the weapon of the Greek god Hercules. In more recent times it was 'an implement for military gymnastics'. In 1866 a British officer in India wrote that 'the wonderful club exercise is one of the most effectual kinds of athletic training'.[1] An important part of *technique* is training, and, as we discuss later, 'deliberate practice'.
- ♠ The Spade in the time of the Greeks was the blade or cutting edge of a sword. In a Biblical analogy the 'sword of the Spirit' is described as being 'sharper than any two-edged sword, piercing to the division of soul and of spirit and discerning the thoughts and intentions of the heart'.[2] The sword needs an effective cutting edge, or Spade, if it is to *discern*.

Our four attribute sets—or suits—have a long history:

- ◆ Talent is about the basic abilities inherent within us. The Greek word 'talanton' was a unit of weight or money and indicated value and worth.
- ♥ Temperament concerns the kind of people we are. It determines our behaviour and derives from the Greek idea of humours or tempers.
- ♣ Technique covers the skills we acquire by practice and experience. It comes from the Greek *tekhne*, meaning skill or art. The words 'technique' and 'technology' both evolved from this root.
- ♠ Discernment is from the Greek *kriticos*, which means 'discerning judgement' as is required in a court of law. It involves the sifting and evaluation of evidence.

We developed the idea of Talent, Temperament and Technique in our work on Entrepreneurs.[3] As a short-hand we use the term '3Ts' to describe them. We have now added a fourth attribute set, 'Discernment'. It directly affects issues of strategy and decision-making and is an important addition. Certainly the entrepreneur, leader and manager each need discernment but for the **entirepreneur** it is this attribute that holds the others together and provides the background for the 3Ts to perform at their top level.

The metaphor of playing cards illustrates several aspects of our approach.

1.   Playing cards have different strengths, as do people. As we explain in Chapter 7 onwards, these strengths are individual and, most importantly, can be measured.
2.   All cards are in one of four suits, just as we have four main 'attribute sets'.
3.   Each suit is made up of different value cards that give the 'hand' a particular strength. The attributes and sub-attributes that we describe each have different strengths, as do the individual cards in a 'hand'.
4.   The values of each card are known only to each player or team. In the text you are given the opportunity to score yourself on the attributes within the four sets or suits. Your hand is personal, derived by you.
5.   In some games the ace is 'high' and a person with a hand of four aces is the winner. A winning hand for the **entirepreneur** is to have four aces.

Taken as part of a whole, these four attribute sets provide a fuller and more balanced description of the 'person dimension' than each is able to do alone. In these chapters we divide them into their component parts and, after a description of each subset, we provide a series of questions for you to consider. These questions form the basis of a self-assessment that you can use to derive a measure of your strength across the four attributes and determine a final **entirepreneur** score.

Whilst we believe there is value in trying to quantify strengths, it is important to see them not so much as a score but as an understanding of where strengths lie and what that says about your abilities and aspirations.

We structure Part 3 of the book around each of the four attribute sets and provide a chapter on each. By way of background, we begin in Chapter 6 with a review of the present understanding of the 3Ts and the debate that surrounds their use. We conclude that they are valid and work quite adequately for what we are trying to explain and evaluate. We do not include any comment on Discernment at this stage because, as far as we are aware, it has not been the subject of the same level of debate.

6

THE 3TS—EXPLAINED

The phrase 'nature and nurture' is a convenient jingle of words, for it separates under two distinct heads the innumerable elements of which personality is composed. Nature is all that a man brings with himself into the world; nurture is every influence from without that affects him after his birth.[1]

Sir Francis Galton, 1874

By way of introduction to the 3Ts we now use our deck of cards metaphor to discuss the age-old question of 'nature and nurture'.

Sir Francis Galton (1822–1911), a half-cousin of Charles Darwin, put a new slant on the 'born or made' question when in 1874 he used the term 'nature and nurture'. Five years earlier he had carried out an analysis of 'eminent men' and their relatives and identified three key factors that together produced this elite group. These were *ability*, *zeal* and the capacity for *hard work*. They have a direct correspondence with our 3Ts.

- *ability* is a *Talent* issue;
- *zeal* comes from *Temperament*;
- and *hard work* is essential in the acquisition of *Technique*.

Galton believed that his three factors were all inherited; our conclusion is shown in Figure 6.1.

Talent we see as an 'all nature' axis, with a person's range of talents marked along it according to their strengths. Rather like a plant, a talent starts as a seed that has to be grown and brought to maturity. Temperament and technique each play a part in that growth process, but the talent seed has to be there in the first place.

Talent	Temperament	Technique
All nature	Part nature, part nurture	All nurture
Has to be grown	Has to be managed	Has to be learnt

FIGURE 6.1 The person dimension

Temperament is the axis of personality and is part nature and part nurture. In *Genes, Environment and Personality*, Thomas Bouchard, at the Centre for Twin and Family Research at the University of Minnesota, reported his findings on identical twins separated at birth and brought up in different environments.[2] He concluded that 'the genetic contribution to "personality" is around 40 per cent'. Earlier work in 1960s by psychologist Hans Eysenck put the ratio at 75/25.[3] A reasonable rule of thumb, we believe, is 50/50: half nature and half nurture.

Research findings apart, people's personal experiences often recognise a genetic 'nature' contribution to personality across the generations.

> Steve Jobs … had long thought his personality was entirely the result of his life experiences until, as an adult, he met for the first time Mona Simpson, the sister he did not know he had. Jobs marvelled at how similar he was to Simpson despite having grown up with a different family. "I used to be way over on the nurture side but I've swung over to the nature side" Jobs told the *New York Times* in 1997.[4]
>
> *David Epstein, 2013*

As we discuss later, temperament is the leader of the 3Ts and must be managed with care. It can be the most positive of the three but it can also be the most destructive. Many a high achiever has been brought low by an addictive personality.

Technique is 'all nurture' and is something that has to be learnt. This is more than just a matter of 'practice makes perfect'. Studies of expert performances have shown that techniques can only be mastered with considerable dedication and hard work. This was first quantified by Simon and Chase in 1973, when they investigated elite chess players.[5] They concluded that 'there appears not to be on record any case where a person has reached grandmaster level without a decade's intense preoccupation with the game'.

We now describe each axis of the Person Dimension in greater detail and explain how the three axes interact together to provide a total picture of the person.

◆ Talent

In our work on talent two issues have stood out. First, we found a growing skepticism around the idea of innate talent. As talent is one of the three pillars of our approach, we present our own views on this debate. Second, in the domain of business we were surprised to find that there was little research that considered talent in any depth. However, in due course we came across the work of Donald Clifton (1924–2003) who spent many years studying talent as it applied to the workplace. When his own company, Selection Research Inc., acquired the Gallup Organisation in the late 1980s he was able to add the study of talent to its portfolio. Their work on 'talent strengths' acquired significant momentum and resulted in the 'StrengthsFinder' questionnaire that we discuss later in this chapter.

The talent debate

In his book *Genius Explained*, Howe concluded:[6]

> The belief that certain individuals can be said to have been born to be geniuses is not one that is supported by firm evidence, and the innate gifts or talents that are commonly believed to be possessed by a minority of individuals who are thereby imbued with a capacity to excel in particular areas of expertise are probably more mythical than real.

The heart of this debate goes back to 'The Role of Deliberate Practice in the Acquisition of Expert Performance' by Ericsson and colleagues, published in 1993.[7] This paper challenged the role of talent in the achievement of elite performance.

> In summary, our review has uncovered essentially no support for fixed innate characteristics that would correspond to general or specific natural ability... . We reject any important role for innate ability... . We agree that expert performance is qualitatively different from normal performance and even that expert performers have characteristics and abilities that are qualitatively different ... However we deny that these differences are immutable, that is, due to innate talent. Instead we argue that the differences ... reflect a life-long period of deliberate effort to improve performance.

Ericsson's anti-talent comments were subsequently picked up by others. Colvin's 2008 book, *Talent is Overrated: What Really Separates World-Class Performers from Everybody Else* is a popular interpretation of Ericsson's academic paper.[8] He concludes that 'at the very least, these talents are much less important than we usually think'.

Gladwell's 2008 book, *Outliers: The Story of Success* quotes Ericsson extensively.[9] Importantly, Gladwell adds the factor of 'opportunity' to the equation. In commenting on the success of Bill Gates and The Beatles he writes that 'what truly distinguishes their histories is not their extraordinary talent but their extraordinary opportunities'. On that basis he concludes that 'extraordinary achievement is less about talent than it is about opportunity'.

The 2009 book by Coyle *The Talent Code: Greatness Isn't Born, It's Grown* has a more positive take on talent.[10] Coyle accepts the role of 'deliberate practice' espoused by Eriksson but adds that 'if we overlay Ericsson's research with the new myelin science, we get something approaching a universal theory of skill that can be summed up in a temptingly concise equation: deep practice x 10,000 hours = world-class skill'.

Coyle then follows that sentence with the significant remark, 'But the truth is, life's more complicated than that.' His book unwraps that complexity in terms of a 'talent code' whose elements match our 3Ts.

Coyle's 'talent code' has three elements. These are:

1. 'Deep practice', corresponding to Ericsson's 'deliberate practice' and our *technique*.
2. 'Motivational fuel', which we class under *temperament*.
3. 'Ignition': 'a hot, mysterious burst; an awakening', which is a *talent* effect.

Despite his anti-talent stance, Ericsson does give a place to what Coyle termed 'ignition'. He acknowledges the importance of new ideas and innovation.

> The criteria for eminent performance goes beyond expert mastery of available knowledge and skills and requires an important innovative contribution to the domain... . In the arts and sciences, eminent achievements involve contributions of new ideas, theories and methods.
>
> *Ericsson, Krampe and Tesch-Romer, 1993*[11]

In other words, Ericsson and his colleagues accept that a creative contribution is required, and expert mastery alone is not enough. Many an 'eminent performance', to use Ericsson's term, has been the result of the special kind of 'creative contribution' that Coyle terms 'ignition'. The more familiar term, 'Eureka moment', corresponds closely to Coyle's 'hot, mysterious burst; an awakening'. We see such moments as clear examples of talent in action.

To strengthen this point we now give three Eureka moments experienced by what Galton would have called 'eminent men', or masters in their own field. Each held the position of Lucasian Chair of Mathematics at the University of Cambridge and made 'an important innovative contribution' to their domain.

Isaac Newton held the Lucasian Chair from 1669 to 1701. His moment of insight is linked with his observation of an apple falling from a tree. The source of this story is to be found in William Stukeley's 1752 *Memoirs of Sir Isaac Newton's Life*:[12]

> After dinner, the weather being warm, we went into the garden & drank tea under the shade of some apple tree; only he & myself. Amid other discourse, he told me, he was just in the same situation, as when formerly the notion of gravitation came into his mind. Why should that apple always descend perpendicularly to the ground, thought he to himself, occasioned by the fall of an apple, as he sat in contemplative mood. Why should it not go sideways, or upwards? But constantly to the Earth's centre? Assuredly the reason is, that the Earth draws it.

Paul Dirac was the Lucasian Professor from 1932 to 1969. He was 29 years old when he took the Chair, just three years older than Newton had been. Dirac was a remarkable mathematician and physicist. With no experimental evidence and only mathematical theory he predicted the presence of antimatter in the universe. In due course others proved him correct. He received the Nobel Prize for physics in 1933. At 31, he was the youngest theoretician ever to receive this prestigious award.

His biographer, Farmerlo, records Dirac's Eureka moment:[13]

> It was during one of his Sunday walks … that Dirac had his first great epiphany. Out of the blue, it occurred to Dirac that he had come across a special mathematical construction, known as a Poisson bracket. In one of his greatest insights Dirac saw that he could weave an entire carpet from this thread… . Within a few weeks of uninterrupted work he had set out the mathematical basis of quantum theory in analogy to the classical theory. Forty-two years later, he remembered, 'The idea first came in a flash … and provided … some excitement.'

The Dirac equation that resulted 'was something miraculous'. A colleague called it beautiful. Dirac was 'jubilant', not a common emotion for him. 'Like Einstein's equation of general relativity, the Dirac equation was universal yet fundamentally simple.' It is now carved on Dirac's commemorative stone in Westminster Abbey.

Stephen Hawking held the Lucasian Chair from 1979 until he retired in 2009. In his autobiography, *My Brief History*, Hawking comments:[14]

> My work on black holes began with a Eureka moment in 1970, a few days after the birth of my daughter, Lucy. While getting into bed, I realised that I could apply to black holes the causal structure theory I had developed for singularity theorems. There was an exciting period culminating in the Les Houches summer school in 1972 in which we solved most of the major problems in black hole theory.

These three 'eminent men' are, for us, clear examples of creative talent. As we discuss later, creativity is just one of a wide range of talents that can be identified and evaluated.

At the heart of the debate about talent is the question of whether or not an inborn genetic component is involved. In 1999, Howe wrote in *Genius Explained*:[15]

> There are no direct one-to-one relationships between genes and psychological characteristics, and the popular idea that there are genes 'for' complex traits is simply wrong.

More recently, in 2008 as we have noted, Geoff Colvin published *Talent is Overrated*, in which he asserts that:[16]

> since talent is by definition innate there should be a gene (or genes) for it. The difficulty is that scientists haven't yet figured out what each of the 20,000 plus genes does. All we can say for the moment is that no specific genes identifying particular talents have been found.

Maybe now, as the results of genetic studies make further progress, Colvin will be proved wrong. David Epstein's *The Sports Gene: Talent, Practice and the Truth about Success*, published in 2013 comes close to doing exactly that. He quotes psychologist Drew Bailey as saying:[17]

> Without both genes and environments, there are no outcomes. A present inability to pinpoint most sports genes doesn't mean they don't exist, and scientists will, slowly, find more of them.

In April 2003 the completion of the Human Genome Project was announced. Early work showed that it was impossible to identify single genes responsible for a specific effect—thus supporting Colvin's assertion. However, Epstein goes on to point out that it is gene sets, rather than individual genes, that are important. He provides some interesting examples in different sporting areas. If 'hundreds of genes are involved in each person's response to exercise' as Epstein asserts, then the task ahead is clearly momentous. Though this will be a long road, it does suggest that the idea of innate talent will not go away.

Talent in the domain of business

The influential educationalist Benjamin Bloom (1913–1999) understood the importance of talent in the learning process. In an interview conducted towards the end of his career he commented:[18]

> I am confident that virtually all people have enormous potential for something. The problem is to find some way of unearthing what that is and to make it possible for them to excel in the things they find most interesting.

Donald Clifton and the geneticist Claude Bouchard both agree that we all have 'enormous potential for something', and that the real problem is discovering that 'something'. Their approaches, however, are quite different.

In *Soar with Your Strengths*, Don Clifton and Paula Nelson outline their 'talent strengths' approach, in which the first step is to discover your strengths.[19] The second step is to 'use your strengths to achieve excellence'. Their extensive interview-based research has shown that we all have our own set of strengths, and that no one is without talent. They have concluded that each person has the potential to 'do one thing better than 10,000 other people'.[20]

Bouchard heads the Heritage Family Study across several universities in the USA.[21] The study seeks to identify the genetic influences associated with the efficacy of aerobic training for a person's well-being. It has also included the study of athletes. In his book *The Sports Gene*, Epstein reports Bouchard's finding that elite athletes must have both an 'elevated aerobic capacity' and be a 'high aerobic responder' to training.[22] He calculates the odds on having the required aerobic capacity as between 1 in 10 and 1 in 20 and those on being a high aerobic responder as between 1 in 10 and 1 in 50. The combined odds, then, become 1 in 100 or 1 in 1,000, which Bouchard describes as 'not pretty'. If this probability is in turn multiplied by a person's inclination for a third factor such as attitude—Epstein refers to an athlete who 'got sick of competing'—then the odds of not succeeding become even greater.

The difference between the approaches of Clifton and Bouchard is important to note. Clifton looks at the one thing a person can do better than 10,000 other people, whilst Bouchard looks at the odds against success and says, 'It's not pretty.'

The Gallup Organisation

Our own work on talent in the business domain was given a head start by the Gallup Organisation and specifically Don Clifton. Clifton had been professor of educational psychology at the University of Nebraska for almost 20 years when in 1969 he founded Selection Research Inc. (SRI). In 1988, following the death of his friend George Gallup, Clifton's SRI acquired the Gallup Organisation. Under his leadership Gallup added the area of 'talent' to its well-established opinion poll work, in which they were already world leaders.

It is important to recognise the significant research base behind Gallup's work on talent. By the early 1990s SRI, and then Gallup, had interviewed 'more than 250,000 successful salespeople, managers, leaders, executives, teachers, doctors, pilots and athletes'.[23] Studies were also conducted in businesses large and small and in more than 1,000 school districts across the USA.

In their 2008 book *Strengths-Based Leadership: Great Leaders, Teams, and Why People Follow*, Rath and Conchie comment that 'nearly a decade ago, Gallup unveiled the results of a landmark 30-year research project' in the area of strengths.[24]

Two important books provide the background to their StrengthsFinder evaluator. The titles speak for themselves:

- *First Break All the Rules: What the World's Greatest Managers Do Differently*[25]
- *Now, Discover your Strengths: How to Develop Your Talents and Those of the People You Manage*[26]

Gallup's contribution has been in two main areas. First, they have focused not just on talents but on talent strengths. Second, they have shown that talent strengths can be measured. As these are central to our own approach, we discuss each in turn.

Talent strengths

In many ways talents are self-evident, but it is also true that they can be hidden and never discovered. The most critical factor here is the availability of opportunity. As is often said, 'I might have been a concert pianist but no one gave me a piano.'

Another factor in the discovery of talent is to know what we are looking for. Gallup uses the term 'talent indicators'.[27] These are:

- 'Spontaneous reactions'—instinctive patterns of behaviour
- 'Yearnings'—inner compulsions often shown at an early age
- 'Rapid learning'—expertise comes naturally and is learnt quickly
- 'Satisfactions'—exercising a talent brings great satisfaction
- 'Timelessness'—talent never goes away

Reviewing these talent indicators in turn, we have:

Spontaneous reactions. Given the right opportunity, our talents come to us naturally. Often, they are so obvious that we take them for granted. The 400-metre athlete Roger Black found running so easy he never thought he was special. In his autobiography he comments, 'Throughout the sixth form I had been wondering, "What am I going to do after school?" And never once did I think, "I'm going to become an Olympic athlete."'[28] Later a friend suggested that in his year out before going to university he should think of joining the Southampton Athletic Club. His friend told him, 'You really are a very talented athlete.' Soon he was to win a 400-metre race and set a new British junior record. His friend and fellow athlete Kriss Akabusi told him, 'You're special. You don't realise it yet but you're going to be a great star.'

Yearnings. These are about strong inner feelings that drive us to do things. Entrepreneurial talents often show themselves at an early age. When, at 14 years old, Michael Dell took on a paper round, he turned it into a business. He made almost $20,000 a year, earning more than some of his teachers.[29] At the age of nine, Bernie Ecclestone, of Formula One fame, saw an opportunity in the wartime shortages. He set up a 'playground' business selling Chelsea buns to his school friends.[30]

Rapid learning. Bill Hewlett and Dave Packard provide an interesting example of 'rapid learning'. Their Stanford University professor, Fred Terman, encouraged them to set up their own business linked with a project that Hewlett had been working on. When interviewed some years later about those early days of Hewlett-Packard, Terman commented that 'any place in which you put them in a new environment they somehow learned what they needed to know very quickly … at a superior level. So when they got into business they didn't need a teacher; they somehow learned as they went along. They always learned faster than the problems built up.'[31]

Satisfactions. Finding you can do something gives great satisfaction. This is often seen in children when taking their first steps or riding a bicycle unaided. There is a 'wow!' factor associated with talent, and people get great satisfaction from exercising it. Joy and fun are important indicators of talent strength.

Timelessness. The urge of a particular talent never seems to go away, but it can be buried for many years. We have often been told by those with entrepreneurial talent that they wish they had started earlier in their lives. Ray Kroc was 52 years old when he bought out the McDonald brothers' business and turned it into an international institution. Talent is timeless, but is often constrained by opportunity.

This list of indicators is by no means exhaustive. Clifton and Nelson have an earlier list that also includes 'glimpses of excellence' and 'total performance of excellence'.[32] The perception of excellence covers both these terms. Often, before we know we have a talent there are moments when we realise we really are good at something. These 'glimpses' move on to continuous performance at a high level. As mentioned in Chapter 3, Mihaly Csikszentmihalyi uses the term 'flow' to describe these moments of excellence.[33] At such times you achieve excellence almost without effort. You are 'soaring with your strengths' and, like a bird in flight, it seems effortless.

This brings us to a conditional definition of talent. We cannot soar if we are not strong in the talent set required for the task.

The manufacturing director of the UK arm of a large engineering multinational was faced with the challenge of reaching production levels he knew would be exceedingly difficult to achieve. He decided on a plan of action that he believed possible, but only if the workforce of 1,000 people really got behind him. If the production target was not reached, there was a real threat from the head office that UK operations would be ended.

The manufacturing director decided that the best way to communicate the serious-ness of the situation to so many people at once was to speak to them over the somewhat impersonal public address system in the factory. This was clearly a high-risk strategy and failure was not an option. Luckily, his short speech was to the point and came across clearly and confidently. Output targets were met and the business survived.

This was an example of a man 'soaring with his strengths'. We knew he was good, but his performance was beyond our expectations. He was truly outstanding as he brought together his various talents—a weakness in any one of them would have meant failure.

Strength in a talent is not just the opposite of weakness—for a talent to be worthy of the name it has to be outstanding. Gallup tells us that 'the acid test of a strength is that you can do it consistently and nearly perfectly'.[34] The bar is set high. Clifton captures this idea in his definition of talent. He saw it as 'any recurring pattern of thought, feeling or behaviour that can be productively applied'.

'Recurring patterns' means that talents are 'enduring and unique'. They come back time and again for that very reason. Talents may be hidden and then discovered but they cannot be invented anew. Training is about building up talent. It does not create it.

Talent, for Clifton, covers 'our thoughts, feelings and behaviour'. For us this is closer to a definition of *temperament* than it is to *talent*. In fact, Gallup's list of 'talent strengths' comprise both talent and temperament attributes. For their analysis this is not a major issue, but for our approach it is. We take the line that true talents are enduring and unique and that temperament attributes can change. In consequence we deal with them differently in our analysis, as we explain later.

'Productive application' implies that talents create positive and useful outcomes, but of course that is only true if the talent involved is strong. Where a required talent is weak, it cannot be productively applied. The best that can be done is to manage it with care.

Gallup has told us of a call centre experiment in which an equal number of best and worst performers attended the same productivity course. The result was that the best performers became even better whilst the worst showed no improvement. It was even suggested to the call centre company that productivity would be improved if these worst performers actually stayed at home! Whilst this might not be the best approach for those concerned, they did appear to be in a job for which they had little talent. However on the basis that we 'can all do something better than 10,000 people' they need to discover their strengths and find a job where their talents can be used.

It is of course one thing to identify the importance of talent strengths but quite another matter to actually measure them. Don Clifton's interest in measuring talent goes back to his time at SRI. There he researched the talent attributes of some 200 different roles and developed evaluation questionnaires around them. One of these evaluation tools was the SRI Entrepreneur Perceiver questionnaire, which assessed the strength of 12 entrepreneur talent attributes through a set of 86 questions. The assessment was carried out by telephone interviews conducted by trained staff.

Gallup's StrengthsFinder evaluator was a subsequent development and is based on the assessment of '34 themes of talent' using 180 balanced questions. 'The StrengthsFinder's purpose is not to anoint you with strengths but to find where you have the greatest potential for a strength.'[35] On completion of the evaluator you are notified of your five most dominant talent themes. Gallup calls these 'your signature themes'. This strength evaluator has proved remarkably popular and has been taken by more than three million people.

In 2008 Gallup introduced StrengthsFinder 2.0 with a distinctive leadership focus.[36] It sets the 34 strengths in one of four leadership domains: executing, influencing, relationship building and strategic thinking. Upon completion of the web-based questionnaire you 'receive a highly customised Strengths-Based Leadership Guide that lists your top five strengths as well as several suggestions for leading with each theme'.

We followed this Gallup line in our work on the strengths of entrepreneurs and produced a balanced questionnaire to evaluate the key attributes we had identified.[37] This has worked well and is used in a number of business schools to identify potential entrepreneurs. We apply this approach to the **entirepreneur** in Chapters 7 to 10 and offer a series of questions so readers can make their own strengths evaluation.

♥ Temperament

Hippocrates (460–370 BC), of 'Hippocratic Oath' fame, promoted the idea that our moods, emotions and thereby our behaviour depended upon the balance of four body fluids which he termed 'humours'. These were blood, yellow bile, black bile and phlegm. This understanding was developed further by Galen (131–200 AD) who made two important steps. First, he linked the four humours with four tempers, or dispositions. In effect he updated the terminology to the extent that they can be understood even today:

- Blood: sanguine—pleasure-seeking and sociable
- Yellow bile: choleric—ambitious and leader-like
- Black bile: melancholy—analytical and literal
- Phelgm: phlegmatic—relaxed and thoughtful

Galen's second important step was to introduce the word temperament as per his dissertation *De Temperamentis*. Galen understood human behaviour to be a mixing or mingling of the humours in different proportions, hence the word *temperament* from the Latin *temperar*, 'to mingle'.

Sir Francis Galton (1822–1911) brought the understanding of temperament and personality into the modern world. He was a man of many interests, of which the new subject of psychology was just one.[38] Galton not only recognised that we all have our own individual characteristics and differences, he was the first to catalogue these and measure them. He developed methods of statistical analysis that are still in use today. He pioneered questionnaires and surveys.

Perhaps Galton's greatest contribution was the idea that language itself was an important indicator of our individual characteristics.

> I tried to gain an idea of the number of the more conspicuous aspects of the character by counting in an appropriate dictionary the words used to express them... . I examined many pages of its index here and there as samples of the whole, and estimated that it contained fully one thousand words expressive of character, each of which has a separate shade of meaning, while each shares a large part of its meaning with some of the rest.[39]
>
> *Galton, 1884*

This approach is now termed the 'Lexical Hypothesis'. In general terms it is the assumption that 'individual differences that are most salient and socially relevant in people's lives become encoded into their language'.[40] When applied to the study of personality traits it is taken down to a further level and the differences understood as being encoded into a single word.

This important observation was taken up by Gordon Allport (1897–1967) who worked through an English language dictionary of 400,000 words and identified almost 18,000 as associated with human personality or behaviour, of which 4,500 described personality traits.[41]

Raymond Cattell (1905–1998) took Allport's list of personality traits and first reduced them down to 171 by combining terms and removing less common ones.[42] He then tested out the list on a large sample of individuals and, using factor analysis, finally reduced it to just 16 personality factors or traits. His final step was to develop his Sixteen Personality Factor Questionnaire (16PF) personality assessment tool.

Other personality assessment tools were developed around the same time, though they had different roots. Carl Jung (1875–1961) identified two psychological types which described attitudes—*introvert* and *extrovert*. He then added four psychological types not unlike those of Hippocrates and Galen mentioned above. These were *thinking* and *feeling*—functions whereby we are able to decide and judge—and *sensation* and *intuition*, which enable us to gather information and perceive.

From this understanding the now well-established Myers-Briggs Type Indicator (MBTI) was developed. Katherine Briggs did the early work in 1940 and was later joined by her daughter Isabel Briggs Myers. They added a fourth dimension, *judging-perceiving*. This gave a total possible type-combination of 16.

Hans Eysenck (1916–1997) analysed personality differences and identified the two factors of neuroticism and extroversion. These two factors with their opposites created a foursome which Eysenck identified with the four Greek humours. He later added a third factor he termed psychoticism.

Whilst these various approaches had their champions and led to a vigorous psychometric-testing industry, none had really carried the day. However over the last two decades researchers have been able to combine Galton's lexical approach to the understanding of personality and the work done by Cattell, Eysenck and Myers-Briggs on measurable traits. 'We at last have a set of personality concepts we can use that is firmly based on evidence and which we psychologists can agree on. This set of concepts is called the five-factor model of personality or the Big Five.'[43]

These 'Big Five' factors are:

1. Extroversion
2. Neuroticism
3. Conscientiousness
4. Agreeableness
5. Openness

In some ways this is a catch-all list and so it has to be applied with care. 'Openness' is termed by some as 'openness to experience' and described as equating to 'creative' with the opposite being 'conforming' or 'practical'. These terms in themselves are fairly general. It can also be argued that the link between these personality factors and behaviour has not yet been established. Despite this lack of precision the Big Five are seen as dimensions of personality that can actually be measured, and a number of new questionnaires have been developed around them.

Gallup's comment on the Big Five is that it 'is a measurement model rather than a conceptual one. It was derived from factor analysis. No theory underpinned it. It consists of the most generally agreed upon minimal number of personality factors.'[44]

In our own work we found it difficult to connect the personality attributes and traits that lie behind the Big Five with a workable description of an entrepreneur personality. As we have reported elsewhere, evaluations of the entrepreneur using the Myers–Briggs Indicator have described the entrepreneur as being variously ESTPs, ENTPs and ENTJs.[45] These classifications mean that entrepreneurs show extroversion (E) and thinking (T) but can use either sensation (S) or intuition (N) and perceiving (P) or judging (J). We find that this is too diverse a set of personality attributes to be of any real value in assessment.

Even the extroversion trait, which does seem to be characteristic of the entrepreneur, is not reliable. The hi-tech 'nerd' entrepreneur who starts a successful business is a case in point—there is often nothing extroverted about him or her. Nor is it true to say that all leaders are extroverts. Susan Cain's book, *Quiet: The Power of Introverts in a World that Can't Stop Talking*, includes a chapter on 'The Myth of Charismatic Leadership'.[46] Some extremely successful enterprises are run by people who shun the limelight. Amancio Ortega, who founded the Zara clothing group and is now one of the world's richest men, shuns publicity. Although he launched his first store in 1975, no one saw a picture of him until 1999. He has only ever given three interviews in his life!

In our efforts to use personality attributes to identify entrepreneurs these ambiguities made us consider whether temperament might be a better area to explore. We were encouraged in this approach when we heard a BBC Radio commentator's review of why England had lost the Ashes cricket series against Australia. He explained that he had ranked the players from both sides in terms of their talent and temperament to see where the difference lay. He found that they were equally matched in talent but were far apart on temperament. The Australian team was committed and aggressive with a determination to win. The English team was the opposite. To them cricket was just a game; to the Australians it was a war!

We heard that radio broadcast in 1998. When in 2003 Michael Vaughan was appointed England captain for the one-day matches, commentator Christopher Martin-Jenkins wrote in *The Times*, 'Vaughan has the talent and temperament to handle pressure.'

We understood from these examples in cricket and other sports that temperament was about attitude and the will to win. It came from something within us.

A temperament model

Whilst temperament and personality are clearly linked, they are not the same. Temperament is highly subjective: it is about who we are and how we see ourselves. Personality, on the other hand, is an objective evaluation that classifies us according to what we are—our characteristics and traits.

To provide a framework for considering temperament we have developed a model that begins with the inner self, or 'Inner Ego' as we prefer to term it. The Inner Ego derives from a person's self-belief and captures those things about ourselves that only we know. As our Temperament Model in Figure 6.2 indicates, these attributes are hidden inside us, below ground.

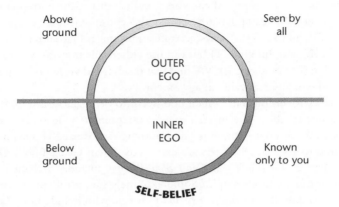

FIGURE 6.2 Temperament model

Within the Inner Ego we place three attributes of the person. These are:

- Self-assurance: the 'I can do it' factor, bringing confidence and audacity
- Dedication: the 'I love it' factor, bringing passion and commitment
- Motivation: the 'I must do it' factor, bringing drive and determination

If these Inner Ego attributes have significantly different strengths, they can create an imbalance within the person. On the whole, however, they tend to have similar strengths because they come from the same source of self-belief. Thus it is unlikely to find that a person is confident and driven but has little passion or commitment.

As we have developed our use of this model we have recognised that behind the Inner Ego there is the element of self-belief that in turn links with issues of self-worth and self-esteem. Where these are strong they provide a solid foundation for the Inner Ego attributes of self-assurance, dedication and motivation. But if they are weak or weakened for any reason, the Inner Ego takes a serious knock.

During his journey to the top of General Electric, Jack Welch observed an effect that he termed 'The GE Vortex'.[47] This occurred because a blame culture had taken hold across the company that destroyed people's confidence and filled them with self-doubt. This even affected senior managers and some never recovered. Once in the vortex it was difficult to escape. Self-doubt had replaced self-belief, and the result was that self-assurance took a serious knock.

Dedication comes from the heart and so is directly linked with self-belief issues. We have found that this link can be a particular problem for social entrepreneurs who espouse a cause. If their dedication is an expression of a belief system or worldview that is also the source of their self-belief then all should be well. For a person with low self-belief, however, their dedication may be about a search for inner meaning as they try to deal with their feeling of inadequacy.

Of the three Inner Ego elements, motivation is the one most likely to be impacted by self-belief. This was very evident in our work with entrepreneurs where the 'achievement' motivation is the driver. The challenge to achieve can be triggered by a number of things from an event such as redundancy to a moment of awakening.[48] One trigger that particularly touches self-belief is being told by an authority figure that you are worthless and will never amount to anything. Though such comments can cripple some people, for others, in particular potential entrepreneurs, it is a call to action. Their motivation to achieve is triggered by such criticism.

> Philip Green has a large retail clothing empire. He is worth over £4.5 billion and is estimated to be Britain's fifth richest man. He went to a "fiercely academic" Jewish boarding school but by the time he reached the fifth form he found himself relegated to the bottom class of only five or six boys. He left school without a single O level. This sense of being an underdog at school … is likely to have been one of the key influences on his determination to prove himself at the highest business level.[49]
>
> *Lansley and Forrester, 2006*

Green certainly proved many people wrong. This motivation works well as long as the person concerned is not struggling with a self-belief problem. It is all too easy to think that you can build your self-belief by succeeding where others had forecast failure. Unfortunately this rarely happens.

The Oxford psychologists Gillian Butler and Tony Hope make the point that

> if you do not value yourself independently of your achievements, you will not value your achievements. Finding within yourself a sense of value that does not depend on your achievements will make you more resistant to crippling self-doubts.[50]

In other words, if your motivation for achieving springs from the desire to build up your own self-belief, you are likely to become over-confident after a success and you will probably fail the next time around. Equally, should you fail first, your already weak self-belief will take a serious knock and you may never recover. Using achievement as a means of building up your self-belief is a double-edged sword.

The Outer Ego completes our model, showing the part of our temperament that is above ground and seen by others. It is generally the basis on which people judge us. These outer characteristics are less enduring and we often adapt them to our environment.

As with the Inner Ego we have identified three attributes within the Outer Ego. These are:

1. Courage: the 'I will succeed' factor. The emotional strength to face up to adversity and win through.
2. Responsibility: the 'we can and we will' factor. Being seen to carry the risks for your team and enterprise, thereby instilling the confidence of success in others.
3. Accountability: the 'it's my fault' factor. This is about 'carrying the can' and having an 'inner locus of control'. You never blame others or the system.

The word 'persona' is from the Latin word for mask, and referred to the mask used by actors in public plays. Jung described the persona as 'a kind of mask, designed on the one hand to make a definite impression upon others, and on the other to conceal the true nature of the individual'.[51] This implies manipulation of which we are often unaware in order to achieve certain ends.

In the balanced self, the Inner and Outer Ego work well together. There is an integrity and consistency about such people. What you see is what you get; they are not acting a part. As Jung put it, 'In the best case, the persona is appropriate and tasteful, a true reflection of our inner individuality and our outward sense of self'.[52]

Whilst our model of the Inner and Outer Ego may have such deeper implications, we are here concerned with the two perspectives of how we see ourselves (our Inner Ego) and of how others see us (our Outer Ego).

The T-groups, pioneered by Chris Argyris in the 60s and 70s, sought to break the rigid authoritarian management style of those days by putting groups of managers together and making them discuss their relationships with each other.[53] For some, this freedom to open up to one another was a liberating experience. However in our experience the benefits were generally short-lived as people went back to their old ways. They reverted to their previous patterns of thought and behaviour, which is in line with our view that Inner Ego attributes are not easily changed. This examination of the inner self within a group context is not for everyone and can have serious emotional consequences, as the following story illustrates.

A major manufacturing multinational once ran a T-group session with its senior factory managers. These people were strong-minded individuals, kings in their own domain. Although they knew each other well, they rarely—if ever—shared their inner feelings. For one man this process was just too difficult. It was as if he had never even thought about his inner self. The result was that his normal confidence disintegrated and he had to leave the group. In due course he resigned and left the company. He was a broken man.

We share this example to illustrate the importance of our Inner/Outer Ego model and the problems that can arise when the two egos are out of balance.

We discuss Inner and Outer Ego attributes in more detail in Chapter 8 and have presented them here as a guide to our Temperament Model.

♠ Technique

When we introduced the idea of the 3Ts we were seeking a 'framework of understanding' for the entrepreneur. In this context we commented that 'techniques that are proven, and linked with a recognised body of knowledge, can make most people reasonably competent in the field to which they relate'.[54] Thus we took technique to be concerned with the know-how required to do the job of starting up and running a business. To point the potential entrepreneur in the right direction, the final chapter was titled 'Techniques for the Entrepreneur', and gave practical advice on product life cycle, the management of cash flow, business plans and so on.

We also noted that entrepreneurs did not sit in classrooms and rarely read textbooks. Instead, they picked things up as they went along and often served an informal apprenticeship of some kind where they learnt the tricks of the trade. This 'learning by doing' is an important part of how business techniques are acquired.

Charles Forte, who built one of the largest hotel groups in the UK, learnt the hard way when his first venture almost failed. In his autobiography he wrote:

> I now learnt a lesson I shall never forget. I realised that until I could find the right balance between income on the one hand, and the cost of raw materials, wages, rent, rates and other overheads on the other, the sums would not add up. In fact there and then I worked out the essential ratios which would guarantee the profits.[55]
>
> *Forte, 1997*

Years later, when he bought the Café Royal in London in 1954 and then the Lyons Hotel chain in 1976, he used his 'tried financial formulae, the ratio of sales to gross profit' to prove to himself that he could turn both ventures into profit.

Thus our understanding of Technique was related to business best practices with an informal approach to its acquisition. Whilst we were able to measure the attributes related to talent and temperament, we were not able to do the same with technique. This was mainly because of the difficulty of identifying the correct parameters and then being able to measure them. A CV, for example, would be of little real use to identify lessons learnt and understood. Nor indeed would the number and even quality of business training courses attended. Success in climbing the management and/or leader ladder is also an uncertain indicator.

Under the title 'The Story of Joe (a Fable)', the Boston Consulting Group's newsletter wrote of how Joe, the outstanding manager, rose to the top of the organisation.[56] It was at that point that he failed and was fired. Joe's 'success formula' was to clear out all the dead wood and cut costs. This earned him promotion and he repeated the process. It was only when he reached the top that his formula failed. His past decisions caught up with him. Joe had moved up at regular intervals, which was enough time to cut but not enough time to build. His technique was fundamentally flawed.

There are many Joes in the business world, and we are therefore somewhat sceptical that the 'deliberate practice' approach can be applied to the business domain. There are many business courses that, like 'deliberate practice', could be described as a 'highly structured activity, the explicit goal of which is to improve performance', but business does not work like that.

Ericsson and his colleagues went further than identifying the importance of 'deliberate practice'—they gave it a timescale. They claimed that their research and that of others showed elite performance to be 'the product of a decade or more of maximal efforts to improve performance'.

Ericsson assembled the following impressive list of domains where he claimed that the 'ten-years' rule applied: chess—Simon and Chase, 1973; musical composition—Hayes, 1981; music—Sosniak, 1985; mathematics—Gustin, 1985; tennis—Monsaas, 1985; and swimming—Kalinowski, 1985.

More recent research has challenged some of these claims. Daniel Goleman's 2013 book, *Focus: The Hidden Driver of Excellence*, has a chapter with the title 'The Myth of 10,000 Hours'.[57] Even so, the idea of deliberate practice and the ten-year rule have found general acceptance. Malcolm Gladwell's influential 2008 book, *Outliers: The Story of Success* contributed to this view. His claim that '10,000 hours is the magic number of greatness' caught people's imagination. The assumption here is that it takes ten years to practice for 10,000 hours. This roughly corresponds to 20 hours a week.

Despite these reservations, we pick out two issues that we feel require much more attention. The first is the need for a greater understanding of business as a domain of human activity. Here we draw parallels to research into chess, which, like business, involves human decisions that require both intellect and intuition. The second issue we address is the transition that seems to take place with experience and enables people to see both the wood and the trees at the same time. It is not 'big picture' versus 'small picture', but both. It is also about the transition from 'knowing' a subject—finance, for example—and actually 'getting it'.

Chess and business

Herbert Simon (1916–2001) pioneered the study of human performance in complex tasks. He was particularly interested in decision-making in organisations, and he took chess as a key domain of study. A psychologist and computer scientist, he sought to use computers to simulate the skills and judgments of the human chess player.

Early in his career Simon wrote an influential book, *Administrative Behaviour: A Study of Decision-Making Processes in Administrative Organisations*, which challenged the mechanistic approach to decision-making that was popular at the time.[58] He observed that 'the "entrepreneur" of economic theory makes static decisions in a fixed framework, bearing little resemblance to the active innovator who launches new enterprises and explores new paths'. He saw this as an impoverished description of organisations and set about providing one in which people made decisions within 'processes molded by limits on their knowledge and computational capabilities'. He termed this effect 'bounded rationality'. This work gave Simon an international reputation and he was later honoured with a Nobel Prize in economics.

Although most of the research behind the 10,000-hour claim comes from sport, its application to chess and language is interesting. In their 1973 paper, 'Skill in Chess', Simon and Chase reference research that investigated the size of the 'chess pattern' computer database required to put it on a level with a human chess master.[59] The answer was 'a vocabulary of chess patterns [or 'information chunks'] of around 50,000'. Simon and Chase then drew a parallel between the chunks required in the mastery of chess and those involved in the mastery of a language. They comment that 'highly literate people have reading vocabularies of 50,000 words or more'.

This is an intriguing observation and suggests that patterns of understanding might be one way of quantifying the technique issues in business. As with chess and language, it is not just a matter of pattern recognition but also of knowing what to do with that recognition. Business situations can be very complex but the issues do come round again and again and can be identified, as many business and management students realise.

We believe Simon's work on 'bounded rationality' and his use of chess as a way of seeing and dealing with complex problems is even more significant, however. Chess of course has a set number of pieces, but each piece has its own rules that define what it can and cannot do. There is also a corporate dimension to this, as the pattern recognition side of Simon's research showed. The chess pieces have to work together, some even being sacrificed for the benefit of the whole.

There is a remarkable learning process involved. Simon tells us it takes 'about a decade's intense pre-occupation with the game' to reach the level of a grandmaster. He calculates that the chess master is able 'to recognize at least 50,000 different configurations of pieces on sight, and a grandmaster even more'. This exceptional ability allows the top chess players to take on many players simultaneously and win every game—the reason being that they can see the best move in just a few seconds, whereas the average time per move in a serious tournament is three to four minutes or longer.

With such proficiency so clearly demonstrated, one would expect grandmasters to have remarkable intellectual powers. Simon found this was not the case. He tells us that 'there is no evidence that masters demonstrate more than above average competence on basic intellectual factors; their talents are chess specific'.

The parallel with decision-making in organisations, noted by Simon, is both interesting and tantalising. At the present stage one can see the parallels between a person's chess database of 'information chunks' and the business experience that is built up over the years. Both require extensive data that also needs to be understood in interactive patterns. Chess and business both involve strategy and tactics and there are theories for different stages of the activity, from openings to endgames.

Another similarity is that there is more to chess and business than proven technique. There has to be innovation. The great chess players have all invented move sequences that then have been named after them. A typical book on chess for beginners lists more than 30 different openings, with names like the 'Alekhine Defence' and 'Evans Gambit'.

This naming of significant innovations is also found in the world of computer programming. We well remember the excitement of a colleague when an algorithm he invented was attributed to him. The nearest we come to this in business is when a particular procedure or approach is named after its originator. A typical management example is the 'HP Way'.

The growth of the company founded by Bill Hewlett and Dave Packard in a garage in 1939 is legendary. In 2007 their biographer Michael Malone wrote:

> A trillion-dollar industry and the largest employer in the developed world is an awful lot to place upon an old, un-insulated wooden structure of less than two-hundred square feet at the end of a dirt driveway.[60]

From that humble beginning Hewlett and Packard not only led a technology revolution but they invented the HP Way, the bottom line of which was trust. They showed it was possible to move away from the 'command and control' style of management to one that treated people as human beings and put people first. Packard described the HP Way in the following terms.

> We have a set of values—deeply held beliefs that guide us in meeting our objectives, in working with one another, and in dealing with customers, shareholders and others. Our corporate objectives are built upon these values. These objectives serve as a day-to-day guide for our decision making. To help us meet our objectives, we employ various plans and practices. It is the combination of these elements—our values, corporate objectives, plans and practices—that forms the HP Way.[61]

Behind this description are what Simon would call 'chunks' covering values, objectives, plans and practices, but Hewlett and Packard understood and applied them in a new way. Primarily they, as an organisation, put people and trust first.

Sadly in more recent times 'HP has been led by a succession of CEOs—some competent, others less so. Few were able even to maintain the fabled company philosophy, the "HP Way".' In chess terms, Bill and Dave were grandmasters.

In the above we have tried to draw a parallel between chess and business, recognising that chess has a strong technique dimension and that it involves both proven knowledge and innovation. It is also a combination of hard and soft data that are not always easy to interrelate or quantify.

From 'knowing it' to 'getting it'

We were once interviewing the General Manager of a social enterprise and questioning her about the costs of the enterprise, which seemed to be spiraling out of control. When challenged, she refused to get involved in the conversation. Despite her seniority her simple answer was 'I don't do finance.' In her case she neither knew it nor got it, but she still ran the organisation.

Most areas of business have a body of knowledge that can be learnt. There are techniques to be understood and qualifications to be obtained. Levels of performance and general competence can be measured. However, head knowledge is important but it is not enough. **Entirepreneurs** need a feel for business and enterprise: the need 'to get it'. Sara Williams believes that many people are stifled by their jobs in big business and have what it takes to 'breakout' and start their own enterprise. In her book *Breakout: Life beyond the Corporation* she gives the example of Tim Waterstone, the founder of the highly successful Waterstones bookshops.[62]

> Waterstone believes he has a number of valuable gifts. He understands that business is basically built on simple principles. He can spot the issues that matter. He can lead and persuade. He is tenacious and courageous. And it helps that he is slightly contemptuous of money!

Because there is often a mismatch between knowing something and really getting it, it is inherently difficult to validate measures of technique. However we wonder if it may be worth picking up on Ericsson's idea of 'deliberate practice' but terming it 'direct experience'. By that we mean experience that comes along and has a direct effect upon a person's business performance. It covers those events in a career that we never forget but are rarely put on CVs. The most effective 'direct experience' that comes along is more likely than not to be accidental—a situation that cannot be planned for or avoided. The following is an example of what we have in mind.

Jack Welch, the very successful CEO of General Electric, tells the story of how, as a young engineer, the pilot plant he was working on exploded. 'It was a huge blast that blew the roof off the building'.[63] Welch ran across the street to see the damage. He found it worse than expected but fortunately no one was injured. The next day he had to drive 100 miles to a corporate group executive and explain himself. He knew he could work out why the explosion had happened but he was sure it would still cost him his job. He was 'prepared for the worst'.

Despite being 'a nervous wreck' Welch was able to put the facts before his boss, who remained calm and objective throughout. 'His concern was that I had learnt from the explosion and if I thought I could fix the reactor process. He questioned whether we should continue on the project.' Assured on these points, his boss commented, 'It's better that we learned about this problem now rather than later when we had a large-scale operation going. Thank God no one was hurt.' His boss's reaction was a lesson in management and leadership that Welch never forgot.

This kind of 'direct experience' is something that we carry with us and which accumulates over time. Eventually some will reach elite performance level. At this point they will not only have a great deal of knowledge across a wide area, but most importantly they will simply 'get it'. They will be able to move back and forth easily between the wood and its various, often competing, trees. They will know instinctively what course of action to take.

When the bus operator Stagecoach announced a tie-up with Virgin Rail, the city was surprised. Virgin was on 'draft number 12' of their Stock Exchange flotation document. Then Brian Souter of Stagecoach moved in. Branson commented, 'I have never seen anyone move as quickly as Brian did.' An investment of £158 million was involved and 'the whole deal was set up within a couple of weeks, which for a deal of that size with bankers involved is amazing'. Souter recalls 'picking up my plastic bag and going to see Richard [Branson]. They opened up their books and we did the deal in record time'.[64]

Both Branson and Souter, though very different people, are elite performers, equivalent to business grandmasters. Souter's biographer Christian Wolmar comments that 'they are both "can do" people eager to do deals'. In our terms they not only 'know it'; they 'get it'.

The 3Ts triangle plus

In concluding this introductory chapter on Talent, Temperament and Technique we present what we have termed the 3Ts Triangle. This has come out of our work

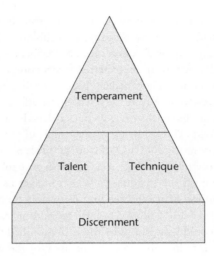

FIGURE 6.3 The 3Ts plus triangle

on the entrepreneur and remains useful for showing the interdependence of the 3Ts. As indicated in Figure 6.3, the triangle can be extended to cover the **entirepreneur** by placing it on a base that represents Discernment, the fourth main attribute group.

The aim of the 3Ts triangle is to illustrate that talent and technique are the basis upon which elite performance rests, with temperament being the operational decider—it is the lead factor without which talent and technique simply go to waste. Temperament is what delivers or, in some cases prevents, delivery. We regularly see examples in sport where weaknesses in temperament destroy promising careers. The same effect can be seen in team games.

Temperament is really the most challenging of the 3Ts. It can bring the drive and motivation that creates world champions but it can also destroy the confidence of the most gifted.

Daley Thompson, the great heptathlon athlete, is an example of the former. He won gold medals at regular intervals throughout his long career but never saw himself as the most naturally talented. He claimed that the difference for him was his desire and expectation of winning every time. He believed in himself to a remarkable degree and his self-confidence—a temperament issue—was always sky high.

In comparison, George Best was the most outstanding footballer of his generation. Playing for the Northern Ireland team, he once won an international match 'single-handed'—the rest of the team just watched him. His biography, *Blessed*, is a story of the tragedy of a remarkably talented man with an addictive temperament.[65] There is the anecdote told of the waiter who, delivering some vintage champagne to Best's hotel room, found him in bed with thousands of pounds in cash from a day at the races and the current Miss World. Looking at the scene, the waiter asked, 'George, where did it all go wrong?' He died an alcoholic.

These are just two examples from sport of the interplay between the 3Ts where the impact of temperament can be seen; one beneficial and the other a disaster. Business also has both successes and casualties, and can mirror these two examples.

Temperament is certainly a central issue for business people, and some are often on the edge of the clinical condition of mania. In *A Mood Apart: The Thinker's Guide to Emotion and its Disorders* the psychologist Peter Whybrow quotes a professional colleague who drew a parallel between his own experience of mania and successful businessmen who fall on hard times.[66]

> I'll bet you that many successful businessmen who have taken risks and almost lost their company can describe something similar to my experiences in early mania. But they edit them out; they decide that such feelings have no relevance to anything but competition and risk and they put them aside.

> I think the "illness" is there, in muted form, in some of the most successful among us—those leaders and captains of industry who sleep only four hours a night.

The 3Ts can strengthen each other, but they can also conflict when one dominates. A balance of strengths in these three areas is essential for the **entirepreneur** but we must also add the important attribute of discernment. This provides a foundation for the 3Ts and contributes to their coherence and collective strength, but it is also essential that it pervades each of them. Without discernment, the 3Ts—Talent, Temperament and Technique—will be less effective.

There also needs to be a balance at the next level down, between the attributes of talent, the Inner and Outer Ego of temperament, and the knowledge and practical experience of technique. In the next four chapters we review this next level down in some detail and provide a series of questions to help you think through and then score yourself against. From this you should be able to build up an understanding of where your strengths lie.

Although it is clearly a first shot, you will be taken through to the point where you have an overall score for the 3Ts and Discernment and can begin to think through the implications of your overall **entirepreneur** score.

Even if you are on the right track, you'll get run over if you just sit there.

Will Rogers

In Chapters 7 to 9 we move from the general understanding of Talent, Temperament and Technique provided in Chapter 6 to consider their practical application. In Chapter 10 we describe 'discernment', the foundation attribute that must lie behind the 3Ts if excellence is to be achieved.

Throughout these chapters we provide you with the opportunity to make a personal assessment of your attribute strengths, using targeted questions as you go through each topic. At the end of Chapter 11 you will be able to put all your scores together and arrive at a final figure for your **entirepreneur** *strength.*

Of course, not everyone who aspires to the top job has the ability to perform outstandingly well at that level. Equally, there are those who miss out on achieving their full potential because they are not aware of their strengths. We hope that by working through the next four chapters you will build up a good understanding of where your strengths actually lie.

7

♦ TALENT—APPLIED

The talent attributes

To bring some order and clarity to the different talent attributes required by the **entirepreneur** we group them into three major areas:

- Creativity
- Focus
- Operations

Each of these does a specific job and has its own outcomes, but they do not stand alone: they influence each other and the other attributes within the temperament and technique groupings. To illustrate this point we show, in Figure 7.1, both the individual attributes and the talent group as a whole within dashed ellipses. Their boundaries are permeable.

Each of the 3Ts and their attributes operate within a particular external context. Thus the talent attribute of 'creativity' is more likely to grow and flourish in an area such as a technology hub where there are other creative people. All talent is directly affected by the availability of opportunity and is most likely to remain dormant if the talent and the opportunity do not meet up. We discuss this and other issues that influence the effectiveness of the 3Ts in Chapter 10.

This talent-based approach to the **entirepreneur** is an important indicator of how the traditional separation between entrepreneur, leader and manager is actually misplaced. Creativity is obviously important to entrepreneurs, but an unimaginative leader or manager who can never see things differently will not do a good job. Focus applies equally to the entrepreneur, leader and manager and is needed

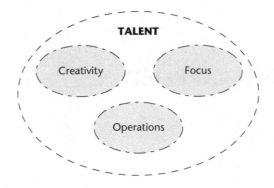

FIGURE 7.1   The talent attributes

across the board. Operations is often seen as the task of managers, but there can be serious problems when entrepreneurs and leaders are weak in this area.

Creativity

The creativity grouping covers a process that begins with *ideas*, then moves through to *opportunity* and on to *innovation*, as indicated in Figure 7.2. In any process, the links between its constituents have to be strong if it is to be effective. This can be a particular difficulty with creativity because each attribute is able to stand alone: thus it is quite possible for a person to be full of ideas and get satisfaction from that alone without taking things further. Equally, they may not be able to make the link between idea and opportunity. Even when the right opportunity is targeted, applying it by effective innovation requires a special talent. In our experience some inventors find it really difficult to turn their idea into a product that actually works and is ready for the market. More often than not they want to keep on adding more improvements—a case of bells and whistles.

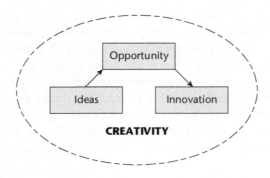

FIGURE 7.2   The creativity group

Ideally the **entirepreneur** should be strong in these three talent attributes, but there are ways around this requirement. 'Ideas' and 'innovation' can be substituted by bringing in the talent from outside. 'Opportunity' however, cannot be handled in this way because it is the talent that selects the one opportunity from the many, and so it must be kept in-house. Even then, for it to progress with the necessary priority it needs strong support from within the company. It is for this reason that the top person, the **entirepreneur**, has to be a strong in this 'opportunity' attribute.

Steve Jobs was a classic example of such an **entirepreneur**. He spent his life going from opportunity to opportunity, taking them to heights no one could anticipate. Young and Simon's book *iCon: Steve Jobs, the Greatest Second Act in the History of Business* provides example after example of how to spot and handle opportunity.[1] This was one of Jobs' greatest strengths.

Of course Jobs' talent is rare, and so we now provide an example of how these talents can be juggled around within the top team. We were once part of a UK Design Council judging panel. The innovative product being considered was presented by the company's Technical Director. Later we met the Managing Director of the company. Together they were a very effective combination. The Managing Director was the source of the idea and in fact he was always coming up with new ones—he just could not help it. Realising this about himself, the Managing Director had recruited a PhD scientist as his Technical Director to help evaluate the ideas and decide which was the best to target. The Technical Director then had to innovate and turn the idea into a saleable product. The outcome was an important step forward in their field and the award they received was well deserved. The following year the Technical Director joined the judging panel.

As we come to consider the three attributes in turn we want to set the bar high, and so we provide each with their own adjective. Thus we have:

- Great ideas
- Real opportunity
- Successful innovation

'Ideas', 'opportunity' and 'innovation' float around companies all the time but only occasionally do they achieve very much. 'Great', 'real' and 'successful' are therefore important qualifiers and it is only people strong in the creativity talent who can make these important adjectives a reality. This is why we see this as the starter talent for the **entirepreneur**. Without it, businesses stagnate and get overtaken by their competitors. Creativity has to be at the heart of any business and, most importantly, it has to reside in the person at the top.

Great ideas

Ideas are the product of a lively mind. Sadly it is often the case that other minds are closed to such creativity. The following quotations are taken from Tim Waterstone's book, *Swimming Against the Stream: Launching Your Business and Making your Life*.[2]

> Everything that can be invented, has been invented.
>
> *Charles Duell, US Commissioner of Patents, 1879*

> There is a world market for six computers.
>
> *Thomas J. Watson, Chairman of IBM, 1956*

> There is no reason for any individual to have a computer in their home.
>
> *Kenneth Olsen, Founder of the Digital Equipment Corporation, 1977*

The last two quotations show why first IBM and then the Digital Equipment Corporation (DEC) missed key opportunities. Their leaders got it wrong.

In the 1950s IBM dominated the computer mainframe business. (Their competitors were known as the seven dwarfs!)[3] It was in 1956 that Thomas J. Watson made his famous forecast about the computer market. In that same year, William Shockley shared the Nobel Prize in physics for the invention of the transistor. A year later Kenneth Olson founded DEC. Watson had not seen these early warning signs (or at least had not taken them seriously).

DEC took on board the new technology and from it created and then dominated the mini-computer industry. Its PDP-8, launched in 1965, was the machine to have. An important innovation was the use of a keyboard to input data, rather than using punched cards.

By 1974 DEC was riding high. Its annual sales were close to a $1 billion. Some people at DEC, notably David Ahl, saw the personal computer opportunity. He even presented a marketing plan to a senior committee, but it failed to get Olson's support. (That was the context in which Olson made the remark quoted above.) Ahl's plan was not accepted and he left the company. But things were already rolling. Earlier in 1968 DEC's PDP-10 machine provided a 13-year old schoolboy with his first access to a real computer. That boy was Bill Gates!

As early as 1964, Gordon Moore had predicted that silicon chips would reduce in price by 30 per cent a year. This happened, bringing component costs down to a level that electronic hobbyists like Steve Wozniak could afford. This in turn enabled Wozniak to build a small computer at home. When he offered it to Hewlett-Packard, his employers at that time, they told him it was not 'a viable product'. His friend Steve Jobs did not agree and together they founded Apple Computer, Inc. in 1976.

Just as Watson at IBM failed to see the opportunity of the mini-computer, so Olson at DEC failed to see the importance of the personal computer as it came over the horizon. We review this 'horizon' issue later when we discuss focus, but here it is important to note the resistance of the large corporation to new ideas.

> Every one of the existing computer companies passed up the chance to bring computers into the home and on top of every work desk. The next generation of computers, the micro-computer, was created by individual entrepreneurs outside the established corporations.[4]

It seems that the greater the idea, the more difficult it is for it to see the light of day. Certainly these ideas have their champions but they are rarely in a position to turn them into real opportunities. Even when they do have influence it can still be a struggle. Akio Morita had status as one of the founders of Sony, yet he still found it hard to get across the idea that there was a market for a product that played music but did not record it, and which could be listened to without disturbing anyone else.[5] The idea had come from his teenage daughter! When he tried to move the idea forward at Sony he was opposed by the engineers because they were already working on a play-and-record device. How could dropping one of its key features make it more successful, they argued? His financial team claimed it would never make any money. Morita prevailed despite this, and when the Sony Walkman launched it took the market by storm, becoming one the most successful products Sony ever produced.

This lack of openness to new ideas can be a serious problem in a company. A business founder can have strong creativity talents that are suppressed as the enterprise grows and other tasks take priority. Equally, it is possible for the founder to feel threatened when other people in the organisation start coming up with new ideas. We have often heard it said that 'the only way to get new ideas across in this company is to make the boss think they were his'.

Being a source of ideas can be a thankless task. Such people rarely get encouragement and can feel that the world is against them. Investors look for proven track records, and start-up money is hard to come by. Even the patent system, which is intended to secure their intellectual property rights, can work against them. We understand from the British Patent Office that only 2 per cent of patented ideas ever get to the marketplace. For the inventor the situation is even more dispiriting: most new patents are close to existing ones, and simply a variant of an existing idea. This can mean that the person with the original idea never gets the benefit.

There is a darker side, too. Some large businesses watch the patent scene very carefully and with their greater expertise 'pepper' the area with new patents close to the one they have spotted. They then approach the inventor and suggest a deal. Others are more direct and just copy the idea. The long tussle that James Dyson had with Hoover is a classic example. When Dyson finally won his patent battle he commented, 'I spent 20 years developing the technology and I am very pleased to see Hoover now found guilty of patent infringement. I am also pleased on behalf of other small businesses and inventors who should be encouraged to take out patents by the result of this case'.[6] Hoover was required to pay Dyson £4 million, in what was believed to be the highest court award ever in a UK patent case.

Another misuse of the patent system is to challenge a patent simply to delay the introduction of a new or improved product into the marketplace. Whilst this can be an expensive strategy for the challenger, a delay of around two years can be achieved. This then gives enough time for the challenger to come up with an alternative.

Real opportunity

The mini-computer and the micro-computer we now call the personal computer (PC) were not just great ideas—they were real opportunities. But IBM and DEC left them at the ideas stage, not convinced that they were all that great. The step from 'great idea' to 'real opportunity' is not an easy one. Many evaluation techniques have been devised and panels of experts set up, but picking winners still remains an art rather than a science in which hindsight rules. In this case talent beats technique every time.

Steve Jobs had this 'opportunity' talent in abundance. At a critical stage in the development of Apple, when their development projects were struggling, Steve Jobs and his team visited the Palo Alto Research Centre (PARC) of the Xerox Corporation. They were shown most of the features that we now take for granted on the computers of today. One of the most exciting was the computer mouse that gave the user independent control of what was on the screen.[7]

Jobs was astounded at what he saw and immediately grasped the potential. He didn't just tell them, he shouted: 'You're sitting on a gold mine. I can't believe Xerox is not taking advantage of this.' Job recalls in his biography that 'it was like a veil being lifted from my eyes. I could see what the future of computing was destined to be'. It was a real opportunity that Jobs grasped with both hands. The things he saw on that visit, and his implementation of them, was what gave Apple its name as the leading innovator in the personal computer industry.

Not everybody is like Akio Morita or Steve Jobs, who both saw a real opportunity and were in a position to do something about it. Others see the opportunity but learn the hard way that it is too early; that the technology is not quite there yet. For example, *Start Up: A Silicon Valley Adventure* tells the story of how Jerry Kaplan had a great idea, but 'six years, hundreds of jobs and $75 million later he had to accept that impossible, final truth: GO was gone'.[8]

It had all started on a flight with Mitchell Kapor, the founder of Lotus Development Corporation. Kapor was using his Lotus Agenda software to enter in the informal notes he had made on odd scraps of paper. He was using 'the most powerful portable computer available', which was bulky and cumbersome by today's standards. Frustrated by the time this was taking him, he mused that it would be great to have some way of entering 'all this stuff directly into the computer and skip the paper'. Kaplan commented that he thought that the real question was 'how small and light you can make a portable computer'. After discussing the problem, Kaplan had a short sleep. He woke up suddenly with the answer. 'Suppose you used a pen instead of a keyboard' he said. As they discussed this idea further they both understood 'that the key to the next wave of computing was to create a device that worked like a notebook instead of a typewriter. The impact of this insight, so obvious and yet so novel, overwhelmed us.' It was a 'unique emotion'.

Kaplan was able to secure funding for the idea that valued the new business at $3 million. He had no business plan and no projection of sales, but investors were convinced that they were seeing the next step of the computer revolution.

This was all true, and the description Kaplan gave to the investors sounds very much like today's tablets (like the iPad) except that the keyboard, now built-in, still prevails in today's models. But that was 25 years ago, and the idea was far from reality.

The question then is at what stage does an opportunity become 'real'. Opportunities do not sit still and can morph into many different forms. Often the first idea is too early and it is the second and third comers who actually bring an opportunity to fruition. Sometimes, as in this case, the original idea of replacing the keypad with a pen was not to become a major feature, but the broader idea of a computer that was not tied to a desk and could go round with the user was absolutely right.

It is easy to compile a list of what makes an opportunity great. Technology, market, finance and competition are all key factors, but the most important by far is the person behind the opportunity. It is their abilities that make all the difference and is why we set the attribute of opportunity centrally within creativity, between ideas and innovation. It is the most important of the three. Ideas and innovation can be contracted out if need be, but not opportunity—it has to be at the heart of the enterprise, with the top person fully behind it. The revival of Apple after Jobs' return shows this clearly. Once he took the helm again, new and very real opportunities like the iPhone emerged.

Successful innovation

In 1979, when Steve Jobs visited Xerox PARC and saw the future, it was fairly clear that Xerox was not exploiting the technology very well. 'In 1981, well before Apple Lisa or Macintosh, they introduced the Xerox Star.' It had all the features that had been shown to Apple but was too expensive, slow in operation and expensive. 'It flopped; only 30,000 were ever sold.' Xerox had failed to deliver. Had they got it right they could have been there before Apple, but they did not.[9]

Poor or slow innovation can stall even the best ideas. As the above example shows, while Xerox were having problems Apple was doing just the right things. Their ability to innovate far exceeded that of Xerox. Not only did they innovate more quickly they integrated the many innovative elements more effectively.

Successful innovation is about getting the details right with the end purpose always in mind. When Apple rolls out a new product they proudly show a video of their manufacturing innovations, rather than only describing the new and innovative functionalities of the product. Not many companies do that.

Edward Stobart's—quite different—innovation was opportunity based. He took advantage of the deregulation of the haulage business in the UK to such effect that the Eddie Stobart trucking company became one of the largest and fastest-growing businesses in the UK. They also became one of the most respected, thanks to successful innovation. Stobart had a passion for clean lorries, smart drivers and serving customers. Each of these was a real innovation for that industry. Lorries are notoriously dirty but he made them clean and shiny. When his drivers turned up for breakfast in transport cafes wearing ties they were at first ridiculed but they soon set the standard. Customers were delighted when orders were delivered on time and competitors had to follow suit or lose business. Stobart succeeded in changing the face of the industry by innovation.

One innovation that really caught the attention of the public, and still does, is the Eddie Stobart Members Club. It has 25,000 members and holds annual Truckfests around the UK.[10] There has even been a popular weekly TV series: *Eddie Stobart: Trucks & Trailers*.

Self-assessment: find your Creativity score

The following questions will remind you of the issues behind the three elements that make up Creativity and enable you to assess your strength in each.

- Are you a creative person, always coming up with new ideas?
- Are you able to see the opportunities behind your ideas and pick out the winner, or is that something you struggle with?
- Do you enjoy taking an opportunity and turning it into a reality?
- Are you able to see the process through, from Idea to Opportunity and then from Innovation to making it happen?

Based on your answers to these questions give yourself a score out of 10 as a measure of your strength in each of the three elements.

My suggested score:

for Ideas: _____ out of 10
for Opportunity: _____ out of 10
for Innovation: _____ out of 10

If the scores are all within one point (plus or minus) of each other, take the average as your overall score for Creativity.

Two issues may require you to move away from your average score:

First, your score for Opportunity is the most important factor of the three, and if it is two or more points above or below your Ideas and Innovation scores, your combined Creativity score needs to be weighted accordingly. We suggest you either add or deduct one point from the average to achieve this.

Second, because the continuity from Idea to Opportunity to Innovation is important, if any of the three differ by more than three points, continuity is likely to be affected. If this is the case, deduct one point from the average.

My overall Creativity score is _____ out of 10

Focus

We use the word 'focus' in the more general sense of 'a point on which attention, activity etc. is directed or concentrated'.[11]

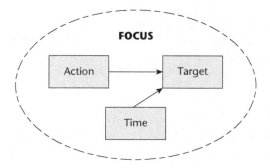

FIGURE 7.3 Focus

Here we are concerned with how to go about achieving and delivering on focus. The simple answer is that we decide on a target, focus on it, line it up and shoot. Things are not that straightforward, however. Defining a target is actually not easy. Some targets are just plain wrong whilst others involve collateral damage. The present interest in setting targets for almost everything can waste time and dilute effort—particularly if the targets are imprecise or cannot be measured easily.

The three elements that make up this talent are *target*, *action* and *time*.

Target focus

This is what is generally understood by the word 'focus'. It is associated with being able to see the target clearly. In the traditional division between entrepreneur, leader and manager, the leader's focus is often at the conceptual level, in line with leaders usually being far-sighted 'horizon' people. The entrepreneur and manager, on the other hand, are strong on hard targets against which they deliver. For the manager the target is fairly easy to identify based on custom and practice, but the entrepreneur is often operating in unknown, more fluid, territory where targets are slippery and not easy to define. The **entirepreneur** has to be able to take these different targets on board, putting them in their correct focus timescales.

In their strength studies, the Gallup Organisation has consistently identified focus as a key attribute for success. They make the important point that people strong on focus filter out anything that does not help them get to their destination. They stay on target and do not wander down false roads.[12]

Achieving simplicity is an essential part of achieving target focus. The more targets you are trying to hit, the more you are likely to miss. Those strong on focus are good at prioritising and keeping things simple. Brian Souter, who built the Stagecoach empire, 'concentrates on major issues, typically no more than three in any situation'.[13] Tim Waterstone, who set up a very successful chain of bookshops that made him a millionaire, has described himself as having 'the gift of simplicity, of being able to lift out the only things that really matter'.[14]

Human vision has both sharp focus and depth of vision. In optical terms—in a camera, for example—this is difficult to achieve, but both are essential. Depth of vision (or depth of field in photography) is the distance over which the object remains in focus. This allows the issues that surround a target to be seen clearly and in context. It is an essential requirement in business if 'target excellence' is to be achieved.

Action and time focus

The ability to focus and thereby deliver on a target is supported by two rather different approaches. These are 'action focus' and 'time focus', and generally one of these tends to dominate as we go for the target.

Action-focused people are doers rather than thinkers—they believe that actions speak louder than words. In their StrengthsFinder, Gallup use the term 'Activator' to describe people strong in this attribute. Activators are 'impatient for action'. They certainly get things done, but working with them can be difficult. They are task-finishers and must achieve completion. They are generally not good at parallel processing and prefer to get one job completed before they start another. Essentially they really enjoy working hard; there is no compulsion about it. Steve Wood, who became the general manager of Microsoft in 1977, says of the early days at Microsoft, 'We were just having fun and working really hard'.[15] They were action-focused.

Time-focused people are able to concentrate and remain productive for long periods. They are not easily distracted and there is an urgency about their work. Time matters to them. They enjoy deadlines and work hard to achieve them. They do not procrastinate. Behind these characteristics lies the 'urgency' that Don Clifton of Gallup noted as an attribute of the entrepreneur.[16] He summarised it as 'no time to waste. Must take action now'. This points to the danger of time- or pressure-induced stress that, for some people, can have serious consequences.

Self-assessment: find your Focus score

We now offer some questions to help you to decide your Focus strength.

- Do you prefer others to define the target for you or do you prefer to make up your own mind?
- Are you able to 'lock on' to a target and not be distracted?
- Does having more than one target bother you?
- Can you stay concentrated over long periods—often self-imposed?
- Is getting tasks done important to you? Do you enjoy completion?
- Are you good at meeting timescales? Do you hate wasting time?

My suggested score:

for Target Focus: _____ out of 10
for Action Focus: _____ out of 10
for Time Focus: _____ out of 10

To derive a score for Focus as a whole, double the score you gave yourself for Target Focus and then add the single scores for both Action and Time Focus. Then divide this total by four to give you a score out of 10. This is in order to give due emphasis to Target Focus.

My overall Focus score is _____ out of 10

Operations

Every business has an operations and a directional side to its activities. The following is an example of an **entirepreneur** who recognised this and developed a dual-management system to handle it. This involved making one person 'responsible for the day-to-day running of the established part of the business' whilst another person 'focused on expansion, evolution and new business'.[17]

Dame Stephanie Shirley started her own business literally 'on her kitchen table'. She grew it with such success that *The Times*' 'Rich List' for the year 2000 placed her as the UK's second-richest self-made woman, with a total wealth of £140 million. Regarding her dual management system she comments:

> My chief executive's approach to the job was quite different to mine. She thrived on making things happen day-to-day. She was organised, strong-minded, calm, principled, a good communicator and good at dealing with pressure. As long as no big strategic innovation was required she was the perfect chief executive.
>
> With me it had been the other way around. My talent is for being an entrepreneur, in the widest sense. I love thinking of new ideas, questioning first principles, sensing new opportunities, starting things, changing things, recruiting new teams, attacking new challenges. That kind of work, for me, is indistinguishable from pleasure.
>
> *Dame Stephanie Shirley, 2012*

For 'Steve' Shirley the operations side of the business with its 'administration, budget-balancing, tax and legal issues, personnel problems, trouble-shooting, making things happen' was a chore. Success came because she was able to delegate that part of the business to someone more capable.

In this section we consider the group of talents involved with operations. As Figure 7.4 illustrates, we place within operations the talents of *administration, organisation* and *people*.

We appreciate that administration and organisation can have similar meanings, but we see administration as concerned with how information is handled across the business. Organisation, on the other hand, is about how people operate and work together to achieve a common aim. It is about the orchestration of the business.

We include *people* as a distinct talent area because ultimately it is this talent that really decides whether the administrative and organisational sides of the business actually work. We also use this section to talk through some of the issues raised by

FIGURE 7.4   Operations

McGregor's X and Y theories of management. Though his book *The Human Side of Enterprise* is now over 50 years old, it is more relevant than ever as society moves further towards a Y-theory approach to life.[18]

Administration

'Admin', as it is often called, runs through every business, whether it is in the private, public or charity sector. Government agencies are always under criticism for the 'red tape' they impose. Every change seems to bring even greater complexity.

Areas such as pensions and personnel are particularly difficult to penetrate and involve specialist staff. Changes over the years have made the administration in these areas ever more challenging. In consequence, separate companies have arisen to handle such matters. Whilst this gets the job done, it is not without difficulties and can certainly increase a company's bottom-line costs.

Businesses that operate on a worldwide basis have to meet international requirements across a wide range, from visas to product quality. The administrative requirements can be huge. We know of a manufacturing company in the UK where documentation for just one contract can take weeks to assemble, and only the boardroom is big enough to assemble all the paperwork involved.

Administration should be an effective means to achieve an end but more often than not it grows over the years until it becomes no longer fit for purpose. The greatest danger is that administration develops a life of its own that no one dare touch in case the business falls apart.

Despite such system problems the most vulnerable part of administration is the people who operate it. This may be because they do not fully understand the overall system and how it works, or it could be simply due to slackness or even laziness. We know of the British arm of a large US company that was struggling to collect the money it was owed by its customers. The 90-day time limit for payment had passed and the American parent flagged it up as a non-payment. An investigation showed that although the invoices had been put into the company's systems, the invoices had never actually been sent out to customers.

These comments are not intended to denigrate administration, but things can certainly go wrong. We believe that only those with talent in this area should really be involved. It requires attention to detail and the ability to spot mistakes. Long memories and effective filing systems can make all the difference.

Self-assessment: find your Administration score

We now offer some questions to help you decide your strength in Administration.

- Are you a person who scans documents to pick out the main points or are you a detail person always spotting mistakes?
- Do you fully understand the administration systems in your company and know how to operate them? Is the person directly responsible sufficiently competent?
- How accurate are your records, and how far back do they go? How good is your memory?

My suggested score:

for Administration: _____ out of 10

Organisation

Here we are concerned not so much with organisation itself as with the talent attribute required to make an organisation work. Some people seem to be born organisers. This can often be seen at an early age when children are at play and one child takes the initiative. It is also seen in communities where just one or two people run all the activities. These organisers are also hands-on doers and set examples that others follow. There is a special integrity about them. They say what they mean and mean what they say. People trust them.

The organisers in the business world have some of these characteristics but, because their area of influence can be much wider, they need to be able to delegate both actions and decisions to others. Some people find this difficult to do. Often, the more competent a person, the less they are able to delegate. Linked to this is the ability to pick able people to whom you can delegate and be sure that the job will be well done. In her biography, Dame 'Steve' Shirley comments that her dual-management system only really worked because she had the ability to select the right person—that is, someone who really enjoyed the operations side of the business and whom she could trust to do a good job. In commenting on the appointment of a new Chief Executive for their operation in the UK she wrote, 'I don't think I have ever made a more inspired appointment. I flatter myself that I am reasonably good at spotting, recruiting and developing talent.'[19]

Trust is an important issue for all organisations. The Boston Consulting Group has pointed out that in hierarchies trust often flows horizontally, not vertically.[20] You trust people on the same level as you, but not those below you (who might be after your job) or those above you (who tell you what to do). Even horizontal trust can be fragile as people compete with one another for promotion or when local issues arise that may, for example, affect status. We were once involved in a major office move from one site to another. When the move was completed we were approached by a normally placid member of staff as to why he had been demoted without consultation. When we assured him this was not the case he pointed out that he was the only person at his level in the organisation who was not sitting next to a window.

Good organisers handle these trust issues well and have the added ability of orchestration. This is more than just team leadership: it is the ability to create harmony with everybody, playing to their strengths and with each person appreciating the contribution made by others.

Any orchestral piece has its own set of musical scores, a range of instruments and people competent in their use. The task of the orchestra leader is to control and manage things in such a way that the music is not only technically correct but also creates the feeling and emotion intended by the composer.

We see the same combination at work in organisations. Some are very mechanistic, with people afraid to show their initiative in case they step out of line. Other organisations, such as Google, are fun places to work and there is a dynamic and drive about them that makes it a joy to go to work.

When the Cambridge phenomenon took off in the 80s, there were many small companies that were both dynamic and fun places to work. But then it seemed that as they became larger and their organisation developed they became slower, heavier and rather dull. It is easy to see this as a growing-up process, but we wonder if it really has to be that way. Companies like Apple, Google and Facebook have tried to maintain their original dynamic and to a degree have succeeded. Even Apple, which lost its charismatic leader, Steve Jobs, for 12 years and became a tired and ordinary company was able, upon his return, to recapture the enthusiasm of earlier years. Apple's 'Think Different' campaign was all it took, but it had to be orchestrated by Jobs himself.

Self-assessment: find your Organisation score

The following questions are to help you to evaluate your strength in Organisation.

- Are you a natural organiser who enjoys taking control and getting things done? Think of examples outside of work where you have done this.
- How easy do you find delegation? Are you able to pick people whom you can trust to do a good job and do it better than you can?
- Can you orchestrate a diverse group of people and get them on board? Is the department or company you run a place that inspires people and brings out the best in them, or is it all rather dull and mundane?

My suggested score:

for Organisation: _____ out of 10

People

Whilst our basic approach to understanding the **entirepreneur** is 'person-centred' throughout, we include this specific section on 'people' because running the operations side of a business requires real 'people talent'. To illustrate this point we now describe how two quite different **entirepreneurs** handled what were very similar people problems.

Ricardo Semler was a young man who took over his father's somewhat static and ageing company and turned it into the fastest-growing company in Brazil, largely by freeing and empowering the workforce with a strongly Y-Theory style. Within almost a decade he took sales from $4 million a year to $20 million and did it with one-third of the original workforce against a difficult business background.

Louis Gerstner, Jr. brought to life an ailing IBM whose demise was likened to the 'brontosaurus that moved deeper into the swamps when the mammals took over the forests, but one day … ran out of swamps'.[21] The large computers that had made IBM famous were seriously outdated. The mainframe revenue of $13 billion in 1990 was predicted to fall to less than $7 billion in 1993, with worse to follow.

Semler's challenge was about taking opportunities and bringing his company into the modern world. Gerstner's was to bring a company back to life. His book, which tells this story, has the title *Who Says Elephants Can't Dance?*—that was his challenge.[22]

The solutions for both companies involved a major change of culture that could only came from the person at the top: the **entirepreneur**. Semler transformed a rigid and controlling management style into one that was free, open and built on trust. In a small but significant step that everybody noticed, he took the security guards off the gates. There had always been a problem with pilfering from the company and this clear example of trust reduced it to almost zero.

Gerstner stayed with the structured management approach of a large multinational and simply put the parts back together again, Humpty-Dumpty style. He stopped the break-up of IBM into individual geographically based companies, which was already underway. He famously said, 'The last thing IBM needs is a vision'.[23] It had to get back to what it was best at doing, which Gerstner saw as servicing other multinational companies.

Using these examples we now make an important connection with Douglas McGregor's X and Y theories of management. Though his book *The Human Side of Enterprise* was published in 1960, its ideas were first made public in a speech he gave under the same title at the fifth anniversary convocation of MIT's Sloan School of Management in April 1957. Even earlier, in 1950, McGregor wrote, 'The ancient concept that people do the work of the world only if they are forced to do so by threat or intimidation has been suffering from a lingering fatal illness for a quarter of a century. I venture the guess that it will be dead in another decade.'[24]

Although McGregor was wrong in his prediction about the early demise of the X-Theory approach to management—it was too much part of human nature—his book marked a watershed in management thinking. Warren Bennis, in his foreword to the 25th anniversary printing, commented that the themes in McGregor's book 'can be seen and are reflected in virtually every book written on management today'. That is how important his thinking was and still is.

McGregor described X-Theory management as being 'The traditional view of direction and control.' Below we give the assumptions about human nature and behaviour that he believed lay behind this approach.

1. The average human being has an inherent dislike of work and will avoid it if he can.
2. Because of this human characteristic of dislike of work, most people must be coerced, controlled, directed, or threatened with punishment to get them to put forth adequate effort towards the achievement of organisational objectives.
3. The average human being prefers to be directed, wishes to avoid responsibility, has relatively little ambition and wants security above all.

Although these assumptions seem a little strong in today's thinking there is no doubt that many companies—we would suggest the majority—do still have a 'direction and control' approach to management. Theory X does allow people to know where they are and what is expected of them. 'Management by objectives' and the present fashion for performance measurement and results tables are alive and well. Theory X certainly has not gone away; it has merely reinvented itself.

McGregor's describes Theory Y as 'the integration of individual and organisational goals'. This suggests a compatibility between what the individual wants out of an organisation and what the organisation requires for it to function effectively. McGregor's assumptions about human nature that lie behind his Theory Y are that:

1. The expenditure of physical and mental effort in work is as natural as play or rest.
2. External control and the threat of punishment are not the only means for bringing about effort towards organisational objectives. Man will exercise self-direction and self-control in the service of objectives to which he is committed.
3. Commitment to objectives is a function of the rewards associated with their achievement.
4. The average human being learns, under proper conditions, not only to accept but to seek responsibility.
5. The capacity to exercise a relatively high degree of imagination, ingenuity and creativity in the solution of organisational problems is widely, not narrowly, distributed in the population.
6. Under the conditions of modern industrial life, the intellectual potentialities of the average human being are only partially utilised.

These accord with our 3Ts approach and the understanding of human potential that lies behind it. We would expect that a majority of people would say that in principle they agree with Theory Y but that in practice they have to live with Theory X. No doubt there are many reasons for this dichotomy. Here we suggest two of them.

First, the strong focus on bottom-line results. The Stock Exchange system puts undue pressure on companies to perform. Even slight rumours can affect share prices quickly and significantly. This, we believe, is not good for long-term business success and creates an environment in which Theory X prevails.

Second, the financial and status rewards for reaching the top echelons of the business world encourage the emergence of X-Theory-type people. In some cases the word 'ruthless' would not be out of place.

To provide some evidence that a way can be found for Theory Y to take root, we return to the example of Semco and IBM outlined earlier. Both Semler and Gerstner inherited X-Theory companies. Semler himself was a Y-Theory person and a strong enough personality to re-create the business in his own image. Such was the difference he effected that his book, which tells the story, was given the title *Maverick*.[25] He created a growing and exciting business with strong employee participation.

Gerstner also inherited an X-Theory business in line with the IBM tradition set by Thomas J. Watson, Sr in 1962. His was a long shadow. Although Watson espoused a number of Y-Theory attributes, such as 'respect for the individual', his approach was paternal. He preferred that employees be married and specified a dress code that became institutionalised. Dark suits and white shirts were the order of the day.

Gerstner recognised that his real problem was that he had to effect a culture change. He had to move IBM from Theory X to Theory Y. He recognised the need to stop people using hierarchy as a crutch and get them to take personal responsibility. Though he wanted people to listen to what he said he needed 'to get them to stop being followers and think for themselves'. He expected this culture change would take at least five years but it took longer. He abolished the outdated dress code in 1995 when two years into the job, but that was relatively easy.[26]

Looking back on his experience at IBM, Gerstner puts his finger on this key point. Moving an organisation from a traditional Theory X position to the more progressive and human approach of Theory Y is all about culture. Gerstner tells us:

> I came to see, in my time at IBM, that culture isn't just one aspect of the game—it is the game. In the end, an organisation is nothing more than the collective capacity of its people to create value.

Though Semco and IBM were quite different businesses, they both showed that Y-Theory management can succeed, but it is clearly not easy and requires strong leadership.

Self-assessment: find your People score

We now provide some questions for you to self-assess the strength of your People talent. However, since that strength is directly affected by your view on McGregor's X and Y theories of management, we provide questions in that context.

- Are you a command and control (X-Theory) person, or do you believe that everybody has potential and is able to take responsibility (Theory Y)?
- When things are difficult do you become an X-Theory person and simply tell people what to do and take full control?
- To what extent is your approach to Operations dictated by X- and Y-Theory considerations? Can you think of examples? Do people enjoy their work because of the environment that you have created?
- Do people see you as a hard person, a soft touch or a bit of both?

Here we suggest that instead of giving yourself a score you try to identify where you sit in the range from Theory X to Theory Y. As an exercise you may then like to add where the companies that you have worked for would sit. Does this tell you anything about how you fitted into the company culture?

Theory X _____|_____ Theory Y

midpoint

To derive an overall figure for Operations we suggest you first take the average of your individual scores for Administration and Organisation.

My first score for Operations is _____ out of 10

To complete the evaluation think how your X/Y balance might affect your operations score once you add a people dimension.

My first score for Operations is _____ out of 10

◆ Your Talent score

First we suggest you bring forward the individual scores you gave yourself so that they are all together.

My previous scores were:

Creativity: _____ out of 10
Focus: _____ out of 10
Operations: _____ out of 10

My average Talent score is _____ out of 10

Now look at your individual Talent scores. If there is a mismatch of four points between any one of the three Talent groups, adjust it one or two points up or down.

My final Talent score is _____ out of 10

8

♥ TEMPERAMENT—APPLIED

The temperament elements

In the previous chapter we grouped talent into the three major groups: *creativity*, *focus* and *operations*. For temperament we use a different model built around the idea of the ego. We appreciate that 'ego' has a number of interpretations and want to make it clear that we are using it in the sense of the 'self of an individual person'.[1] We are not using it as a measure of selfishness or self-indulgence, although we are aware that those who rise to the top of an organisation can face challenges in this area.

For convenience we reproduce Figure 6.2 renumbered here as Figure 8.1.

As explained in Chapter 6, this model distinguishes between the Inner Ego and Outer Ego, wherein the Inner Ego is the part of ourselves that only we can

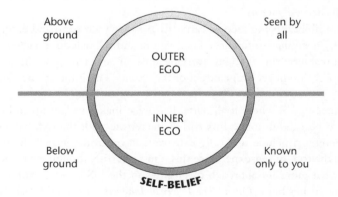

FIGURE 8.1 Temperament model

know and the Outer Ego is the part that others see. In researching the work of McGregor on Theory X and Theory Y management styles, we discovered that he had similar ideas to our own on this ego component. He came to it through Maslow's Hierarchy of Needs and concluded that the social needs were 'of greatest significance to management and to man himself'.[2] He called them 'egoistic needs' and said they were of two kinds:[3]

1.   Those that related to one's self-esteem: needs for self-respect and self-confidence, for autonomy, for achievement, for competence, for knowledge
2.   Those that relate to one's reputation: needs for status, for recognition, for appreciation, for the deserved respect of one's fellows

Although we came at it from a different angle, there are clearly similarities with needs related to one's self-esteem and our Inner Ego, and needs related to one's reputation and our Outer Ego.

We now consider the Inner and Outer Egos in more detail and describe the elements of which they are composed. In Chapter 6 we listed them in the following terms.

Inner Ego elements:

1.   Self-assurance: this is about inner assurance and draws on the deeper factor of our self-belief. Its output is self-confidence. It is the 'I can do it' factor.
2.   Dedication: passion and emotional commitment are important here. The 'I love it' factor.
3.   Motivation: what drives us to do things is the issue. The 'I must do it' factor.

Outer Ego elements:

1.   Courage: the emotional strength to face up to adversity and win through. The 'I will succeed' factor.
2.   Responsibility: being seen to carry the risks for your team and enterprise and thereby instilling confidence. The 'we can and we will do it' factor.
3.   Accountability: this is about 'carrying the can' and having an 'inner locus of control'.[4] You never blame others or the system. This is the 'it's my fault' factor.

The Inner Ego is where it all starts. It is what makes us 'get up and go'. Here we need to be careful not to link this characteristic with the extrovert personality and thereby conclude that only extroverts have strong enough Inner Egos to make it to the top. In our experience this is just not true, though we do accept that the somewhat gung-ho approach to business in the USA can certainly give that impression. In her book *Quiet: The Power of Introverts in a World That Can't Stop Talking*, Susan Cain quotes an informal conversation with students at the Harvard Business School, who told her that 'this school is predicated on extroversion'.[5] She then makes a good case for the 'quiet' people.

Outer Ego comes from and builds on the Inner Ego, or at least it should do. A person with a strong Inner Ego strengthens their Outer Ego over time as they respond to and learn from their environment. Its three elements of courage, responsibility and accountability are all tested and grow through involvement in the day-to-day activities of a business.

In interview research with our 'efacets' questionnaire we found that, for most people, the Inner Ego is stronger than the Outer Ego.[6] We see this as being the correct way round because a strong Inner Ego provides a solid foundation for a sound temperament, as experience strengthens the Outer Ego. On the other hand, a strong Outer Ego on a weak Inner Ego suggests a person who appears to be confident but is essentially fragile. This was borne out when we interviewed a person that our questionnaire had shown to have that profile. At that time we had not seen many people with this level of imbalance and so we asked her if she thought the result was correct. Her response was that it was exactly right. She was aware that she came over as a confident and able person but knew that deep down she had many doubts as to her abilities. Her self-belief and thereby her self-confidence was low. She commented that she always did badly at interviews because she tended to talk herself down.

The Inner Ego elements

Self-assurance

This important element of the Inner Ego stands between self-belief, the source, and self-confidence, the output. Self-belief we see as something that is deep within us and provides the foundation for not only self-assurance but all three of the Inner Ego elements.

Self-assurance is among Gallup's 34 StrengthsFinder themes.[7] 'In the deepest part of you, you have the faith in your strengths. You know what you are able to deliver.' This is an interesting definition in that it is circular, depending upon itself. It is a strength that has faith in other strengths. Here we make two points. First, that self-assurance is a temperament issue and not a talent one. It is therefore possible to have both a strong temperament (self-assurance) and strong talents (your strengths). By seeing them as different entities the circularity of Gallup's description disappears.

Second, we believe that our Inner and Outer Ego model clarifies the Gallup understanding of self-assurance significantly. 'In the deepest part of you … you know what you are able to deliver.' The 'deepest part of you' corresponds to the Inner Ego and 'what you are able to deliver' is found in the Outer Ego. Taking it further, Gallup's description goes on to refer to the outcomes of self-assurance as having 'confidence not only in your abilities but in your judgement'. From this, Gallup says we gain a personal 'authority' and have 'final accountability'. We agree. Our Outer Ego includes accountability as one of its elements.

Self-assurance is something that grows within us as we go through life. Our early years are particularly important. We have already referenced, in Chapter 7,

Jack Welch and the 'blame culture' at General Electric which resulted in the 'The GE Vortex' that destroyed people's confidence and permanently damaged their self-assurance.[8] Welch was acutely aware of how important this confidence was. As a child he had suffered 'with a speech impediment, a stammer that wouldn't go away'.[9] His mother solved the problem by telling him the reason why he stuttered. 'It's because you're so smart. No one's tongue could keep up with a brain like yours.' This may not have been medically accurate but that didn't matter. He stopped worrying about it and his stammer left him.

The title of the first chapter in Welch's biography is 'Building Self-Confidence'. It is significant that one of the most powerful business leaders of his day should begin his biography in this way. He clearly saw it as the foundation of all that he was able to achieve and remained ever grateful to the part his mother had played. 'Perhaps the greatest gift she gave me was self-confidence. I didn't understand for many years just how much confidence she poured into me. My mother never managed people, but she knew all about building self-esteem'.[10]

Self-assurance is the 'I can do it' factor. This is not so much a matter of ability—a talent issue—as one of an inner belief that whatever it takes, you can deliver. You may not know how difficult the road ahead really is—none of us ever do—but you have an assurance within that you will get there.

Self-assessment: find your Self-Assurance score

Here are some questions you might like to think about regarding Self-Assurance.

- Were you a confident child? —you might like to think of examples—Have you grown more self-assured as you got older?
- Are you a 'can do' or a 'what if' person? If you are a bit of both, try expressing it as a percentage.
- Now think how that ratio might change if the 'chips were down'. Would you go for it or would you hold back?

My suggested Self-Assurance score is _____ out of 10

Dedication

This Inner Ego element is about the heart. It is concerned with being wholly committed to something with a passion and emotional commitment that is unstoppable. It is easy to understand why such characteristics would sit well with people dedicated to a social cause. People like Dame Cicely Saunders, who founded the modern hospice movement that enabled people to die with dignity.[11] Starting as a nurse, then an almoner and finally qualifying as a doctor, it was a long and difficult road to even get people to listen to her. Finally she changed professional opinion about the use of drugs to relieve the physical pain of the dying and pioneered the provision of special homes that could handle terminally ill patients. Her dedication was remarkable.

Anita Roddick was an outstandingly successful businesswoman whose life from a young age was dominated by causes. Even so, it took her some time to make the link between business and her passion for the just cause. It was only when her company had gone public 'that it began to dawn on Gordon and me that The Body Shop actually had the potential and power to do good'.[12]

In the same vein, many wealthy business people give large sums of money to good causes.[13] Under 'Values in action' in Chapter 10 we term them 'Today's philanthropists.' Their remarkable generosity is in marked contrast to the general view of the business world as being heartless and driven by personal gain. On that basis it would be easy to conclude that the Inner Ego element of Dedication does not apply to those involved in business. In fact, research shows otherwise. Whatever goals we have for ourselves, whether altruistic or mercenary, we need the passion and emotional commitment that the dedication element of the Inner Ego brings.

In his book *The Millionaire Mind* Thomas Stanley provides some interesting insights.[14] His research ranked 'loving my career/business' as the sixth most important 'Millionaire's Success Factor', ahead of 'having strong leadership qualities'. Stanley comments that 'the more wealth they have, the more likely they are to say "My success is a direct result of loving my career or business"'.

Sam Walton of WalMart fame has commented, 'If you love your work, you will be out there every day trying to do the best you possibly can, and pretty soon everybody around you will catch the passion from you—like a fever.'[15]

Tim Waterstone has said of the bookshop chain he created, 'I did love Waterstone's and I very much still do, for Waterstone's made my life, and defined my life. We believed we had a winner … and at least for me personally, committing myself passionately and unswervingly to that win was as necessary to me and as instinctive as breathing itself'.[16]

This Inner Ego element is the easiest to spot and be sure about because such dedication changes your life. You talk about it and think about it all the time. Your business idea—or more accurately your business opportunity—takes you over.

Dedication is the 'I love it' factor. It is much more than simply 'liking' to do something. Here we are talking about something that is all-consuming of time, effort and thinking. It generates a passion that never goes away. It is from the heart and not the head. This factor means that you really love what you do and would not have it any other way.

Self-assessment: find your Dedication score

The questions you need to think about here are:

- Do you get passionate about things and maintain that passion when things are not going well? Can you think of examples?

- Do you think you are ready for the high level of dedication and commitment involved?
- Are you a person who likes to have several interests and keep everything in balance?

As with this last question you may have noticed that the expected answer can be a 'no'. We have tried to avoid 'apple-pie' questions where the answer is both obvious and a 'yes'. This is to help you think about the question and, in doing so, give yourself a more accurate score.

My suggested score for Dedication is _____ out of 10

Motivation

This third element of the Inner Ego is about what drives us to do what we do. Duncan Bannatyne, of Dragons' Den fame, was wasting his life. He had no qualifications and no profession to follow. He was an unemployable, aimless drifter. Then he read an article about Alan Sugar and how he had grown a business from scratch and made his first million.

> As I sat on that beach, I decided that this was my wake-up call. I was going to do exactly what Alan Sugar had done; I was going to change my life and make myself a million. At the age of 30, I was a penniless beach bum. At the age of 37, I was a millionaire.[17]

Bannatyne's motivation was to make himself 'a million'. That was his target. It was what he wanted to achieve and he directed all his efforts to that end.

Most motivations are expressed in terms of outcomes. They are all 'I wants' and represent desires and ambitions. Typically they are:

- I want to make a difference; to leave footprints.
- I want to be rich.
- I want to show the world (or a specific person) that I am worth something.
- I want a better life for myself and my family.
- I want to be in charge of my life, to be independent.
- I want to run a large enterprise or organisation.

It is all very well wanting these things but that is not enough. Motivation is about *musts*, not wants. Wants only get you halfway there; musts get you the whole way.

A somewhat different approach to motivation was presented by David McClelland.[18] Rather than looking at individual motivations linked with wants and musts, he considered a mix of three primary motivations that are present at different strengths within a person. This fits well with our understanding of motivation as an element of the Inner Ego. The strength of the motivation decides whether it really is a must or simply a want.

In *The Achieving Society*, McClelland showed that there was a direct link between the economic growth of a society and the strength of its 'achievement' motive.[19] This he found was true whether the society was advanced or primitive, developed or developing. He also found that there were two other motivations that had to be considered: the motivation to 'affiliate', meaning to join with others, and the 'power' motivation that was about authority and control. Different economic situations arose depending upon the relative strength of these factors. For example, he concluded that 'a combination of low affiliation and high power is particularly likely to lead a country to pursue its economic or other ends by totalitarian means'.

McClelland identified the entrepreneur as being a person high on 'achievement' and thereby the key to successful economic development. However, at the end of a chapter called 'The Characteristics of Entrepreneurs' he asks the question, 'What kind of men are available for leadership positions in economic organisations in various countries?[20] For in the long run it is they, and their primary concerns, whether for achievement, affiliation, power or something else, that determines the rate at which the economy of their country develops.'

Here it is quite tempting to make a simple connection between McClelland's three motivations and the traditional business threesome of entrepreneur, leader and manager. Thus the motivation of the entrepreneur would be *achievement*, of the leader *power* and the manager *affiliation*. This clearly works to a degree but, as McClelland shows, even the pairing of two strong motivations when the third is weak can produce a particular effect. Thus a person strong on achievement and power and weak on affiliation will operate in an authoritarian manner and will get results that way. This corresponds to McGregor's X-Theory approach. Equally, someone strong on achievement and affiliation but weak on power will succeed by using a team-based approach and behaving as a Y-Theory person.

Andy Law showed how this could be done. He ran an outstandingly successful advertising agency in London with a deep personal commitment to his handpicked team. When the US advertising agency Chiat/Day (of which his company had become part) was merged with another large agency, he had a decision to make. This merger was going to be big. It would create a £2 billion global operation, but as Law put it

> we were mutinying. En masse. And the strangest thing was that all we cared about was each other and sticking together. Exactly how we were going to succeed as a standalone company seemed a distant hurdle.
>
> Earlier Andy had got his team together. Speaking slowly and carefully he had challenged them 'Just look at the view from this window. It's a great view. It offers all sorts of ideas for the future. Some of you, and I understand why, might not be as interested in this view as me. If you're not, don't be

afraid, don't compromise yourself. Just walk out now. We are about to enter uncharted territory and I can make absolutely no promises for a safe journey.'

No one moved or spoke as Andy looked around at his team. 'All brilliant, loyal and un-fireable in anyone's book' he thought. The whole company stood silently still. Rock solid.

Well, it looks like we're all in it. Now it's action stations.[21]

Whilst a weakness in either power or affiliation matches X-Theory and Y-Theory people respectively, unless there is a strong achievement motivation, progress will be slow and no heights will be scaled. Thus, the real decider and essential requirement for the **entirepreneur** is to be strong on achievement.

Self-assessment: find your Motivation score

As with the elements of Self-Assurance and Dedication, we now offer some questions to help you assess your Motivation profile.

Here you need to consider the three Motivations and think through which is likely to be your strongest and which your weakest. Remember that:

- 'Achievement' is about 'must do or have'.
- 'Affiliation' involves building strong relationships.
- 'Power' is concerned with being in control.

Rank these three Motivations in order of their importance to you as energisers and drivers. Give them each a strength score out of 10.

My suggested score:

for Achievement motive: _____ out of 10
for Affiliation motive: _____ out of 10
for Power motive: _____ out of 10

We suggest you now pick out your top two scores and take an average.

My Motivation score is _____ out of 10

Your Inner Ego score

The three Inner Ego elements of Self-Assurance, Dedication and Motivation all work together and all must be present.

To give yourself an overall score for Inner Ego, look at the scores you gave for each of the three elements. If they are similar then simply take an average score out of ten. If they are widely different, drop the average by one point as it suggests imbalance somewhere in your profile.

My suggested Inner Ego score is _____ out of 10

In considering your scores it is important to see them as not so much a score but rather as an understanding. You may also find it helpful to check your scores through with a close colleague or partner, but bear in mind that these are about your Inner Ego so you have the last word.

The Outer Ego elements

The Outer Ego elements are an outcome and expression of the Inner Ego elements, but there is not a one-to-one correlation. Thus *courage*, the first element we consider, draws mainly on self-assurance and motivation. However, depending on the situation, dedication can also be involved, bringing tenacity and commitment.

The second and third elements of *responsibility* and *accountability* both draw strongly on dedication, though here too, the other Inner Ego elements play their part.

Courage

People strong in courage have the emotional strength to confront difficult situations and deal with them. They do not avoid or procrastinate; they face up to situations. They 'bite the bullet'.

Although the Gallup Organisation's StrengthsFinder does not include 'courage', it was identified in Don Clifton's earlier work on the entrepreneur. In that context courage was described as being 'determined in the face of adversity' and 'an ability to use emotion to overcome resistance'.[22]

There are two subsets here: *practical courage* and *emotional courage*.

Practical courage is the ability to face reality and take appropriate action. People with a strong Inner Ego but a weak Outer Ego can find this particularly difficult. Their strong self-assurance, dedication and motivation can make it very hard for them to realise that they might actually be wrong. People who have never failed at anything in their lives can come to believe too much in themselves and find failure difficult to accept, let alone face up to.

A Cambridge student who set up in business on graduation had to learn the hard way. The 3i Group, a leading venture capital company in the UK, provided him with funding and he seemed set for a good start. Two years later the business failed. He had debts, which meant that bailiffs came to his flat and took away everything of value, including his hi-fi equipment.

This was a humiliating experience for the young man but he dusted himself down and started again. He was not defeated. His practical courage had seen him through. He faced reality and moved on.

This strength in adversity is what *practical courage* is all about. It is needed when hard decisions have to be made, which is how valuable experience is gained.

Sir Richard Branson faced what seemed an impossible situation when Mike Oldfield of *Tubular Bells* fame pulled out of the concert that Branson had specifically set up for him. For Branson it was to be the launch of Virgin Records and the solution to a serious debt crisis just days away.

Oldfield's call to Branson to cancel the performance came through on the morning of the concert. At this point you might like to think what you would have done—call your lawyer, pay Oldfield more money. Branson did neither. Oldfield's emotions were obviously high. The roller coaster success of his record had drained him. He was emotionally spent. Branson's solution was to put some positive emotional pressure on Oldfield, in what on Branson's part was a remarkable example of *practical courage*. He did not just push emotion aside, he used it in what was essentially a hard-nosed commercial approach.

> Branson said that they should talk the situation through and although Oldfield told him he had made up his mind he agreed to Branson's suggestion that they meet. Branson drove over to see Oldfield in the vintage Bentley that his in-laws had given him as wedding present and which he knew Oldfield admired. They went for a ride, drove past the concert venue and then some way on Branson stopped the car and asked Oldfield if he would like a drive. Unsuspecting, Oldfield took the wheel and no doubt began to relax. When Oldfield parked the car and passed the car keys back, Branson asked him if he would like to keep them. The deal was that he could keep the car if he did the concert. Oldfield agreed and the concert went ahead.[23]

Emotional courage is required when people and personal situations have to be confronted and dealt with. In most cases the winner is the one who puts the emotion aside and goes for a practical solution. Although we do not know Branson's inner thoughts, it seems as if he was able to put aside his emotional attachment to his wedding present and any emotional impact his action might have on Mike Oldfield. The latter proved to be significant. After the concert Oldfield refused to speak to the press and described the onstage experience as like 'being emotionally raped'.

This kind of tussle between emotional and practical courage often arises when close friends are involved in difficult and personal decisions. Both know that one of them will lose out. The interview in which John Sculley, Apple's CEO, dismissed Steve Jobs is a classic example. Sculley chooses the prologue of his book, *Odyssey: Pepsi to Apple*, to tell us this part of his story.[24] He may have been following board instructions, but the deep emotions involved come through.

> Only a year ago, I had raised a toast: "Apple has one leader, Steve and me." He had become my closest friend, a soul mate and a constant companion. But there were no smiles. We spoke quietly and sadly. A break in our partnership seemed inevitable. It would destroy our friendship, it might destroy the company, and it had already destroyed my confidence.
>
> For over an hour, Steve pleaded with me for a second chance … for more time. Over and over. Again and again. I refused to relent.
>
> Then, overcome with emotion, he suddenly burst from the room. I was left, wanting only to hide… . I wept there, wondering how it had come to this.

This example shows how the two Inner Ego motivations of affiliation and achievement can clash. Jobs and Sculley had developed a remarkable personal bond but when the results were not forthcoming the achievement motivation took over and affiliation was sacrificed. Handling that situation produced some deep emotional hurts and Apple became virtually unmanageable. The new management tried to change the ethos of the company but it failed. What they did not seem to have realised is that despite, or perhaps because of, his personal idiosyncrasies, Jobs had created an affiliation that extended beyond the employees to the customers as well. It had a cult status. There were Apple 'believers': that's how strong the affiliation motivation was. Steve's return after a 12-year absence was like a second coming to them.

'I will succeed' is courage's statement of intent. For practical and emotional reasons, failure is not an option. If courage fails, it is not easy to recover. This is because its roots are in the Inner Ego and defeat challenges those roots deeply. Self-assurance is the element most deeply affected and has the knock-on effect of negatively impacting the other Outer Ego elements of responsibility and accountability that we consider next.

Self-assessment: find your Courage score

Before we continue, we offer the opportunity for you to score yourself on Courage.

- Think of those times when you have had to summon up courage to do something. How hard were those times for you, and how frequent? What did you learn from them?
- Have you ever had your self-confidence seriously damaged? If so, did you take any specific action, such as counselling, to help you through, or did you just tough it out?
- Would you say that you are a naturally courageous person, in that facing difficult issues and making tough decisions does not bother you? If you fail, do you simply lick your wounds and get on with the next challenge?

My suggested score for Courage is _____ out of 10

Responsibility

People strong in responsibility take initiative without waiting to be told. It comes out of a strong self-assurance. This can, of course, create conflicts in a highly structured organisation that does not expect or permit people to step out of line.

A university student in a summer job worked for the local council in the house maintenance department. There had been a burglary in a house and the fitting of a new lock on the back door had been approved. When the student went to check that all was going according to plan, the householder pointed out that the front door lock also needed replacing. As the workman was on site and he could just as well fit two locks, the student authorised the action. It seemed obvious to him. When his boss found out, however, he was in trouble. He was told that only one lock had been approved and he had no authority to change the order. He tried to explain that his decision had saved the council the cost of a second call out but he got nowhere. The student had demonstrated he was a natural responsibility taker. He is now the CEO of a listed company and enjoying it.

Responsibility is one of the Gallup Organisation's 34 'themes and ideas for action' evaluated in their StrengthsFinder. The person strong on responsibility is the one that people 'will look to first when assigning new responsibilities because they know the job will get done'.[25] This is the element of the Outer Ego that others can see the most clearly. Where there is a job to be done in any organisation or group of people someone strong in responsibility will emerge. If it is not the person officially in charge, however, it can create real problems. This is one of the major weaknesses with hierarchy management structures and more often than not an informal structure operates around the person strong in responsibility.

Some years ago, when trade unions were particularly strong in the UK, the directors of a large aluminium foundry became concerned that instructions from the board were not getting through to the workforce. They engaged outside consultants to investigate the matter. When reporting back, the consultants asked the simple question, 'Who runs your company?', 'We do!', came the reply. 'You are mistaken,' they were told. 'It is the Chief Shop Steward.'

It was then decided to offer the Chief Shop Steward early retirement in the hope that then the problem would go away. When the offer was put to him he jumped at the chance and commented that it was time for his son to take over his father's job. At last the directors got the message and set about dismantling the informal organisation structure that had arisen around the shop steward.

People strong on responsibility can carry amazing loads and really enjoy it. This is an essential requirement for the **entirepreneur**, and it comes about when high self-confidence combines with a strong achievement motivation. One such person was J Arthur Rank.

> "J. Arthur" emerged from the shadow of his father, Joseph Rank, the miller, at the ago of forty-one, to almost single-handedly build the British film industry. Rank knew very little about acting or the theatre and yet he was the man who stepped forward and took the responsibility for the fledgling industry. He carried it on his shoulders for twenty years and gave the British Industry its finest hour. But the starting point was that he took responsibility and people trusted him to deliver.[26]

Self-assessment: find your Responsibility score

The questions you need to think about here are:

- When something needs to organised or sorted out do you jump into action or wait for someone else to take the initiative?

- Do you often find the official lines of authority to be restrictive and even annoying? Are you sometimes regarded as a 'maverick'?
- Are you able to carry responsibility with ease and actually enjoy it or do you stay awake at night worrying about things?

My suggested score for Responsibility is _____ out of 10

Accountability

This is normally understood as the process of being measured against targets and having a judgment made as to your performance. Who sets the targets, who does the measurement and how accurate that measurement is make this a somewhat uncertain process. This we see as 'external accountability', but our interest here is in what might be termed 'internal accountability'. It is about those people who are strong on self-accountability. They judge themselves all the time and do not wait to be told.

A person's sense of accountability derives from the dedication element of the Inner Ego. It is dedication that brings passion and commitment to an activity and in turn makes people self-accountable. They are always trying to do better and are their own harshest taskmaster. In the extreme they can become perfectionists.

Making such a person accountable within a system just does not work for them. In fact, it often challenges their dedication. Teaching and health care are both professions in which people have a sense of calling. Too strong a focus on external accountability can be very demoralising and make people give up on self-accountability.

Self-accountability may at first sight appear relatively rare in Western culture. We seem to be swamped by systems that make everybody accountable to somebody somewhere. However, there are many indicators that show we are more introspective than ever. Positive psychology is now arguing that it can change the workplace for the better. Instead of hard work leading to success and thence to happiness, the process is being reversed: happiness comes first and that breeds success. Tom Rath, whom we have quoted in connection with the Gallup Organisation and their StrengthsFinder 2.0, is now offering a WellbeingFinder. This scores individuals against five areas of well-being, from 'Career Wellbeing' to 'Community Wellbeing'.[27] Shawn Achor, in his book *The Happiness Advantage: The Seven Principles of Positive Psychology that Fuel Success and Performance at Work*, references a website, www.viasurvey.org, that gives you your top five 'signature strengths' from a list of 24 cross-cultural character strengths that most contribute to 'human flourishing'.[28]

Self-accountability works well if it is set in the context of one's Inner Ego strengths, as we have sought to do, but it is not recommended for those with low self-belief because any evaluation that they make of themselves will be downbeat and negative.

Sport psychologists have had some interesting things to say in this area because athletes are performance driven but likely to lose more events than they win. Athletes carry failure in two ways: they either blame external forces or they take responsibility for the failure. Thus a sprinter, eager to get a good start, can sometimes take off too early and the race has to be restarted. False starts can be blamed on external things such as the starting block or the official with the starting gun. Athletes can also see it as being their own mistake: maybe it was their nervousness or a lack of concentration.

Psychologists have described this 'who can I blame' effect in terms of one's 'locus of control'.[29] People with an external locus of control believe that their lives are controlled by things outside themselves. They often feel society is against them; that they are always the victims. Nothing is ever their fault. Those with an internal locus of control are exactly the opposite. They see themselves as self-accountable for their own lives and believe that it is their own actions that dictate events. If something goes wrong they look for the mistakes that they have made and put them right.

On the downside, people with a strong internal locus of control can often be too harsh on themselves.

> Jonathan Edwards is an outstanding holder of the triple-jump world record. Set in 1995 at the World Championship in Gothenburg the record still stands today. Three years earlier he had failed badly at the Barcelona Olympics, not even reaching the finals. Edwards was very harsh in his judgement of his performance at the time. His biographer comments that for top athletes "there is a necessary harshness of self-judgement" in such situations. "They work to a balance sheet with a bottom line that is defined as sharply as any financial institution in the City. There is one column marked 'Win'; there is another column marked 'Loss'. The truth cannot be laundered."[30]

Though it is an Outer Ego element, accountability can put great pressure on the Inner Ego when it challenges self-assurance. Edwards again provides an interesting example.

> Just before his world record achievement Edwards went down with a serious virus and spoke with fellow athlete Roger Black who had had the same illness. Black comments, 'I heard the tiredness and detachment in the voice, and became aware of his lack of confidence. You can always hear that doubt in an athlete.'[31]

A person strong on self-accountability and weak on self-assurance can easily get caught in a downward spiral of guilt. This kind of mismatch between the Inner and Outer Ego is difficult to live with. Thankfully for most people it is not a permanent condition and the confidence required for self-accountability returns once things get back to normal or the particular pressure is dealt with.

Self-assessment: find your Accountability score

When considering these questions remember that they are about Self-Accountability and not accountability on general. They relate to the 'it's my fault' factor.

- How easy do you find it to admit to yourself and to others that you have made a mistake?
- How do you rate workplace assessments of performance? Do you treat them with disdain or look for areas where you could improve?

• Does failure spur you on to get things right and try harder? Do you really learn from your mistakes? Are you a perfectionist?

My suggested score for Accountability is ＿＿＿ out of 10

Your Outer Ego score

The three elements of Courage, Responsibility and Accountability are equally important, and on that basis we suggest you take an average of your three scores. If however you gave yourself a score of four out of ten for any of the three, think a bit more carefully and see if they are linked with any of the Inner Ego elements. For example, a low score for Dedication could be why you have a low score for Accountability.

My suggested score for Outer Ego is ＿＿＿＿ out of 10

Since these Outer Ego scores are about how others see you, you may like to talk over your score with a good friend. In this case they, rather than you, should have the last word.

♥ Your Temperament score

First, bring forward your Inner and Outer Ego scores:

My Inner Ego score was ＿＿＿＿＿＿＿ out of 10
My Outer Ego score was ＿＿＿＿＿＿＿ out of 10

A typical **entirepreneur** score would be eight out of ten or more for both Inner and Outer Ego. If you are at a lower level in an organisation, seven for Inner Ego and six for Outer Ego would be on the limit.

It is now important for you to consider any imbalance between your Inner and Outer Egos.

1. If your Inner Ego is stronger than your Outer Ego, there is not likely to be a problem as long as the difference between the scores is not greater than two points. This is because the strength of Outer Ego generally increases with experience.
2. If your Outer Ego is stronger than your Inner Ego, this could represent a problem. This is because the Outer Ego will be driving the Inner Ego. This can occur when you are playing a role and not being your true self. Equally, it may be that you are driven by what others think about you rather than by your own inner strengths. The danger then is that you may be tempted to compensate for your weaker Inner Ego by bullying or by using your status to gain authority and get things done.

9

♣ TECHNIQUE—APPLIED

Of the 3Ts, technique is at first sight all about application. Technique, as we have already noted in Chapter 6, has to be worked at hard, indeed very hard. The 10,000-hour rule of 'deliberate practice' is not an exaggeration. But there is a major difference between business and those areas such as music, sport and chess from which the 10,000-hour rule emerged. The difference is that in business the rules of the game are changing all the time. What worked last year will not work this year. Products, services and ways of doing things are short lived. This, as we have discussed earlier, is the 'New Normal'.

Our first technique element is *teams plus*. We use this term because we want to cover not only the *team* itself but the additional elements of *using experts* and *networking*. A key change here is the move from Theory X to Theory Y that is already affecting how people relate to each other. The remarkable growth and influence of social media networks is one such factor influencing that shift.

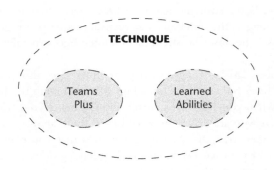

FIGURE 9.1 The technique elements

The second element is *learned abilities* and these are certainly affected by the changes in the business environment. The knowledge base and skills of yesterday have been replaced by what to some is a bewildering range of computer-related competences. A working knowledge of Excel and the ability to search the Internet quickly and efficiently are essential tools today.

Teams plus

Entirepreneurs are only as good as their teams, whether that be their direct-report team or teams throughout the organisation. We start by considering the team itself and then bring in the use of experts and networking, as in many ways they are an extension of the team approach. It is not practical or cost-effective to employ a range of experts in areas where their help and advice is only required occasionally. Networking is often the first step to finding experts but it is also a way of building up connections with others at the top of their organisations. Being an **entirepreneur** can sometimes be a lonely occupation where true friends are difficult to find. We have observed in reading the stories of **entirepreneurs** how often golf comes up as the sport they enjoy playing. It is competitive, has strong individual challenges but is also a way to get to know other people. It is a networking opportunity.

Teams

Getting people to work together is a complex issue. It involves each of our 3Ts in different ways. Talent can be a basis for competition, friendly or otherwise, whilst temperament can give rise to clashes of personality or group cliques. Technique, on the other hand, offers the possibility of overcoming some of these hurdles and of building shared values and strengths. Team activities within companies are now run on a regular basis and appear to be popular.

The personality structure of a team is important if incompatibilities within it are to be avoided. A certain amount of difference is of course helpful so that team

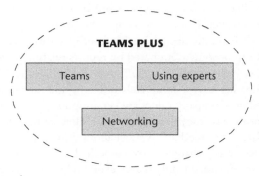

FIGURE 9.2 Teams plus

members can challenge each other, but too many big egos just do not work. In our own experience with team-building, personality clashes are the most difficult area to deal with. We were able to resolve this only when we insisted upon personality profiling each participant in a programme. For this we used a combination of Myers-Briggs profiling and Belbin's team roles.

The team roles and their importance were brought to prominence through the research of Meredith Belbin and his book *Management Teams: Why They Succeed or Fail*.[1] His research showed that people take on roles when they are in teams that are independent of their official function. The balance, or otherwise, between these roles is a strong decider of the team's effectiveness. Belbin identified nine team roles, including 'Plants' who provide ideas, 'Shapers' who give form to the team's efforts, 'Team Workers' who smooth the way and 'Completer-finishers' who get the job done. Whilst these are helpful to explain a team's strengths and weaknesses, it is rarely possible to rebuild a team.

We were once involved in evaluating a board of directors that was thought to be out of balance. The Belbin analysis confirmed this to be the case. Three of the five directors were Plants. There were plenty of ideas but little progress. Whilst the analysis explained the problem, it was difficult to solve. It was not possible to replace any of the directors, and the suggestion that one of the Plants should take the role of being a Shaper and another a Completer-finisher made little sense as these were not their natural roles.

Another issue in trying to achieve a balanced board using Belbin's model is that the members of the board are generally department heads appointed for their functional skills and not their boardroom roles. It is also most likely that in any discussion the individual directors will speak as functional heads and 'look after their own'.

Team events can be about improving company performance or boosting morale. The approach companies adopt will depend upon whether they take an X- or a Y-Theory stance. For X-Theory companies this would be a top-down exercise with the challenge of meeting the aspirations and targets set by senior management. The only debate would be on how to achieve the targets rather than whether the targets were the right ones. Team training would be practical and to the point. People would be instructed in what was expected of them. The motivational speaker would encourage the group to achieve their aims. Our experience with public sector boards confirms this can be a danger for them; the agenda can become dominated by reports relating to performance and compliance.

Y-Theory companies have a completely different understanding of what motivates and drives teams. Company values are very important to them and they make great efforts to ensure that they are understood. They want believers. The Body Shop, under the late Anita Roddick, was all about values. Their aim to 'make the world a better place' was a shared vision embodied in a company charter.[2] They saw themselves as an extended family where everybody works together responsibly and efficiently:

- The Body Shop's goals and values are as important as our products and profits.
- Honesty, integrity and caring form the foundations of the Company, and should flow from everything we do.
- We embrace everyone who works for The Body Shop and with The Body Shop as part of our extended family. We are all the Company: it is up to all of us to make it work.

Andy Law (whom we referenced earlier) of St Luke's Advertising Agency took things further.[3] He believed that it was only possible for a company to share a common vision if they had shared ownership. He introduced this into his new company believing that it produced the following advantages:

- Endemic involving of everybody
- Deep loyalty
- Increased productivity
- Increased responsibility
- Breeding 'high trust'
- Better than empowerment
- Releasing of a trapped spirit

This list is typical of the aspirations of teams based on Theory Y management. They result in a different kind of workplace—one that brims over with social capital.

Using experts

Three steps need to be taken here, and none are easy. The first is to recognise when you need help from an expert, the second is to know where to find one and the third is to assess the expert's competence.

The resources available depend very much upon the size of the business. Large companies will have their own lawyers and patent experts for example, but small businesses will need to hire them. Finding so-called experts is not too difficult, but knowing their worth is another matter. When the hi-tech scene developed in Cambridge in the 80s there was a sudden influx of experts of all kinds. When we were involved in setting up the St John's Innovation Centre, lawyers, accountants, venture capitalists, banks, business advisers, recruiting and advertising agencies all came knocking. We could have easily filled the Centre with these advisers rather than the start-up businesses that it was intended to serve.

As to competence, it is always best to have a personal recommendation of some kind, which is why the networking we discuss in the next section is so important.

Despite these comments, advisers and consultants are an important support group and can become part of a kind of 'extended team'. In some cases we know of them being given non-executive board positions.

Banks are also an important source of help and advice, but they seem to have developed a bad image in this area. The following advertisement was placed in the

Financial Times in 2001 and we believe that the frustration of the managing director who placed the notice is still felt by many. The image and reputation of the leading banks has not improved in the intervening years.

WANTED

A Progressive, Understanding and Positive Bank

Frustrated, knowledgeable, ambitious and totally fed up Managing Director of a £6 million turnover company employing 175 people URGENTLY seeks a supporting bank.

A bank that has vision, is supportive and positive and knows how to provide support without weakness and has a good business sense and has the foresight of a Richard Branson/Margaret Thatcher type person.

A bank that can recognise and encourage potential and help to achieve success rather than generate negative attitudes and fear of failure, is URGENTLY required.

Currently the majority of high street banks fail to provide the correct level of support to companies like ourselves and have lost their drive and direction and generally lack initiative and interest.

Networking

McClelland, whose work we discussed in Chapter 8, identified achievement, affiliation and power as a person's primary motivations. Of these, networking's main link is with affiliation. The need to be together, to affiliate with others, is what drives 'social capital'. This term has been coined by sociologists to describe the relationship of co-operation, based on trust, that can exist between people and within groups. Teams that really work are examples of social capital in action.

Francis Fukuyama has defined social capital as 'a set of informal values or norms shared among members of a group that permits co-operation between them'.[4]

In recent years this need to affiliate and the networking capabilities of the Internet have combined to give us MySpace and Facebook. With their millions of members, these organisations are the largest sources of social capital the world has ever known.

Behind this phenomenon is what Kevin Kelly has called 'The Law of Plenitude'.[5] This law determines the number of communications that can arise when people are linked together in a network. If 100 people are connected on a social network, there will be 9,900 gateways open between them along which messages can be sent. Although it is unlikely that all the gateways will be used at the same time, it does make networking via social media sites a powerful tool for linking people together.

LinkedIn has been a very successful business network for connecting people with the same professional interests. It has become a powerful recruitment tool where both jobs opportunities and CVs can be shared. Membership, which is free of charge, has now reached 175 million and is still growing.

Emails are another important Internet-driven networking tool. This needs to be handled in a sensible manner if it is not to get out of control. We know of cases in both health care and education where emails are sent on the basis that the recipient will not be able to argue later that they had not been informed.

Another problem is that people who enjoy socialising also enjoy networking, and that can both be a serious distraction and encourage office gossip. We think Jack Welch of General Electric fame was quite right when he said that 'everyone you meet is another interview'. For him, networking had to have a purpose and a focus.

Places that have seen the emergence of business clusters all have extensive informal networks. Silicon Valley, particularly in its early days, was like a big village where people networked easily. As time went on, informal groups like the Homebrew Computer Club were formed. The main talking point in these networks was the latest technology and they were a very effective of disseminating information and more. 'If a Homebrew member knew about a secret chip design at Intel, he'd be happy to share the details'.[6]

Networking also stimulated the spin-off of new businesses as ideas were born and developed. 'The Fairchild spin-offs were often projected, discussed and decided in a nearby restaurant in Mountain View, Walker's Wagon Wheel Bar and Grill, frequented by the company's engineers.'[7]

These last few examples show that networking is most effective when it is done with a purpose. Chance meetings can, of course, always be important, but having something in mind or key people to see is always the best way to approach networking.

Self-assessment: find your Teams Plus score

You now have the opportunity to score yourself on the three areas covered by the Teams Plus aspect of Technique.

- Are you a team player or do you see yourself as something of a loner?
- Have you ever found yourself leading a team and at the same time being part of a more senior team? If so, think through how you dealt with the conflicts and the opportunities involved and whether you followed an X- or Y-Theory approach.
- Do you feel vulnerable when deciding on an expert in an area in which you have little knowledge? On what do you base your selection decision?
- How often has the advice of experts been really helpful to you?
- Are you a casual networker or do you really make an effort to get to know the people who can be of value to you?
- Do you think that most networking is of little value and wastes time?

Based on your answers to these questions give yourself a score out of ten as a measure of your strength in each of the three elements.

My suggested score:

for Teams: _____ out of 10
for Using Experts: _____ out of 10
for Networking: _____ out of 10

To derive a score for Teams Plus, calculate the average of twice your Teams score and the single values for Using Experts and Networking.

My overall Teams Plus score is _____ out of 10

Learned abilities

In their earlier work, the Gallup Organisation placed their 'life themes' at the centre of two concentric circles as shown in Figure 9.3 below.[8] These central themes determined a person's 'strengths' pattern or signature, and are identified in Gallup's StrengthsFinder questionnaire. In our terms these life themes include both talent and temperament attributes.

Skills are built around the central life themes and give them structure as enhancing techniques are learnt. In due course, as experience builds, the person moves steadily towards performance excellence.

This model emphasises the key point that a person's skills and experience must match and connect with their life themes, ideally being driven by them.

We were once involved in assessing an individual for a 'new business' programme. His personality profile showed him to be an introspective and cautious individual but his CV told us that he had spent most of his career working in sales.

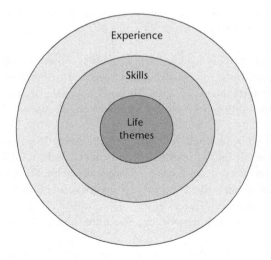

FIGURE 9.3 The Gallup performance model

We were rather puzzled by this mismatch. When we asked him about it he explained that the only job he could get when he was younger had been in sales and he had got stuck there. He told us he had never liked selling and felt he had no aptitude for it. He was delighted that we had come to the same conclusion. 'Why did no one ever tell me that before?' he asked.

Gallup later extended their model to include 'knowledge' that covered both factual and experiential knowledge.[9] This, we believe, completes the picture and is our basis for now using the three elements of *knowledge*, *skills* and *experience* to describe learned abilities.

Knowledge

Careers generally begin with a speciality of some kind and then develop more broadly as responsibility increases. The disciplines most likely to lead to CEO status are finance and marketing. Jack Welch was a chemical engineer and so faced a difficult journey to the top of GE. There were 29 levels of hierarchy to negotiate! He felt he was well on his way when he reached level 27, but then hit a knowledge barrier. His new job was to run the Consumer Appliances sector, in which he had little interest or knowledge. This sector was responsible for around 20 per cent of GE's total sales but it seemed to be going nowhere. He also knew his boss was not on his side.

Within his new portfolio was GE Credit. 'It was the orphan in a manufacturing business.'[10] It had been set up in the 30s to help finance appliance dealers during the Depression. In the 60s it began to finance Caterpillar construction equipment. In the 70s they were into real estate, commercial loans and credit cards. Welch realised this small operation, by GE standards, was a potential 'gold mine'. 'My gut told me that compared to the industrial operations I did know, this business seemed an easy way to make money.' But he had a problem: he was an engineer and knew very little about finance.

> In those early days, I didn't understand the intricacies of finance. I had the staff prepare a book that translated all the jargon into layman's terms. I called it 'finance for little folk', but it was just what I needed. I studied it like I was back in grad school.
>
> *Welch, 2001*

Welch also asked lots of questions and would grill his team about the ins and outs of their business. '"Let's pretend we're in high school" I said. "Take me through the basics."' When questioning one of his insurance specialists he got the reply 'How do you expect me to teach you in five minutes what it has taken me 25 years to learn!'

Knowledge is about gaining understanding, and in that sense learning is an ongoing process. Welch did not avoid this and made the effort to acquire the knowledge he needed.

Skills

Skills are about being able to do things, and they are learnt from seeing other practitioners in action. This is the best way to learn the subtleties involved.

Gallup gives the example of public speaking.[11] Skills, they say, 'Will help you perform but not excel.' It is possible to learn the skills of public speaking so that you will become a better speaker than before and achieve a reasonable level of competence. 'But lacking the necessary talents, you will never be as good as General Powell. The General is blessed with a talent that enables him to be more articulate when he is on stage.'[12]

To take a business example, there is an important skill dimension in the understanding and handling of cash flow issues. There is certainly an important knowledge base involved in drawing up a company's monthly accounts and understanding how cash flow drives a business, but that is not enough. It is, after all, history. The running of the business on a day-to-day basis calls for skill rather than knowledge. Certainly formal procedures have to be learnt, but essentially it involves a skill base. Juggling the money around so employees and suppliers get paid at the right time and debts get paid off is no easy task. It requires great skill to get it right and it can make or break a business.

As with the public speaking example, outstanding achievement in this area can only be attained if the person responsible has a real talent for finance. They must not only understand it, they must also 'get it'.

Experience

The third factor, experience, is ongoing. Over time, experience can contradict or at least modify both knowledge and skills. This is because things move on and, as we argue in Chapter 2, a 'New Normal' arrives so that we have to think differently. John Sculley discovered this the hard way when he took over from Steve Jobs as CEO of Apple. Sculley had an MBA from a prestigious US business school, had top-level experience as Vice-President of Pepsi-Cola and been featured in the front cover of *Business Week* at the age of 34.[13] Despite all this, he tells us that at Apple 'I had mistakenly thought … what I hadn't realised was … I should have understood … I discovered.'

It is possible that the mistakes Sculley made were because he applied the thinking that had worked at Pepsi-Cola in a newly born and dynamic computer company. Two differences stand out, the first concerning culture and the second the market strategy. Pepsi-Cola's board meetings were a very formal affair—people all wore ties—at which the main topic was the latest research data on their market share compared with that of Coca-Cola, their main competitor. Apple's board meetings were the opposite. They were informal and unstructured with no clear agenda. 'They spent the day arguing with each other' according to Sculley's account.

The cultural difference of formal versus informal meant that the leadership styles were very different and not transferable. The market-share approach of an established company with a standard product bore no relation to what was needed in a new and growing market that was not easy to define. Again, Sculley's experience was not transferable and so it is not surprising that he got it wrong.

Experience, then, can provide steady growth in competence as people progress along a learning curve but it can also lead to mistakes when the environment is changing rapidly and people try new tricks. In recent years the traditional rules of business have been challenged on many fronts. The book *Barbarians at the Gate* tells the story of the $25-billion battle for control of RJR Nabisco in 1988, when the normal protocols of Wall Street were brushed aside. The new rules were 'Never pay in cash, Never tell the truth, Never play by the rules'.[14]

The book *Pipe Dreams* carries the sub-title *Greed, Ego and the Death of Enron*.[15] Enron was a giant company that in 2001 bought and sold nearly $3 billion worth of natural gas, electricity and other commodities every day. In early December 2001 Enron declared bankruptcy. Behind it there were unethical deals, offshore accounts and accounting irregularities. Enron took Arthur Andersen, the respected accounting firm, down with it.

Self-assessment: find your Learned Abilities score

Your score here is about the extent to which you have the necessary expertise for the top job in your own or someone else's organisation.

* To what extent has your career to date given you the Knowledge, Skills and Experience base required to successfully run a business? Are there any serious gaps that you can identify?
* Do you think you have the Knowledge base for the top job? If not, how prepared are you to learn and perhaps swallow your pride?
* Work through your Skills. How many do you 'sort of' understand and how many do you really 'get'?
* Can you recall examples of when you have really learnt from Experience?

Here we ask you to score yourself separately on Knowledge, Skills and Experience. My suggested score is:

for Knowledge: _____ out of 10
for Skills: _____ out of 10
for Experience: _____ out of 10

The next two questions are intended to help you rethink the scores you have just given.

* How much are you impacted by the uncertainties and change within the sector that you work? Has this seriously reduced the value of the Experience that you have gained over the years?
* Have your ever considered or made a career change? If so, how much value to you was the expertise you had gathered over the years?

We now suggest you give yourself an overall score for Learned Abilities by taking the average of your scores for Knowledge, Skills and Experience.

My overall Learned Abilities score is _____ out of 10

♣ Your Technique score

To determine your overall score for Technique simply average your scores for Teams Plus and Learned Abilities. If, however, one of the scores is more than three points above the other, take the higher of the two. This is because the two areas are quite different and it is important to recognise that you have strong performance in at least one area.

My final Technique score is _____ out of 10

10

♠ DISCERNMENT—APPLIED

> The mature are those who have the powers of discernment trained by constant practice so that they can distinguish.[1]

We see Discernment as a Talent that is strengthened and matured by experience. Constant practice is a theme that we discussed under Technique in Chapter 6. In the quotation above there is the idea of a lawyer in training who builds up a level of understanding based on previous cases. This of course is only one aspect of discernment. Here we consider the clarity of *vision*, the foundation of *values* and the *perception* that results in sound decision making.

We show these three attribute groups in Figure 10.1, describing them as the 'elements of discernment', where:

- *Vision* is about the ability to see clearly at different time distances, from the horizon to the immediate (the 'Now').
- *Values* provide the ethical underpinning without which Discernment will almost certainly be compromised.
- *Perception* enables the recognition, understanding and evaluation of what *vision* and *values* reveal.

The plus sign in Figure 10.1 indicates the need for the integration of the three elements so that the whole is greater than the sum of the parts.

In 2007 Chris Nassetta was appointed CEO of the hotel group Hilton Worldwide. He brought it through the difficult recession period that saw its value drop by 70 per cent and its debts rise to $20 billion. Six years later, the picture is

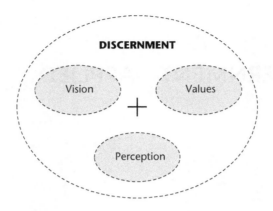

FIGURE 10.1 The elements of discernment

quite different. In 2013 Hilton's IPO valued the company at $33 billion and its debt had been reduced to $12 billion.[2] These impressive numbers were the outcome of Nassetta's person-based approach. He had first overhauled his senior management and then integrated that team 'around a common *vision* and set of *values* to get people working around a set of key *priorities*'.

His vision, values and priorities approach match the three elements that we discuss in this chapter. He and his team had focused on the right things, operated on a foundation of shared values and moved forward against carefully discerned priorities (further information on Chris Nassetta and Hilton Worldwide can be found on their website www.hiltonworldwide.com).

We now discuss our three 'elements of discernment' in turn and provide you with the opportunity to evaluate your strength in each of them.

Vision

The human eye is a remarkable device for focusing clearly at different distances. Once we have decided what we want to look at, the eye muscles change the focal length of the eye accordingly depending on whether the objects are far away or near. With two eyes working together there is the added bonus of three-dimensional vision.

This provides an interesting metaphor for business. As we show in Figure 10.2, business has to have a clarity of focus—and thereby vision—from the distant horizon to the day-to-day, or the 'Now' as we have termed it. The 'middle' distance must also not be neglected, for it is here that strategic mistakes are often made, though by then it may be too late.

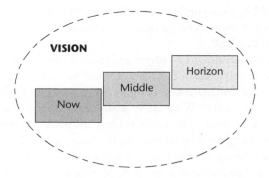

FIGURE 10.2 Vision

Most commonly the word 'vision' is about seeing the future direction of the company. Vision statements are written to try and capture where the business hopes to be in, say, 20 years. That is, they look at the horizon. The problem here is that in many fields 20 years is just too long. These days, very few companies can control what comes over the horizon and discernment is required to know whether what is emerging is something to merely keep an eye on or something that requires immediate action. Sadly, business history is littered with companies that have failed to see what was just coming over the horizon.

We now consider the three elements of vision in turn, starting with the Horizon and then considering the Middle distance and the 'Now'.

Horizon distance

Focusing on things a long way off (in distance or in time) is all about horizons and the ability to see what is coming. Horizons, of course, are very deceptive. Ellen MacArthur, who sailed round the world single-handed, was asked how much sleep was she able to get when sailing. Her answer was a surprise: 'No longer than 20 minutes at a time.' She explained that this was how long it took for two yachts to collide that were coming directly towards each other but out of sight just below the horizon.

In effect, 'horizon watchers' can never sleep—they cannot afford to. In his book *Focus: The Hidden Driver of Excellence*[3] Daniel Goleman describes how Research in Motion (RIM) achieved amazing success with their BlackBerry mobile phone. It was RIM's launch of its BlackBerry wireless email service in January 1999, combined with the PDA functions of a calendar, address book and more, that made it a real winner. In its first year sales reached $185 million and it became a status-symbol product. In two public listings the company raised $1,155 million.

By mid-2007 RIM had nine million subscribers with three million new ones being added every three months. The company reached a valuation of $42 billion in 2007; this doubled in 2008.

RIM added a camera and media player and moved into the smartphone market. Then suddenly over the horizon came the Apple iPhone. It redefined the product area by removing the hardware keyboard. As Steve Jobs put it when he launched the iPhone in January 2007, 'What we're gonna do is get rid of all those buttons, and just make a giant screen.' The keyboard had just become a piece of software.

In his book *Research, No Motion: How the BlackBerry CEOs Lost an Empire*, Jesse Hicks tells us that 'things reached crisis point in 2011, The Year of the Open Letter'.[4] This letter, attributed to a senior RIM executive, described things in the company as 'chaotic' with a 'demotivated workforce. We missed not boldly reacting to the threat of the iPhone when we saw it in January, over four years ago. That is the painful truth. It was a major strategic oversight and we know who is responsible.'

RIM had failed to maintain an horizon focus and then missed the middle ground as Apple closed in on it. At the end of those missed four years Apple was so far ahead that there was little RIM could do. RIM is still in the smartphone market, though in 2014 its UK market share was only 1 per cent.[5]

Living and succeeding in this kind of environment is an amazing challenge. The secret is clarity of vision by focusing on the right things at the right time—but that is easier said than done.

Andy Grove was the CEO of the Intel Corporation and knew all about horizons. In his book *Only the Paranoid Survive* he comments:[6]

> The ability to recognise that the winds have shifted and to take appropriate action before you wreck your boat is crucial to the future of an enterprise.

Running a company has been likened to driving a car in the fog whilst looking out of the rear window. Clarity of vision is always limited, no matter how near or far the problems or opportunities are. Whilst those at the top of the organisation should be able to see the most clearly, this is generally not the case. In fact, the people on the shop floor or in the sales room are often the first to spot the problems. They do not need the accounts department to tell them. The idle machines or lack of customers make it all too obvious.

When Marks & Spencer was in trouble in the late 90s the situation was evident 'to the humblest part-time check-out assistant. Out there on the sales floor it showed.'[7]

Entirepreneurs who are strong on vision-focus are able to move seamlessly and swiftly back and forth between Horizon and the Now and still take account of what is going on in the Middle distance. Effectively they blend strategy (which is Middle to Horizon distance and directional) and tactics, which are more focused on the Now and often affected by competitor activity. This ability to move 'back and forth' between the future and the present is essential in today's fast-moving world, but it is no easy task. We have already noted the case of Xerox in Chapter 7 and how 'they fumbled the future'. Another example is Marks & Spencer.

The Rise and Fall Of Marks & Spencer by Judi Bevan is a remarkable story.[8] The Marks and Seif families produced some amazing **entirepreneurs** over several generations. When things began to fall apart in the late 90s, only David Seif, one of the old guard, seemed to see what was happening.

> David Seif, the lone family member left on the board feared for the old values. "Nobody talked to the young trainees anymore", he said. "Nobody was listening; nor were they watching the market place."

> By the time of the half-year results in November (1999) Peter Salsbury (CEO) had destroyed the spirit of the company and the trust of its suppliers and staff. "Peter had absolutely no vision for the future", said a director. "In a situation like that he needed to map out the future."

The struggle for survival began when senior management stopped looking at the far horizon and turned their attention to what was happening close at hand. However, they did this so ineptly that, as Bevan puts it, 'Like busy fools, Salsbury and his new team rushed around changing, consulting, revamping to little purpose.' They could not see what was going on right under their noses.

Middle distance

Focus at this distance can be the most confusing of all. There is plenty of activity going on, so the picture is often somewhat blurred. It is not easy to identify key issues, but if these are missed there can be serious consequences.

At this point strategies have to be hardened up to the point where tactics can be decided. When an industry that has been dominated by a few companies for many years suddenly begins to open up, clarity of focus becomes essential. It is all too easy for the 'middle' distance to become something of a 'muddle' distance.

The fashion industry provides an interesting example of this effect. The advent of market segmentation and 'fast fashion' found once-dominant companies like Britain's Marks & Spencer and Holland's C&A floundering with no clear focus. They did not seem to be aware of what was happening in the middle distance. Although fast fashion is seen as emerging in the 90s, the signs were there in the 70s and 80s and they should have been spotted. To cite three of today's top fast-fashion companies, Zara led the way, followed by H&M and Gap. They all saw the opportunity and were able to forge ahead as they moved from the concept of the middle distance to the practicalities of the now.

The origins of fast fashion can be traced to two people, both **entirepreneurs**, who founded businesses that dominated their sector with billion-dollar sales. They were Amancio Ortega Gaona, who founded Zara, and Liz Claiborne in the USA.

Ortega set up a clothes design and manufacturing company in Spain in 1963. He opened his first Zara store, also in Spain, to sell directly to the public in 1975. Real growth began when he expanded internationally. By 1985 sales were approaching $1 billion. A decade later they were $5.3 billion and by 2005 had reached $16 billion. It is now the world's largest fashion retailer, having overtaken Gap in 2008.

Claiborne has been described as 'a fashion designer' and a 'pioneering business executive'. As a 'fashion designer' she increased the frequency of fashion releases from two a year (summer and winter) to six a year and put the 'fast' into 'fashion'. Today's fast-fashion companies have followed her lead and are now able to 'introduce interpretation of runway (catwalk) designs to the stores in a minimum of three to five weeks'.[9]

As a business executive, Claiborne took her company to annual sales of more than $1 billion and a Fortune 500 listing in fewer than ten years. She became the first woman to be the founder, chair and CEO of a Fortune 500 company. Sales reached $2.2 billion in 1989, making her company the largest women's retailer in the USA. It enjoyed great success throughout the 70s, 80s and 90s.

The middle distance is the most challenging of the three focus distances, but it is where the greatest opportunities are found.

The Now

There is generally a full and complex picture at this close range. As the earlier examples from Marks & Spencer and RIM indicate, when things go wrong, near-panic can ensue. This is the operational side of things, and handling change can be very difficult if there is not a clear focus that is integrated well with middle and horizon vision. Ideally the clear-sightedness and tangible targets required will have come out of the possibilities of the middle distance and the dreams of the horizon, but these do need to be kept up to date and together.

Conrad Hilton famously said that 'to accomplish big things you must first dream big dreams' but he then explained that he did not mean idle daydreams or wishful thinking, nor even a visionary revelation.[10] 'What I speak of', he wrote, 'is a brand of imaginative thinking backed by enthusiasm, vitality and expectation'.

Hilton's 'dream' came from a photograph of the newly built Waldorf Astoria hotel in New York. He rated this hotel as 'the greatest of them all' and dared to believe that one day he might own it. This seemed highly unlikely at the time: Hilton was heavily in debt as he struggled with a hotel chain hit by the recession of the 30s. To ensure that this dream never left his sights, he placed the photograph of the hotel under the glass top of his desk. He spent 15 years looking at that picture, until in October 1949 the 'the greatest of them all' became a Hilton Hotel. His dream had come true.

Hilton's dream became a reality because he changed a dream into a target that he could see clearly and always keep before him.

Self-assessment: find your Vision score

Rather than giving yourself an overall score for Vision, we suggest you rank Horizon Distance, Middle Distance and The Now according to which you find the most enjoyable. Maybe you are a Horizon-watcher, or perhaps you see yourself as a strategist and prefer the Middle Distance when things are beginning to take shape. Equally, you may enjoy the tactical detail and action of The Now.

Don't forget, of course, that **entirepreneurs** are able to switch from one vision to another as needed.

My Vision of choice is first _____ , then _____ and finally _____.

Values

In the business world value is usually associated with monetary worth, but there is increasing interest in the less tangible—but equally important—area of human values. Francis Fukuyama's book *Trust: The Social Virtues and the Creation of Prosperity* is an interesting study in the important, but often hidden, role of trust in how companies grow and develop.[11] He links this with the idea of the creation of social capital, which, as noted in Chapter 9, he defines as 'a set of informal values or norms shared among members of a group that permits co-operation among them'.

Values become norms when they are accepted by members of a group and go on to form the basis for that group's culture. Businesses, whether large or small, have their own cultures. HP and IBM both developed strong cultures around shared values, as we have already noted. At the other end of the scale, the small technology businesses of the Cambridge phenomenon in the 80s formed a remarkable network cluster with common values of openness and trust. There was plenty of social capital about.

In this section we consider the three areas indicated in Figure 10.3. We begin with the *beliefs* from which values derive, then we consider *ethics*, an expression of those beliefs, and finally we give examples of *values in action*, covering the Quakers, today's philanthropists and cause-driven **entirepreneurs**.

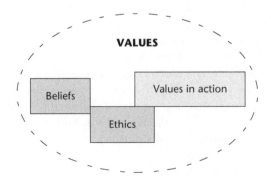

FIGURE 10.3 Values

These key areas directly affect how **entirepreneurs** run their businesses, and what they stand for, as well as how they use (some of) the monetary wealth they acquire for doing good in the world.

Beliefs

We all believe in something: even the belief in nothing is itself a belief. Faith belief has been a main source of human values over the years. The work ethic that came out of the Protestant Reformation proved a remarkable driver. Max Weber's *The Protestant Ethic and the Spirit of Capitalism* linked the Protestant faith—Puritan ethics in particular—with the development of capitalism.[12] Whilst Weber's work has generated much controversy over the years, there is little doubt that among such groups as the Huguenots in France and the Quakers in England there was a remarkable work ethic. The Quakers, whom we discuss later, played a major part in the Industrial Revolution, and Coalbrookdale and the neighbouring Ironbridge where it all began are now recognised as World Heritage Sites.

Perhaps the most common belief is the belief we have in ourselves. As we discussed in Chapter 8, self-belief is the basis for a strong Inner Ego. Norman Vincent Peale's 1952 book, *The Power of Positive Thinking*, and the more recent 'positive psychology' movement have made a big impression on Western thinking. Positive psychology became 'official' when it was taken as the theme of the inaugural presidential address of the American Psychological Association (APA) by Martin Seligman in 1998. Don Clifton, whom we have already referenced, was one of the pioneers of the positive psychology movement. In 2002 he was honoured by the APA with a Presidential Commendation as the 'Father of Strengths-based Psychology'.

In his book *The Happiness Advantage*, Shawn Achor reports a study of 112 entry-level accountants that found that those who believed they would be successful 'were the ones who ten months later scored the best job-performance ratings'.[13] Achor concluded that 'their belief in their own ability was an even stronger predictor of job performance than the actual level of skill or training they had'. If we believe in ourselves we are happier people and achieve more. In this context we can understand something of the popularity of 'How-To' management books that promote self-belief.

This *Gung Ho!*, 'I can do it' approach can have an empowering effect but, as we discussed in Chapter 8 when describing the Inner Ego, if self-belief is seriously challenged there can be real problems.[14] People with low self-belief have little confidence in themselves and simply telling them to 'pull their socks up' does not work. What we believe about ourselves, and the way in which we fit into the great scheme of things, really does matter.

It is from our belief system that our values derive, both as a society and as individuals. As Tom Rath puts it in his book *StrengthFinder2.0*, 'If you possess a strong Belief Theme, you have certain core values that are enduring.'[15] Whilst we agree that our values come from our beliefs, this connection is not a straightforward one. We all know from experience that, when under pressure, people do not always live up to the values they espouse. They take shortcuts, are economic with the truth, turn a blind eye, put themselves first and so on.

The business world presents a particular challenge and it is quite possible for a person to have one set of values for family and friends but a quite different set in the workplace. In today's target-driven, competitive world it is all too easy to argue that the end justifies the means. The examples of RJR Nabisco and Enron—discussed below but first mentioned in Chapter 9—show that greed can be a very strong motivation that seriously challenges our values.

Ethics

Value and mission statements are now common in the world of business, yet the public view is that many businesses are unethical and their values do not count for much. This opinion has been fuelled by large payments made to senior executives even when their companies have underperformed. *Barbarians at the Gate: The Fall of RJR Nabisco* was the well-chosen title of the book and subsequent film that exposed corporate and executive greed on a grand scale in the $25 billion leveraged buyout of RJR Nabisco in the late 80s.

More recently in 2001, the Enron scandal unfolded. *Fortune* Magazine had ranked Enron as 'America's Most Innovative Company' for six consecutive years as it grew to become the seventh largest company in the US. When it filed for bankruptcy and the truth came out, the name Enron became 'synonymous with greed, deceit, fraud, earnings manipulation, forgery, unbridled capitalism and an insatiable desire for money.'[16] The prestigious accounting firm Arthur Andersen lost its credibility when, amongst other things, it shredded important Enron documents. Their subsequent indictment for obstruction of justice destroyed this international company.

These well-publicised events confirmed for many the view that greed and corruption are endemic in the business world, and that it goes with the territory. This makes the values-stance of businesses like Anita Roddick's The Body Shop and, in recent times, Google all the more remarkable. As we commented in Chapter 9, Roddick created a value-driven business. The Company Charter stated that 'honesty, integrity and caring form the foundation of the Company, and should flow from everything we do'. These values became one of their 'unique selling points' (USPs).

Google put values at the centre of their approach to business with the phrase 'Don't Be Evil'. Larry Page and Sergey Brin, the founders, included it in their 2004 IPO letter.[17] Under that heading they set out their 'values' bottom line: 'We believe strongly that in the long term, we will be better served—as shareholders and in all other ways—by a company that does good things for the world even if we forgo some short term gains.'

The next section in the IPO letter was headed 'Making the World a Better Place' and described programmes that Google was initiating.

> Last year (2003) we created Google Grants—a growing program in which hundreds of non-profits addressing issues, including the environment, poverty and human rights, receive free advertising. And now, we are in the process of establishing the Google Foundation. We intend to contribute significant resources to the foundation, including employee time and approximately 1% of Google's equity and profits in some form. We hope someday this institution may eclipse Google itself in terms of overall world impact by ambitiously applying innovation and significant resources to the largest of the world's problems.

A decade later Google was a very large company indeed. It generated $15.42 billion in the first quarter of 2014 and had $59.38 billion in the bank. Any company of this size is going to challenge the status quo as it creates new markets and threatens old ones. In that context it will have enemies who inevitably belittle their altruistic values. It is a soft target.

In September 2014 *The Times*, reporting on a major criticism of Google's activities by Rupert Murdoch's News Corp, asked, 'Has Google gone from "don't be evil" to a "vast, powerful, often unaccountable bureaucracy" that stifles competition and promotes piracy?'

Despite such difficulties the belief in and application of values, are essential in the achievement of true excellence. This is because excellence in business is more than just shareholder value, as those who have championed the idea of a Triple Bottom Line (TBL) have been saying for some time. The first steps towards this TBL approach was a broadening of the idea of capitalism to include social capital in addition to economic capital. Fukuyama's book, quoted above sees the 'values or norms' upon which social capital is based as including 'truth telling, the meeting of obligations and reciprocity'.[18] The ethic of reciprocity, or the 'golden rule' as it is also called, is that we should 'do as we would be done by'.[19]

In 1994 John Elkington added the third component to the TBL: 'environmental value'.[20] Thus the TBL becomes economic, social and environmental, or as it is sometimes expressed, though in a different order, 'people, planet and profits'—the 3Ps. The main theme behind Elkington's approach is 'sustainability', which emphasises the environment and planet aspects. Though this is important, care has to be taken to balance the three components.

It is also important that the 3Ps are quantified as far as possible. Whilst profit involves hard measurable data, 'people' and 'planet' have softer measures. However some organisations, such as the micro-lending charity Opportunity International, has included in its annual report parameters such as 'the number of lives transformed' and 'the number of jobs created' as a means of quantifying their social impact. In *Bread of Life* Ronald Sider reports that 'from 1981 to 1993' the organisation 'made (micro) loans to 46,000 third-world entrepreneurs and created 77,700 jobs among the poor'.[21]

Whilst the TBL and 3P's are useful in evaluating a company's performance on a broader basis than simply profitability, it is important to recognise that these are not the only indices that can be used. In their book *Business Ethics*, Andrew Crane and Dirk Matten describe the 'ethical challenges facing business' as being 'corporate citizenship, globalisation and sustainability'.[22] Whilst these may not form so convenient an alliteration as 'people, planet and profits', they do provide a sound basis for a consideration of the ethical issues.

Values in action

Whilst we have argued that the link between belief and values can be difficult to sustain, under some circumstances there is no doubt that strong values do derive from strong beliefs. Here we look at three examples of values in action. First we review the unusual combination of business and welfare of the Quakers. Next, we look at the modern business philanthropists who give away vast sums of money to areas of need. Finally, we consider those **entirepreneurs** who have pursued particular causes because of the values they hold dear.

The Quakers

The Quakers of the eighteenth and nineteenth centuries provide a remarkable example of how beliefs created a set of values that transformed society, combining business and welfare. The Quaker Abraham Darby I is credited with founding the Industrial Revolution when he established an iron foundry in Coalbrookdale, Shropshire in 1709.

From this starting point, Quaker businesses grew to encompass 'a huge section of British Industry and commerce from brewing to banking, engineering to cotton, chemicals to china'.[23] Names like Barclays, Cadbury, Carrs, Clarks, Fry, Lloyds, Price Waterhouse and Rowntree all have Quaker roots.[24, 25, 26] In the nineteenth century George Cadbury built the town of Bournville on the edge of Birmingham for his employees and Elizabeth Fry pioneered the reform of women's prisons.

It was their Quaker beliefs that gave them the values of honesty, fair dealing, hard work and social equality that they pursued diligently and with enthusiasm. In his book *The Quakers: Money and Morals* James Walvin tells us of the Quakers' 'fierce commitment to honesty'.[27]

> They took Jesus' words "Let your yea be yea and your nay be nay" (Matthew 5:37) with a literal seriousness, and were accepted as honest even by those who disliked them. During the eighteenth century, when there was a growing demand for financial services and the number of banks mushroomed, this reputation made the public ready to trust the Quakers with their money. Honesty also stood them in good stead in other areas of commerce. Their word could be trusted, their goods were what they purported to be, and their prices were both fixed and reasonable.

The Quakers combined social responsibility with business in a special way. In his book *Quakers in Science and Industry*, Arthur Raistrick explains that 'the unification of life among the Quakers, their refusal to separate business activities from the principles and disciplines which regulate their religious life, gave them a stability and soundness of practice that was unusual in their day'.[28]

In describing 'The Quaker Enterprise', David Burns Windsor puts this down to 'the lack of priests and dogma and the practice of contemplation' that 'forced the Friends to a degree of self-awareness and discipline that is essential to the entrepreneur.[29] The tradition of inner strength to cope with both the assaults and temptations of the external world was responsible for creating the great Quaker Entrepreneurs.'

Of course Quakers were not the only dissident Christian group to be involved in business. Others groups were the Mennonites and the Huguenots.

Today's philanthropists

Philanthropy has a long history and comes from those who have strong personal values and generous natures. Many of today's philanthropists have created their own wealth rather than inherited it, though their motivations are the same. These 'new money' **entirepreneurs** often feel that life has been kind to them, and that they want to 'give something back'. One such individual who was interviewed on a BBC programme suggested that perhaps we should use the word millionaire to describe a person who has given away £1 million rather than made £1 million.

In October 1977, Bill Hewlett attended the opening of the $9.1 million Terman Engineering Centre on the Stanford University campus, built using donations from him and Dave Packard. This was a thank you to Professor Fred Terman for suggesting that they should think of going into business together and helping to get them their first business loan. In his speech at the ceremony, Hewlett reminded Terman of the time, some 40 years earlier, when they had walked out of the old engineering building together and Terman had remarked that he was looking forward to the day when Hewlett would give his first million dollars to the laboratory. Hewlett recalled that at the time he had thought that such an idea 'was incredible'.[30]

As individuals, both Hewlett and Packard have, through their foundations, given away more than $1 billion, though according to their biographer Michael Malone, this is only a fraction of the overall impact that their example has made. In his 2007 book *Bill & Dave: How Hewlett and Packard Built the World's Greatest Company*, Malone comments that this kind of philanthropic giving was 'the single most important non-governmental source of philanthropy of the last half of the [twentieth] century'.[31] But it was the dot-com generation that really took Hewlett's and Packard's example to heart. Pierre Omidyar and Jeff Skoll of eBay, Sergey Brin and Larry Page of Google and Bill and Melinda Gates are all referenced as giving in billion dollar terms.

Others, such as Facebook's Mark Zuckerberg and his wife Priscilla Chan have joined this group. In 2013 they donated $1 billion and topped The Chronicle of Philanthropy's list of the most generous donors.

The Giving Pledge is a commitment by the world's wealthiest individuals and families to dedicate the majority of their wealth to philanthropy. Their website www.givingpledge.org has details of 126 people who have pledged in this way. Bill and Melinda Gates' reason for making an explicit commitment to The Giving Pledge states clearly what philanthropy is all about:

> We have been blessed with good fortune beyond our wildest expectations, and we are profoundly grateful. But just as these gifts are great, so we feel a great responsibility to use them well.

Cause-driven entirepreneurs

Our beliefs directly affect our values, which in turn influence our behaviour. This can be seen in the way we run our businesses, as with the early Quakers, or in how we dispose of our wealth, as per the philanthropy movement, but perhaps above all it is seen in those who are driven by a cause. An entrepreneur committed to a single cause can achieve amazing things.

William Booth (1829–1912), who founded the Salvation Army, was such a man. In his lifetime the organisation spread around the world bringing hope to the downtrodden and the very poor. In Roy Hattersley's book *Blood and Fire: William and Catherine Booth and the Salvation Army* we see Booth to be an **entirepreneur** who built an organisation that 'swept through the world', a leader who 'inspired unquestioning loyalty in men of great talent and strong opinion' and a manager who 'played a crucial part in changing the social climate in Victorian Britain' by the practice of 'constructive compassion'.[32] They practiced what they preached.

> General Booth followed his calling with absolute confidence and conviction. The Church of England denounced him. The Wesleyans ostracized him. The establishment derided him. The brewers and the publicans assaulted him. But he never flinched from his vocation. His physical courage was immense and his moral courage even greater. General Booth's life was a triumph of certainty. The creation of the Army—measured by numbers alone—was, in itself a triumph.

This same kind of focus and determination shown by William Booth is seen also in Dame Cicely Saunders, mentioned in Chapter 8. Through the personal experience of nursing a dying man, she saw the need of a new approach to the care of people in the last stage of life. But it was an uphill struggle, and it was ten years before the medical world would take her seriously. In that time she had to qualify as a doctor and begin a campaign, backed by her own careful research, for the use of what were regarded as addictive drugs. Eventually what came to be termed 'palliative care' became the norm and was conducted in the context of special centres for the dying. The first such centre in England was St Joseph's Hospice in Hackney, London, which was founded in 1905. However, it was not until 1969, when Saunders set up St Christopher's Hospice, that others caught the vision and hospices were set up across the country.

Like Booth, Saunders brought new creative thinking to an area of real need and built a movement that spread around the world. Despite great opposition she changed the way people thought about the dying and did something about it. She made things happen.

Many people are driven by causes of one kind or another. They want to make the world a better place, they want to help others. They have values drawn from their beliefs but more often than not the causes are in general terms. Here we have in mind specific causes that take over a person's thinking and dominate their whole life. Such was the case with William Booth and Cicely Saunders.

Self-assessment: find your Values score

- How important are beliefs and values to you? Do you link the two together or see them as separate?
- How do you express your values on a day-to-day basis? How consistent are you?
- Think through how evident your values are at home and in the workplace. Are they consistent? Are you in fact a value-driven person, or more of a pragmatist?
- How interested are you in philanthropy? Do you really want to help others financially who have been less fortunate than you?
- Do you have a specific cause that you base your life around or would like to one day? If so, what are you actually doing about it?

This section is unlike the others in that here we suggest you think through the questions and give yourself a general score for Values. First take account of their importance to you. Second, consider what you have actually done about them. If your answers on importance and action do not match, take the average.

I give myself a score of _____ out of 10 for how important Values are to me and a score of _____ out of 10 for what I have done about them.

Think through what combined Values score you would give yourself. Since actions speak louder than words, give a combined score that is nearer to your action-based score (the second blank in the sentence above). If you cannot decide, simply take the average. Make sure you benchmark yourself with the people we have described, as in our experience it is easy to award yourself a values score that is higher than you truly deserve.

My overall Values score is _____ out of 10

Perception

Perception has two meanings. The first relates to our senses, as when we become aware of something or someone by sight or hearing. The second meaning goes deeper and is about understanding, interpretation and comprehension. Here we use it in this second sense. It is necessarily subjective, and determines how a person sees a situation. This is extremely important for **entirepreneurs** who carry heavy responsibilities. How they perceive things can be critical. This is especially relevant in the respect of 'getting it' and appreciating what needs dealing with, and the 'how' and 'when'. This, naturally, links to the ability to prioritise and to also appreciate what to do and what not to do.

Hence, our first element of perception is *judgement*. Over time, as experience builds, this inner perception becomes *wisdom*, the second element. Taken together, judgement and wisdom form the basis for effective decision making; thereby moving things forward in the right *direction*, the third element.

Judgement

This is the practical side of perception, which directly affects decision making. Here it is important to recognise that, however much we would like it to be, decision making is not a purely mechanistic process. There are always too many unknowns and variables for that to be the case.

The book *Freakonomics* gives an example of how the USA arguably got its understanding of the soaring crime rate completely wrong.[33] In 1995 all agreed that things were bad and getting worse. President Clinton said there were only about six years left 'to turn this juvenile crime thing around or our country is going to be living with chaos'. Things then began to turn around very dramatically. Teenage murder rates fell by more than 50 per cent in five years against a predicted rise of 100 per cent. In New York City, murders fell from 2,245 in 1990 to 596 in 2003.

All this was great news brought about, it was said, by an improving economic situation, effective policing strategies especially in New York City and tighter gun laws. This all made sense, but according to Levitt and Dubner the authors of

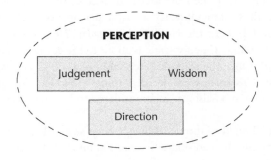

FIGURE 10.4 Perception

Freakonomics, 'There was only one problem: they were not true.' Their own investigations had found a quite different and independent cause, which had happened years earlier. 'A poor, uneducated, unskilled, alcoholic, drug-using 21-year-old woman who had already given up two children for adoption wanted an abortion' but she lived in Texas where abortion was illegal. The case finally reached the US Supreme Court and in 1973 it ruled in her favour, making abortion legal not only in Texas but throughout the country. The result was that over time 'the pool of potential criminals had dramatically shrunk'. Many reasons had been put forward on the pro-abortion side but this was not one of them.

This is an interesting case of unexpected but positive consequences. It is why making the right decisions is never easy. Perceptions can easily be based on prejudice and the traditional view of things. In reality, there is often something that comes up that no one ever thought of, as in the above example. This needs to be recognised far more than it is, and is why we picked up on the term 'bounded rationality' discussed in Chapter 6. Data and its analysis can only get us so far. It is bounded and beyond that point we have to make a judgement. This can come from experience under the general heading of wisdom, which we discuss shortly, or from a hunch or intuition. This is why we class judgement as a talent. Rather like the Eureka moment, sometimes one just knows the answer—though we need to be careful that it is not just an excuse for intellectual laziness. We should never give up the discipline of thinking things through as deeply as we can.

People who are good at making the right decisions do so because they are also good listeners. They pick up information and attitudes from those around them and then sift things carefully. They exercise perception. However, this talent is often muted by temperament issues. At a senior level in companies there are often some big egos on show. In organisations with major departments there can be deep rivalry in the boardroom. This can turn into seriously clouded judgements and create major confrontations. Looked at from the outside the issues often seem petty and almost childlike, but they do matter to people. One of the major mistakes that the person at the top of an organisation can make is not to deal with these kind of conflicts early enough. Too often people are not challenged when they should be or they are given the benefit of the doubt.

We have already mentioned the problems that were experienced at Marks & Spencer. Behind those difficulties lay a major personality problem between the chairman and the CEO. In the late 90s the *Sunday Times* business section front page carried the headline 'Open warfare is about to break out in the boardroom of Marks & Spencer'. Once the roles of Peter Salsbury as CEO and Rick Greenbury as Non-Executive Chairman were decided, things exploded. Greenbury had been seen as an able leader and Salsbury was considered to be a safe pair of hands but:[34]

> they had reckoned without Salsbury's deep-seated loathing of Greenbury, which until then he had skillfully disguised under a pleasant, quietly-spoken exterior. One of the non-executive directors commented that "Peter changed dramatically from the day he was made chief executive. None of us were

prepared for his hatred of Rick, or the irrational behaviour that supported that hatred." Within the rank and file of M&S Salsbury soon earned himself the nickname "Pol Pot".

This example is important because it happened in a large and influential company loved by many. The mistakes made seem almost too obvious to be true, but sadly they are.

Wisdom

> 'Wisdom is found on the lips of the discerning'.[35]

This is a somewhat old-fashioned word but clearly there was not much of it about in the Marks & Spencer example quoted above. Wisdom brings together not only knowledge, understanding and experience but also insight and common sense. Although we see it as a talent, the need for experience links it also with technique. Of course we all have a wide range of experiences in life, but wisdom is about what we can learn from these experiences and how well we apply them.

In the English language, words like 'sage', 'guru' and 'pundit' all point us to the wise and thoughtful teacher from whom we can all learn. They are seen as a source of wisdom. We see this attribute as essential for the **entirepreneur**, though we accept that it is a rare quality. John Adair has provided us with important insights into the thinking of Confucius, a sage of world renown. In *Confucius on Leadership* Adair makes the point that leadership is both a role and an ability, and that there can be a serious mismatch between the two.[36] To show that this is nothing new, he quotes first from Plutarch from the second century AD and then Confucius from 700 years earlier.

> Plutarch described Gaius Antonius, a politician elected to the highest office in Rome, as "a man with no aptitude for leadership in any direction, either good or bad".

> When Confucius was asked "what about men who are in public life in the present day?" he replied, "Oh, they are of such limited capacity that they hardly count."

In business-speak the word 'guru' is generally preferred over 'sage' when referring to a person of great wisdom. Peter Drucker is an obvious example of a business management guru. John Wiley, the publisher, picked up on this theme and produced a 'wisdom series' edited by Peter Krass. Their titles all have the same format: *The Book of Business Wisdom: Classic Writings by the Legends of Commerce and Industry*. Areas covered by other books in the series are entrepreneurs, leadership, management and investing. In all cases the books describe the wisdom as coming from 'classic writing' by 'legendary' individuals. Clearly people who are 'legends' are not necessarily 'gurus', and 'wisdom' is perhaps not the right word to describe their writings. Nonetheless they are clearly people with experience from whom we can all learn and be inspired.

A more appropriate list can be found in *Business: The Ultimate Resource*, which offers a 'quick guide to the key thinking of the world's most famous management gurus and leading managers'.[37] They call 50 management gurus 'business thinkers' and 51 leading managers 'management giants'. We associate what we mean by wisdom with the term 'business thinkers', and that list does indeed include Peter Drucker and John Adair, though not Confucius.

There is of course a danger with this guru approach, in that we look to others to provide us with insights and experience rather than thinking things through for ourselves and learning from our own experience. It is the individual who needs to grow in wisdom; no one else can do it for us. It is not enough to be aware of the views of the 'gurus'. The transfer from experience to understanding is a special talent and is how wisdom is built up. Failure, probably more than success, is what helps to build wisdom.

People who are strong on wisdom never stop learning and always feel that there is more to know. Like the grandmaster chess players mentioned in Chapter 6, they can identify patterns and over time can see many moves ahead and know which is the best one. They appear to make decisions quickly but behind the speed of decision there is a great deal of experience. Their wisdom has been built up over many years. Often it is so embedded that it looks like instinct.

Direction

Here we are concerned with the horizon and middle distance aspects of direction. Dame Stephanie Shirley, whom we referenced in Chapter 7, found this direction side of the business 'indistinguishable from pleasure'. She loved it—a sure sign of talent. She was playing to her strengths. 'Only when I was exploring ways of doing things better did I fling myself into the work with joy.'

Direction is fundamentally a focus and strategic issue. It is about being able to see the future and knowing how to use that visibility to your advantage. We have already given the example of how Xerox was well ahead with its research on what became the PC and how Steve Jobs was able to take their technology and beat them to the market. Jobs was strong on direction; Xerox was not. The title of the book that tells this story from the Xerox perspective was aptly titled *Fumbling the Future: How Xerox Invented, Then Ignored, the First Personal Computer*.[38]

Many companies have 'fumbled the future' because they were not strong in this direction attribute. The mobile-phone sector has seen the demise of Nokia and BlackBerry, once both very strong leaders. Before that was the Palm Pilot PDA which was also a great product. In Chapter 7 we cited the example of the GO company whose product idea was way ahead of the technology that was needed for its success. Apple's version of the same product concept, the Newton, also got nowhere.

Whilst there is something of the wisdom of hindsight in these comments, we see it essentially as a weakness in the direction talent. There has to be something of a prophet in people strong on direction, but they must also be strategic thinkers able to bend the future to their will. Here we are not talking about people who are in the right place at the right time but those who discern the future and can make it happen. Steve Jobs was one such. Trip Hawkins, an early associate of Jobs, has commented, 'Steve has a power of vision that is almost frightening. When Steve believes in something, the power of that vision can literally sweep aside any objections, problems, or whatever. They just cease to exist'.[39] This effect, known as Jobs' 'distortion reality field' became legendary. Andy Hertzfeld, another close associate of Jobs, has described it as 'a confounding mélange of a charismatic rhetorical style, an indomitable will, and an eagerness to bend any fact to fit the purpose at hand'.[40]

An important determinant in deciding the strength of your direction talent is whether you are more interested in concepts than in realities. We were once involved in a UNESCO/UNITWIN project in Latin America. This required visiting universities to encourage them to develop technology transfer and innovate with a view to the generation of new technology-based businesses. One element of this was the role that science parks could play in that process.

During a visit to a university in Brazil we were invited to lunch with a recently appointed State Minister for Technology. There had been some key university personnel on a science-park planning committee, but the new Minister had dismissed them. The purpose of the lunch was to try and persuade the Minister to reinstate them. We assumed that, because of his actions, he was probably more interested in the practicalities involved in building a science park than in the concept itself. Accordingly we told him the story of our experiences in Cambridge, England. This involved both the Cambridge Science Park and the St John's Innovation Park and also our experience with other science parks in Europe through the SPRINT project.

After lunch, the Minister said that he had found the discussion interesting but made no comment about the academics he had taken off the committee. He stayed on in the afternoon for our presentation to the staff and students in which we explained the key concepts that lay behind the projects that had been discussed over lunch. To our surprise and delight after the lecture he thanked us for our presentation and said he would be inviting the academics back onto his committee.

Our assumption had been that, having dismissed the academics, he was more likely to be a pragmatic person who wanted to know the facts; hence our approach over lunch. However, this proved not to be the case. He was clearly a man strong in the direction talent, and was more interested in concepts and the 'why' of things rather than the 'what'. He had not been the pragmatic, 'get things done' person that we had assumed.

Self-assessment: find your Perception score

Reflecting on these points you may find it helpful to consider whether you are a 'concept person' who enjoys handling ideas or a pragmatist who likes to get on and do things within the inevitable constraints. This is something of a 'bottom line' question, as it affects our understanding and approach not just to Vision but to life in general.

I score myself ___ per cent a concept person and ____ per cent a pragmatist.

We now offer some questions to help you to decide your overall score for Discernment. They cover the three elements of Judgement, Wisdom and Direction.

- What is your approach to decision making? Do you weigh all the facts carefully or do you have a nose for the right answer? How often are you not just wrong but badly wrong? Think of some examples.
- Do you feel that you have grown in wisdom over the years? Can you now see most situations coming or do you still get taken by surprise? Do people seek your advice?
- Are you a concept person who thinks strategically or are you more pragmatic and just seek to get the job done? Are you good at seeing the future and turning it into reality? Again, try to think of examples.

My suggested score:

    for Judgement: _____ out of 10
    for Wisdom: _____ out of 10
    for Direction: _____ out of 10

♠ Your Discernment score

To derive a score for Discernment we suggest you average the scores you gave yourself for Judgement, Wisdom and Direction.

    My overall Discernment score is _____ out of 10

In assessing your scores it may be helpful to relate them to your 'concept person v pragmatist' score and check for any anomalies. We would see Judgement as neutral, Wisdom as related to a concept person and Direction as characteristic of a pragmatist. Thus, those who see themselves as concept people are likely to score higher on Wisdom and lower on Direction. Equally, a pragmatist would be expected to be higher on Direction and lower on Wisdom.

If you scoring shows otherwise, it may be that your understanding of what it means to be a concept or pragmatic person is different to ours. This does not mean that you are wrong, but we would expect your difference in understanding to be reflected in the scores you gave yourself for Wisdom and Direction.

11

♦ ♥ ♣ ♠ THE FINAL SCORE

Although there is now the opportunity to derive an overall **entirepreneur** score, we would like to stress that your own understanding of how you measure up to being an **entirepreneur** is more important than the score itself. The actual numbers are important indicators, but we hope that you will have really gained an understanding of your strengths across Talent, Temperament, Technique and Discernment.

Combining your scores

Here you will probably find it helpful to go back to the earlier chapters and transfer your scores to Table 11.1.

The relative value of these scores is important. Temperament and Discernment are the most important because if either or both are the lowest in the Attribute set then it is a warning sign of what could become points of serious weakness. As we have already noted, Temperament can make the greatest talent ineffective and Discernment directly affects strategy and decision making. Equally, too much emphasis on technique can reduce the effectiveness of natural talent.

With these comments in mind we have, in the formula we recommend in Table 11.1, doubled the Temperament and the Discernment scores; by this double weighting you will have amassed a score out of 60. We suggest you adjust this to a score out of 100 (the maximum you can achieve)—to do this you simply multiply by 10 and then divide by 6.

We also offer two ways of seeing the results as a whole. The first follows from Table 11.1 and uses the main attribute scores under the heading Direct Score Evaluation. The second approach takes these direct scores and using the metaphor of a hand of cards derives a value for 'your hand'. In both cases we consider four examples ranging from outstanding to borderline.

TABLE 11.1 Entirepreneur scores

Attribute	Score	Attribute set	Score	Main element	Score
Ideas		CREATIVITY			
Opportunity					
Innovation				♦	
Target		FOCUS			
Action				TALENT	
Time					
Administration		OPERATIONS		♦	
Organisation					
People					
Self-assurance		INNER EGO			
Dedication				♥	
Motivation					
Courage		OUTER EGO		TEMPERAMENT	
Responsibility				♥	
Accountability					
Team		TEAMS PLUS			
Using experts				♣	
Networking					
Knowledge		LEARNED ABILITIES		TECHNIQUE	
Skills				♣	
Experience					
Horizon		VISION			
Middle distance					
The 'Now'				♠	
Beliefs		VALUES			
Ethics				DISCERNMENT	
Values in action					
Judgement		PERCEPTION		♠	
Wisdom					
Direction					
Final formula : (♦ + 2 ♥ + ♣ + 2 ♠) x 10/6			**ENTIREPRENEUR**		

Direct score evaluation

Here results can be tabulated as in Table 11.2 and also expressed diagrammatically as in Figure 11.1 (re Person B). Figure 11.2 is for your own use. Note that from the centre outwards, each ring represents the scores 2, 4, 6, 8 and 10.

TABLE 11.2 The direct score tabulation

	Talent	Temperament	Technique	Discernment	Final score	Comment
Person A	9	10	8	9	91.7	Outstanding
Person B	8	9	7	8	81.7	Very good
Person C	7	8	6	8	75.0	Good
Person D	7	6	7	6	63.3	Borderline

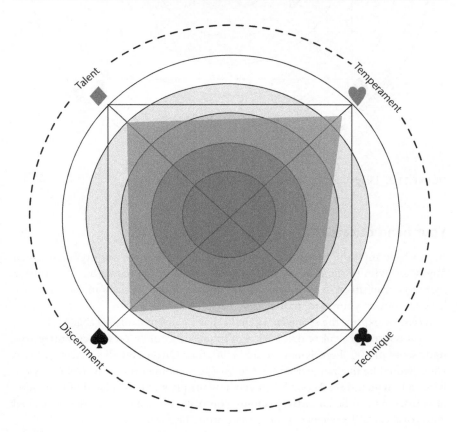

FIGURE 11.1 Diagrammatic framework—person B

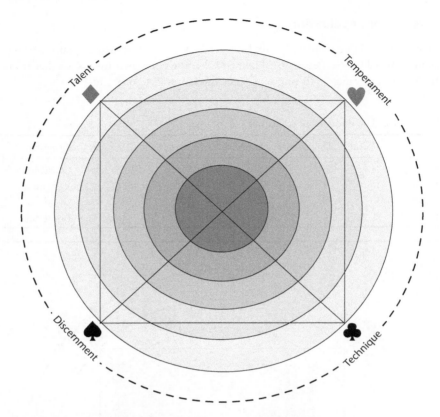

FIGURE 11.2 Diagrammatic framework—your personal profile

Your hand of cards

As we have used the metaphor of playing cards to illustrate our arguments, you might also wish to think of yourself in terms of a hand of four cards. As you have scored yourself from 0–10 (a scale of 11) and there are 13 cards in each suit, we have to convert your score in line with Table 11.3, below.

We now express the scores in Table 11.2 as a hand of cards—Table 11.4.

You can soon calculate that a hand of four aces would represent an **entirepreneur** score of 100. Four Kings would be 90; four Queens 80. Two Aces and two Kings would be in a range from 93.3 to 96.7, depending on which attributes were Kings and which were Aces. Only a very few people will hold a hand of four Aces, of course—but to be an **entirepreneur** you really do need a hand that is stacked with royal cards! Excellence is more than strong performance.

TABLE 11.3 Converting your score

Score	10	9	8	7	6	5	4	3	2	1	0
Card	Ace	King	Queen	Jack	10	9	8	7	6	4	2

TABLE 11.4 Your hand of cards

	Talent	*Temperament*	*Technique*	*Discernment*	*Final score*	*Comment*
Person A	King	Ace	Queen	King	91.7	Outstanding
Person B	Queen	King	Jack	Queen	81.7	Very good
Person C	Jack	Queen	10	Queen	75.0	Good
Person D	Jack	10	Jack	10	63.3	Borderline

*

We have now reached the end of our book. We began with a number of **entire-preneur** stories to bring these important people to life. They are around, they have been around for a long time, and they can be found in both business and elsewhere. They are people who see and seize opportunities, sometimes chasing a personal vision for improving the world in some way. They have direction as they set out to accomplish their dreams; they gather the various resources they need and they get on with it; they sort out the operational details and deliver.

We have discussed the context of the 'New Normal' and argued that this turbulent and uncertain world calls for fresh thinking vis-à-vis the people who are likely to be most effective. We explained why we believe the conventional approach that separates the entrepreneur from the leader from the manager fails to capture the all-round holistic contribution of the **entirepreneur**, who is able to naturally and seamlessly blend the contributions of those people we tradi-tionally call entrepreneur, leader and manager. Finally we provided an attrib-utes profile for the **entirepreneur** and offered you the opportunity to evaluate yourself.

Once you have done this and calculated your **entirepreneur** score we encour-age you to think about what will be required to 'strengthen your hand' in order for you to become increasingly 'fit for purpose' in the challenging, turbulent and exciting world of the 'New Normal'. The important thing is to make effective use of your strengths. The line below might usefully be evaluated against the Will Rogers quotation that appeared between Chapters 6 and 7.

You can't deal me the aces and think I wouldn't play.

From Aces *by Cheryl Wheeler, 1990*

NOTES

Chapter 1

1 A container ship that carries over 19,000 containers is now operational—but the very large ships may not be able to use the Panama and Suez canals and would also only be able to load and unload at selected ports.

Introduction to Part Three

1 The quotation is from the website www.ihpra.org, which describes the history of 'war clubs', linking them with India and Persia.
2 The Bible: Ephesians 6:17 and Hebrews 4:12.
3 Bolton, B. and Thompson, J. *The Entrepreneur in Focus: Achieve Your Potential*, Thomson, 2003.

Chapter 6

1 Galton, Sir F. *English Men of Science: Their Nature and Nurture*, Macmillan, 1874, p. 12.
2 Bouchard, T. Genes, environment and personality, *Science*, 264, 1994, pp. 1700–1. The quotation is from Peter Whybrow's excellent book *A Mood Apart*, 1997, p. 83.
3 Woods, B. *Applying Psychology to Sport*, Hodder & Stoughton, 1998, p. 16.
4 Epstein, D. *The Sports Gene: Talent, Practice and the Truth about Success*, Yellow Jersey Press, 2013.
5 Simon, H. and Chase, W.G. Skill in chess, *American Scientist*, 61, 1973, pp. 394–403. (The quotation is from p. 402.) Also see Simon, H. and Chase, W.G. Perception in chess, *Cognitive Psychology*, 4, 1973, pp. 55–61.
6 Howe, M.J.A. *Genius Explained*, Cambridge University Press, 1999.
7 Ericsson, K.A., Krampe, R.T. and Tesch-Romer, C. The role of deliberate practice in the acquisition of expert performance, *Psychological Review*, 100, 1993, pp. 363–406.
8 Colvin, G. *Talent Is Overrated: What Really Separates World-Class Performers from Everybody Else*, Nicholas Brealey Publishing, 2008.
9 Gladwell, M. *Outliers: The Story of Success*, Allen Lane, Penguin Books, 2008.
10 Coyle. D. *The Talent Code: Greatness Isn't Born, It's Grown*, Arrow Books, 2009.
11 See note 7.

12 Stukeley, W. *Memoirs of Sir Isaac Newton's Life*, 1752. See Royal Society website and *The Independent* 15 October 2014.

13 Farmelo, G. *The Strangest Man: The Hidden Life of Paul Dirac, Quantam Genius*, Faber & Faber, 2010.

14 Hawking, S. *My Brief History*, Bantam Press, 2013.

15 See note 6.

16 See note 8.

17 See note 4.

18 Brandt, R.S. On talent development: A conversation with Benjamin Bloom, *Educational Leadership* 43(1), 1985, pp. 33–5.

19 Clifton, D.O. and Nelson, P. *Soar with Your Strengths*, Bantam Books, 2010. (Originally published in 1992.)

20 See note 19, p. 36.

21 The Heritage Family Study. See website www.pbrc/heritage/home.htm and Bouchard et al. The Heritage Family Study: Aims, design, and measurement protocol, *Medicine and Science in Sports and Exercise*, 27, 1995, pp. 721–9. This is not to be confused with The Heritage Foundation, which is a Republican think tank.

22 See note 4.

23 See note 19, p. 21.

24 Rath, T. and Conchie, B. *Strengths-Based Leadership: Great Leaders, Teams, and Why People Follow*, Gallup Press, 2008. Quotation is taken from the front cover.

25 Buckingham, M. and Coffman, C.W. *First, Break All the Rules: What the World's Greatest Managers Do Differently*, Simon & Schuster, 1999.

26 Buckingham, M. and Clifton, D.O. *Now, Discover Your Strengths: How to Develop your Talents and Those of the People You Manage*, Simon & Schuster, 2001.

27 See note 24, pp. 240–1; and note 26, pp. 69–75.

28 Black, R. *How Long's the Course?*, Andre Deutsch, 1998.

29 Dell, M. *Direct from Dell: Strategies that Revolutionised an Industry*, HarperCollins, 1999.

30 Steiner, R. *My First Break: How Entrepreneurs Get Started*, News International, 1998.

31 Brown, G. *Interview with Fred Terman*, Hewlett-Packard Archives, 1973. Referenced in Rogers, E.M. and Larson, J.K., *Silicon Valley Fever*, Unwin Counterpoint, 1986.

32 See note 19, pp. 52–6.

33 Csikszentmihalyi, M. *Flow: The Psychology of Optimal Experience*, Harper & Row, 1990.

34 See note 26, pp. 56, 48.

35 See note 26, p. 78.

36 See note 24, pp. 24–7, 99.

37 For further information see our website at www.efacets.co.uk.

38 Sir Francis Galton was a prolific writer. He wrote at least 24 books and made a major contribution to statistics. His writings included:

Hereditary Genius: An Inquiry into Its Laws and Consequences, Julian Friedman Publishers, 1979. (Originally published in 1869.)

The history of twins as a criterion of the relative powers of nature and nurture, *Fraser's Magazine*, 12, 1875, pp. 566–76 and *Journal of the Anthropological Institute*, 5, 1875, pp. 391–406.

Inquiries into Human Faculty and its Development, 2nd ed., Macmillan, 1892. (Originally published in 1883.) This was the first use of the word eugenics that Galton saw as an obvious development of evolution.

Memoirs of My Life, Methuen, 1908.

39 Galton, Sir F. Measurement of character, *Fortnightly Review*, 36, 1884, pp. 179–85. (Quotation is from p. 181.)

40 *The Lexical Hypothesis and Factor Models,* Psychometric Resource Centre, EnAct, Dublin, retrieved from www.psychometric-assessment.com.

41 Allport, F.H. and Allport, G.W. Personality traits: Their classification and measurement, *Journal of Abnormal and Social Psychology*, 16, 1921, pp. 6–40.

42 This number is debated and could be 181. For a full review, see John, O.P., Angleitner, A. and Ostendorf, F. The lexical approach to personality: A historical review of trait taxonomic research, *European Journal of Personality*, 2, 171–203, 1988.

43 Nettle, D. *Personality: What Makes You the Way You Are*, Oxford University Press, 2007.

44 See note 26, pp. 249–50.

45 Bolton, B. and Thompson, J. *Entrepreneurs: Talent, Temperament and Opportunity*, 3rd ed., Routledge, 2013, pp. 87–8.

46 Cain, S. *Quiet: The Power of Introverts in a World that Can't Stop Talking*, Penguin, 2012.

47 Welch, J. *Jack: What I've learned Leading a Great Company and Great People*, Headline Book Publishing, 2001. Reference to the 'GE Vortex' is found on p. 29.

48 In our book on entrepreneurs referenced in note 45 we give examples of a number of 'trigger events' that have driven entrepreneurs to action. See pp. 32–3, 116–7, 122–3, 207.

49 Lansley, S. and Forrester, A. *Top Man: How Philip Green Built his High Street Empire*, Aurum Press, 2006. Comments are taken from pp. 13, 17, and 18 of the paperback edition.

50 Butler, G. and Hope, T. *Manage Your Mind: The Mental Fitness Guide*, Oxford University Press, 1995. Quotation is from 'The Chef's Tale' on pp. 15–6.

51 Jung, C.G. *Two Essays on Analytical Psychology*, Meridian Books, 1953, p. 190.

52 Hopcke, R.H. *A Guided Tour of the Collected Works of C.G. Jung*, Random House, 1989, pp. 87–8.

53 Argyris, C. *Understanding Organisational Behaviour*, Tavistock, 1960. There is also a useful review of T-groups in *Business: The Ultimate Resource*, A&C Black, 2006, p. 1650 under the heading 'Sensitivity Training'.

54 See note 45 and the 1st or 2nd edition of our *Entrepreneurs* book. The chapter on 'Techniques for the Entrepreneur' was omitted from the 3rd edition because there are now a number of books that deal solely with this topic.

55 Forte, C. *Forte*. Pan Books, 1997.

56 Henderson, B. The Story of Joe (a Fable). Boston Consulting Group Newsletter, January 1, 1977. This can be found on the website www.bcgperspectives.com.

57 Goleman, D. *Focus: The Hidden Driver of Excellence*, Harper, 2013.

58 Simon, H.A. *Administrative Behaviour: A Study of Decision-Making Processes in Administrative Organisations*, 4th ed., The Free Press, 2013. (Originally published in 1947.)

59 Simon, H.A. and Chase, W.G. Skill in chess, *American Scientist*, 61(4), July–August 1973, pp. 394–403.

60 Malone, M.S. *Bill & Dave: How Hewlett and Packard Built the World's Greatest Company*, Portfolio, 2007. See Foreword: Restoration.

61 Packard, D. *The HP Way: How Bill Hewlett and I Built our Company*, HarperCollins, 1995, p. 82.

62 Williams, S. *Breakout: Life Beyond the Corporation*, Hamish Hamilton, 1993.

63 See note 47, pp. 25–9.

64 Wolmar, C. *Stagecoach*, Orion Business, 1998. Reference is from a 2013 edition published by Kemsing Publishing Limited and an interview in November 2012 with Sir Brian Souter.

65 Best, G. *Blessed: The Autobiography*, Random House, 2001.

66 Whybrow, P. *A Mood Apart: The Thinker's Guide to Emotion and its Disorders*, Picador, 1997.

Chapter 7

1 Young, J.S. and Simon, W.L. *Icon: Steve Jobs, The Greatest Second Act in the History of Business*, John Wiley & Sons, 2005.

2 Waterstone, T. *Swimming Against the Stream: Launching Your Business and Making Your Life*, Macmillan, 2006.

3 Wallace, J. and Erickson, J. *Hard Drive: Bill Gates and the Making of the Microsoft Empire*, John Wiley & Sons, 1992, pp. 42, 59.

4 Freiberger, P. and Swaine, M. *Fire in the Valley: The Making of the Personal Computer*, McGraw-Hill, 1984.

5 Morita, A. *Made in Japan*, HarperCollins, 1994.

6 Buncombe, A. and Arthur, C. James Dyson spent years fighting Hoover: Now he intends to clean up, *The Independent*, 4 October 2000.

7 Isaacson, W. *Steve Jobs*, Little, Brown & Company, 2011.

8 Kaplan, J. *Start Up: A Silicon Valley Adventure*, Warner Books, 1997.

9 See note 7, p. 99.

10 For further details of the Eddie Stobart Club visit their website www.stobartclubandshop.co.uk.

11 From the *Collins English Dictionary*.

12 Buckingham, M. and Clifton, D.O. *Now, Discover your Strengths: How to Develop Your Talents and Those of the People You Manage*, Simon & Schuster, 2001.

13 Wolmar, C. *Stagecoach*, Orion Business, 1998. Reference is from a 2013 edition published by Kemsing Publishing Limited and an interview in November 2012 with Sir Brian Souter.

14 Williams, S. *Breakout: Life Beyond the Corporation*, Hamish Hamilton, 1993.

15 See note 3.

16 Personal communication with Don Clifton about his SRI Entrepreneur Perceiver questionnaire, 1986.

17 Shirley, S. *Let IT Go*, Andrews UK Limited, 2012.

18 McGregor, D. *The Human Side of Enterprise*, McGraw-Hill, 1960. (We recommend the annotated edition published in 2006.)

19 See note 17.

20 Boston Consulting Group Newsletter entitled 'Trust'.

21 Ferguson, C.H. and Morris, C.R. *Computer Wars: How the West Can Win in a Post-IBM World*, Times Books, 1993.

22 Gerstner, L. *Who Says Elephants Can't Dance?: How I Turned Around IBM*, HarperCollins, 2003.

23 See note 22, p. 71.

24 See note 18. 'Foreword to the Twenty-Fifth Anniversary Printing', on p. xx, quoted Warren G. Bennis from a personal communication with McGregor.

25 Semler, R. *Maverick: The Success Story Behind the World's Most Unusual Workplace*, Warner Books, 1993.

26 See note 22. (Quotation on p. 184.)

Chapter 8

1 This definition of 'ego' is from the *Collins English Dictionary*. We use the term in as straightforward a way as possible and are not concerned with Freud's terms that distinguish between the *id,* our primitive instincts in the unconscious mind, the *ego*, our conscious self, and the *superego*, our conscience.

2 Maslow, A. A theory of human motivation, *Psychological Review*, 50, 1943, pp. 370–96. A key book probably read by McGregor is *Motivation and Personality*, Harper & Brothers,

1st ed. 1954. A more recent issue is *Motivation and Personality*, 3rd ed., Harper & Row, 1987. A popular version that describes Maslow's 'hierarchy of needs' is *A Theory of Human Motivation*, Wilder Publications, 2013.

3 McGregor, D. *The Human Side of Enterprise*, McGraw-Hill, 1960. Here we recommend the Annotated Edition published in 1960. The quotations are taken from p. 50 of that edition.

4 Rotter, J.B. Generalised expectations for internal versus external control of reinforcement, *Psychological Monographs: General and Applied*, 80(1) whole no. 609, 1966.

5 Cain, S. *Quiet: The Power of Introverts in a World That Can't Stop Talking*, Penguin, 2012, p. 44. Another book to read is Badaracco, J.L. *Leading Quietly*, Harvard Business School Press, 2002.

6 *Entrepreneurs: Talent, Temperament and Opportunity* 3rd ed., Routledge, 2013. See also our website, www.efacets.co.uk.

7 Buckingham, M. and Clifton, D.O. *Now, Discover Your Strengths: How to Develop your Talents and Those of the People You Manage*, Simon & Schuster, 2001. The quotations are taken from the description of the 'Self-Assurance' strength on p. 113.

8 Welch, J. *Jack: What I've Learned Leading a Great Company and Great People*, Headline Book Publishing, 2001. Reference to the 'GE Vortex' is found on p. 29.

9 See note 8, pp. 5–6. Quotations re Welch's stammer.

10 See note 8. Quotations re Welch's mother as his source of self-confidence.

11 du Boulay, S. *Cicely Saunders: The Founder of the Modern Hospice Movement*, SPCK Publishing, 2007.

12 Roddick, A. *Business as Unusual*, Anita Roddick Books, 2005, p.181.

13 Malone, M.S. *Bill & Dave: How Hewlett and Packard Built the World's Greatest Company*, Portfolio, 2007.

14 Stanley, T.J. *The Millionaire Mind*, Bantam Books, 2002. See Table 21 and p. 186.

15 Quotation from Sam Walton, the founder of WalMart, which in 2013 was the world's second largest company by turnover. Royal Dutch Shell was slightly larger.

16 Waterstone, T. *Swimming Against the Stream*, Macmillan, 2006.

17 Bannatyne, D. *Anyone Can Do It: My Story*, Orion Books, 2007.

18 David McClelland (1917–1998) was a professor of psychology at Harvard for 30 years.

19 McClelland, D. *The Achieving Society*, Free Press, 1961.

20 See note 19, p. 300

21 Law, A. *Open Minds: 21st Century Business Lessons and Innovations from St Luke's*, Orion Business Books, 1998.

22 Personal communication with Don Clifton about his SRI Entrepreneur Perceiver questionnaire, 1986.

23 Branson, R. *Losing My Virginity*, Random House, 1998.

24 Sculley, J. *Odyssey: Pepsi to Apple, a Journey of Adventure, Ideas, and the Future*, Collins, 1987.

25 Rath, T. *StrengthsFinder 2.0*, Gallup Press, 2007, p. 149.

26 Wakelin, M. *J. Arthur Rank: The Man behind the Gong*, Lion Books, 1997.

27 Rath, T. and Harter, J. *Well Being: The Five Essential Elements*, Gallup Press, 2010, p. 6.

28 Achor, S. *The Happiness Advantage: The Seven Principles that Fuel Success and Performance at Work*, Virgin Books, 2011.

29 See note 4.

30 Folley, M. *A Time to Jump: The Authorised Biography of Jonathan Edwards*, HarperCollins, 2001, p. 120.

31 Black, R. *How Long's the Course?* Andre Deutsch, 1999, p. 196.

Chapter 9

1 Belbin, M. *Management Teams: Why They Succeed or Fail*, Butterworth-Heinemann, 1996.
2 The Body Shop Charter. This was issued to all members of staff in the 90s. It included an 'employee handbook' giving terms and conditions of service.
3 Law, A. *Open Minds: 21st Century Business Lessons and Innovations from St Luke's*, Orion Business Books, 1999. See Chapter 15 on ownership.
4 Fukuyama, F. *Trust: The Social Virtues and the Creation of Prosperity*, Hamish Hamilton Ltd., 1995.
5 Kelly, K. *New Rules for a New Economy: 10 Ways the Network Economy is Changing Everything*, Penguin Books, 1999. See also the magazine *Wired* Sept. 1997
6 Rose, F. *West of Eden: The End of Innocence at Apple Computer*, Business Books, 1989.
7 Castells, M. and Hall, P. *Technopoles of the World: The Making of the 21st Century Industrial Complexes*, Routledge, 1994.
8 Garrett, J. 'Gallup's Discoveries about Leaders' at 'Work Together' conference, Spring Harvest Conference, Sheffield, 1998.
9 Jill Garrett's lecture, note 8, was given three years before Gallup's book, *Now, Discover Your Strengths* was published in 2001, see note 11.
10 Welch, J. *Jack: What I've Learned Leading a Great Company and Great People*, Headline Book Publishing, 2001. See Chapter 6, 'Swimming in a Bigger Pond', p. 71.
11 Buckingham, M. and Clifton, D.O. *Now, Discover Your Strengths: How to Develop Your Talents and Those of the People You Manage*, Simon & Schuster, 2001, pp. 41, 46. See chapter titled 'Knowledge and Skills'.
12 See note 11, p. 39. General Colin Powell was Commander-in-Chief of NATO's forces during Desert Shield and Desert Storm. The comments quoted are based on a speech he gave to 1,000 Gallup Organisation leaders.
13 Sculley, J. *Odyssey: Pepsi to Apple, a Journey of Adventure, Ideas, and the Future*, Collins, 1987.
14 Burrough, B. and Helyar, J. *Barbarians at the Gate*, Arrow, 2010. (The quotation is taken from the back cover of the book.)
15 Boyce, R. *Pipe Dreams: Greed, EGO, and the Death of Enron*, Perseus, 2008.

Chapter 10

1 The Bible, Hebrews 5:14 ESV.
2 *The Times*, 20 September 2014.
3 Goleman, D. *Focus: The Hidden Driver of Excellence*, Bloomsbury Publishing, 2013. See Chapter 18, 'How Leaders Direct Attention' and the section titled 'The Telling Detail on the Horizon'.
4 Hicks, J. and Houston, T. *Research, No Motion: How The Blackberry CEOs Lost An Empire*, 2012 Kindle Edition.
5 This 1 per cent figure comes from the research firm Kantar Worldpanel. Despite these small sales RIM has recently (2014) launched the Blackberry Passport.
6 Grove, A. *Only the Paranoid Survive: How To Exploit the Crisis Points that Challenge Every Company and Career*, HarperCollins, 1998.
7 Bevan, J. *The Rise and Fall of Marks & Spencer, and How it Rose Again*, Profile Books, 2007.
8 An earlier version of the reference in note 7 was published in 2002 under the title *The Rise and Fall of Marks & Spencer* before their recovery.
9 Barnes, L. and Lea-Greenwood, G. Fast fashioning the supply chain: Shaping the research agenda. *Journal of Fashion Marketing and Management*, 10(3), 2006, pp. 259–71.
10 Hilton, C. *Be My Guest*, Prentice-Hall, 1991. (Originally published in 1957.)
11 Fukuyama, F. *Trust: The Social Virtues and the Creation of Prosperity*, Hamish Hamilton Ltd, 1995.

12 Weber, M. *The Protestant Ethic and the Spirit of Capitalism*, Acherson Press, 2012. It was originally published in German in 1905 but the first edition in English was not published until 1930.

13 Achor, S. *The Happiness Advantage: The Seven Principles of Positive Psychology that Fuel Success and Performance at Work*, Virgin Books, 2010, p. 74.

14 Blanchard, K. and Bowles, S. *Gung Ho! Increase Productivity, Profits, and Your Own Prosperity*, HarperCollins, 1998.

15 Rath, T. *StrengthsFinder 2.0*, Gallup Press, 2007.

16 Stiles, J. *Enron: A Lesson in Corporate Governance*, 2012 Kindle Edition.

17 Search under Google IPO 2004 Founders' letter. Quotation is from 'An Owner's Manual' for Google shareholders.

18 See note 11.

19 This description of reciprocity comes from the Bible, in Matthew 7:12. There is a similar reference in James 2:8 where it is called the 'Royal Law'.

20 Elkington, J. *Enter the Triple Bottom*, 2004, KMH Associates. See also his book *The Breakthrough Challenge: 10 Ways to Connect Today's Profits with Tomorrow's Bottom Line*, Jossey-Bass, 2014.

21 Sider, R. *Bread of Life: Stories of Radical Mission*, Triangle, 1996.

22 Crane, A. and Matten, D. *Business Ethics: Managing Corporate Citizenship and Sustainability in the Age of Globalisation*, 3rd ed., Oxford University Press, 2010.

23 Kennedy, C. *Business Pioneers: Family, Fortune and Philanthropy: Cadbury, Sainsbury and John Lewis*, Random House, 2000.

24 Milligan, E.H. *Biographical Dictionary of British Quakers in Commerce and Industry 1775–1920*, William Sessions Limited, 2007.

25 Raistrick, A. *Quakers in Science and Industry*, William Sessions Limited, 1993.

26 Windsor, D.B. *The Quaker Enterprise*, Frederick Muller Ltd., 1980.

27 Walvin, J. *The Quakers: Money and Morals*, John Murray, 1997.

28 See note 25.

29 See note 26. Quakers also call themselves 'Friends' as in the term 'Friends' Meeting House'.

30 Malone, M.S. *Bill & Dave: How Hewlett and Packard built the World's Greatest Company*, Portfolio, 2007.

31 See note 30.

32 Hattersley, R. *Blood and Fire: William and Catherine Booth and the Salvation Army*, Abacus, 2000.

33 Levitt, S.D. and Dubner, S.J. *Freakonomics: A Rogue Economist Explores the Hidden Side of Everything*, 2005.

34 See note 7 pp. 192, 197, 199, 120.

35 The Bible, Proverbs 10:13 NIV.

36 Adair, J. *Confucius on Leadership*, Pan Macmillan, 2013.

37 *Business: The Ultimate Resource*, A&C Black Publishers Ltd., 2006.

38 Smith, D.K. and Alexander, R.C. *Fumbling The Future: How Xerox Invented, then Ignored, the First Personal Computer*, iUniverse, 1999.

39 Young, J.S. and Simon, W.L. *Icon: Steve Jobs, The Greatest Second Act in the History of Business*, John Wiley & Sons, 2005, p. 62.

40 Kahney, L. *Inside Steve's Brain*, Atlantic Books, 2008, p. 167.

BIBLIOGRAPHY

Whilst there are biographies and autobiographies for many of the people whose stories we have told, we have found the following references particularly useful.

Preface and Introduction

Brady, K. *Strong Woman: Ambition, Grit and a Great Pair of Heels*, Collins, 2012.

Collins, J.C. and Porras, J.I. *Built to Last*, Random House, 1997.

Colvin, G. *Talent is Overrated: What Really Separates World-Class Performers from Everybody Else*, Nicholas Brealey, 2008.

Fox, E.A. *Winning from Within: A Breakthrough Method for Leading, Living and Lasting Change*, Harper Business, 2013.

Gladwell, M. *Outliers: The Story of Success*, Little, Brown & Company, 2008.

Peters, T.J. *Thriving on Chaos*, Pan Books, 1989.

Toffler, A. *The Third Wave*, Pan Books, 1981.

Chapter 1

Ashton, B. England need entrepreneurial coach who will free players for competition, *The Independent*, 26 November 2011.

Clarke, M. and Joyner, A. *The Bear Necessities of Business*, Wiley, 2006.

Craner, S. *Business the Jack Welch Way*, Capstone, 2001.

Davies, H. *The Eddie Stobart Story*, HarperCollins, 2001.

Elberse, A. and Ferguson, A. Ferguson's Formula, *Harvard Business Review*, October 2013.

Gerstner, L. *Who Says Elephants Can't Dance? How I Turned Around IBM*, HarperCollins, 2003.

Maani, K. and Benton, C. Rapid team learning: Lessons from Team New Zealand's America's Cup Campaign, *Organisational Dynamics*, Spring 1999.

Roddick, A. *Business as Unusual*, Thorsons/HarperCollins, 2000.

Schultz, H. and Yang, D.J. *Pour Your Heart Into It*, Hyperion, 1997.
Welch, J. *Jack: What I've Learned Leading a Great Company and Great People*, Headline Book Publishing, 2001.

Chapter 2

Branson, R. *The Virgin Way*, Virgin Books, 2014.
Collins, J.C. and Porras, J.I. *Built to Last*, Random House, 1997.
Collins, J.C. *Good to Great*, Random House, 2001.
McGrath, R.M. *The End of Competitive Advantage*, Harvard Business School Press, 2013.
Peters, T.J. and Waterman, R.H. *In Search of Excellence*, Harper & Row, 1982.
Peters, T.J. *Thriving on Chaos*, Pan Books, 1989.
Peters, T.J. *Re-imagine*, Dorland Kindersley, 2003.
Porter, M.E. *Competitive Strategy: Techniques for Analyzing Industries and Competitors*, The Free Press, 1980.
Porter, M.E. What is Strategy?, *Harvard Business Review*, November–December, 1996.

Chapter 3

Bennis, W. and Thomas, R. *Geeks and Geezers: How Era, Values and Defining Moments Shape Leaders*, Harvard Business School Press, 2002.
Bracken, R. Comments on McKinsey website, November 2013.
Brady, K. *Strong Woman: Ambition, Grit and a Great Pair of Heels*, Collins, 2012.
Csikszentmihalyi, M. *Good Business*, Coronet, 2003.
Haslam, S.A., Reicher, S.D. and Platow, M.J. *The New Psychology of Leadership: Identity, Influence and Power*, Psychology Press, 2011.
McGregor, D. *The Human Side of Enterprise*, McGraw-Hill, 1960.
Mintzberg, H. *The Nature of Managerial Work*, Harper & Row, 1973.
Mintzberg H. *Managing*, Berrett-Koehler/FT Prentice Hall, 2009.
Peter, L.J. and Hull, R. *The Peter Principle: Why Things Always Go Wrong*, William Morrow, 1969.
Read, S. et al. *Effectual Entrepreneurship*, Routledge, 2011.

Chapter 4

Gerber, M.E., *The Power Point*, Harper Business, 1991.

Chapter 5

Gerber, M. *The E-Myth Revisited: Why Most Small Businesses Don't Work and What to Do About It*, University of North Carolina Press, 1996.

Our earlier books

Bolton, W. and Thompson, J. *Entrepreneurs: Talent, Temperament, Opportunity*, 3rd Edition, Routledge, 2013.
Bolton, W. and Thompson, J. *The Entrepreneur in Focus: Achieve Your Potential*, Thomson, 2003.

INDEX—A QUICK GUIDE TO THE ENTIREPRENEUR ATTRIBUTES

Talent attributes—Chapter 7

Creativity 140
      Ideas 141
      Opportunity 144
      Innovation 145

Focus 146
      Target 147
      Action 148
      Time 148

Operations 149
      Administration 150
      Organisation 151
      People 153

Temperament attributes—Chapter 8

Inner Ego 158
      Self-Assurance 159
      Dedication 160
      Motivation 162

Outer Ego 165
      Courage 165
      Responsibility 167
      Accountability 169

Technique attributes—Chapter 9

Teams Plus 173
    Teams 173
    Using Experts 175
    Networking 176

Learned Abilities 178
    Knowledge 179
    Skills 180
    Experience 180

Discernment attributes—Chapter 10

Vision 184
    Horizon 185
    Middle Distance 187
    The Now 188

Values 189
    Beliefs 190
    Ethics 191
    Values in Action 193

Perception 197
    Judgement 197
    Wisdom 199
    Direction 200

SUBJECT INDEX—MAIN REFERENCES

Note that we do not index 'entirepreneurs' and 'entirepreneurship' because they appear in every chapter

accountability 169
aces 113, 206
action focus 148
administration 150

Belbin team roles 174
beliefs 190
'Big picture' vision xvi
business model, the 100

cause-driven entirepreneurs
    195
change 75
chess and business 132
Chief Executive Officers (CEOs) 86
Chief Operating Officers (COOs) 91
Clubs (card suit) 112
communications entirepreneurs 41
community entirepreneurs 45
competing 74
conventional wisdom (critique) 78
courage 165
creativity 140
cycle of growth, the 107

dedication 160
Diamonds (card suit) 112

direction 200
directional excellence xiii, 7
discernment 112, 183

entertainment entirepreneurs 63
entrepreneurs xiii, 83
entrepreneurship 83
ethics 191
experience 179
expertise 80
experts 175

failing businesses 101
final score (your) 203
flexibility 74
flow 81
focus 146
followers 80

Gallup Organization 121, 178
Gallup StrengthsFinder (Donald Clifton) 124
growing businesses 105

Hearts (card suit) 112

ideas 141
influence 87

Inner Ego 127, 158
innovation 75, 145

judgement 197

knowledge 179

leaders 86; entrepreneurial leaders xi;
    transformational leaders xv
leadership 86
learned abilities 178
luck 102; hard luck 102; smart luck 102

managers 89
managing 89
motivation 162; achievement motivation
    163; affiliation motivation 163; power
    motivation 163

nature–nurture (debate) 85,
    115
networking 176
new businesses 104
'New Normal', the x,
    67, 97

operational excellence xiii, 7
operations 149
opportunities 144
organisation 151
Outer Ego 129, 158, 165

people 153
perception 197
person dimension 111
personality tests 125
Peter Principle 82

philanthropists 194
progression 80

Quakers 193

responsibility 167
retail entirepreneurs 28

self assurance 159
skills 178
social capital 176
social entirepreneurs 47
Spades (card suit) 112
speed 74
sports entirepreneurs 58
strategic thinking 74
successful businesses 99
sustainability 109

talent 112, 115, 117, 139
target focus 147
teams 173
Teams Plus 173
technique 112, 116, 130, 172
temperament 112, 116, 124, 157
time focus 148
transformational entirepreneurs 5
trust 87, 176

values 189, 193
vision 184; horizon vision 187; middle
    distance vision 185; 'now' vision 188

wisdom 199

X and Y styles (of leading and managing)
    92, 153, 174

ENTIREPRENEURS INDEX— MAIN REFERENCES

Ainslie, Sir Ben (*America's Cup*) 60

Barnum, P.T. 64
Berners-Lee, Sir Tim 41
Bezos, Jeff (*Amazon*) 22
Booth, William and Catherine 52, 195
Brady, Dame Karren xiv, 89
Branson, Sir Richard (*Virgin*) 20, 69, 135, 165
Bussau, David 49

Clarke, Maxine (*Build-a-Bear*) 30
Club Med 26
Coca-Cola 101
Conran, Terence 17
Coutts, Russell (*America's Cup*) 60

Dambusters, The 102
Davies, George 18
Disney, Walt 20
Dorsey, Jack (*Twitter*) 43
Dubrule, Paul (*Accor*) 26
Durrell, Gerald 63
Dyson, Sir James 19, 143

Eastman, George (*Kodak*) 19

Ferguson, Sir Alex 58, 76
Ford, Henry 19

Gerstner, Lou (*IBM*) 40, 153

Hande, Harish (*SELCO*) 53
Hewlett-Packard 122, 133, 194
Howard, Ebenezer 56

Jobs, Steve 10, 116, 141, 145, 166, 180, 200

Kamprad, Ingvar (*IKEA*) 28
Kelleher, Herb (*Southwest Air*) 20
Kroc, Ray (*McDonalds*) 14, 195

Laguiole knives 45
Laliberté, Guy (*Cirque du Soleil*) 63
Lusher, Caroline Redman 83

M-Pesa 23
Marks & Spencer 187, 198
Masterchef 8
McLean, Malcolm 33
Morita, Akio (*Sony*) 11, 143

Nightingale, Florence 51

Packer, Kerry 59
Pelisson, Gerard (*Accor*) 26
Pony Express, The 37

Roddick, Dame Anita (*The Body Shop*) 47, 161, 174, 191

Saunders, Dame Cicely 195
Schultz, Howard (*Starbucks*) 13
Shirley, Dame Stephanie 'Steve' 25, 149, 200
Shoen, Sam (*U-Haul*) 36
Silicon Valley 45
Sinclair, Sir Clive 83
Smit, Tim (*The Eden Centre*) 5
Smith, Fred (*Federal Express*) 35
Soros, George 21
Soros, Paul 22

Stephenson, George 32
Stobart, Edward 34, 145

Trippe, Juan (*PanAm*) 20

Walton, Sam (*Wal-Mart*) 29
Wedgwood, Josiah 16
Weinstock, Lord Arnold 95
Welch, Jack 39, 160, 195
Williams, Evan (*Twitter*) 43

Young, Michael 54
Yunus, Mohammed (*Grameen Bank*) 48

Zuckerberg, Mark (*Facebook*) 42

ABOUT THE AUTHORS

Bill Bolton

Bill Bolton spent 25 years in industry in both the public and private sectors. He has worked in large and small companies at board level. He was the UK Technical Director of a Swedish Multinational and is currently a non-executive director of a manufacturing SME. He began the academic side of his career at Cambridge University where he headed what was then the Production Engineering Group. In that time he was closely involved in the Cambridge Phenomenon, serving as a non-executive director of a seed-capital fund. He was also the Founding Director of the St John's Innovation Centre in Cambridge. This experience with university spin-offs led to a major university/industry project in Latin America for which Dr Bolton held a UNITWIN (UNESCO) Chair in Innovation and Technology Transfer.

His first publication *The University Handbook on Enterprise Development* (1997) came out of this project. More recently he has jointly authored with John Thompson *The Entrepreneur in Focus: Achieve Your Potential* (2003) and *Entrepreneurs: Talent, Temperament, Technique* now in its 3rd edition (2013).

John Thompson

John Thompson started his working life in book retailing and then, after a number of years in sales and marketing in the steel industry, he joined the academic world. He is currently Professor of Social Entrepreneurship at Anglia Ruskin University (part time) and Emeritus Professor of Entrepreneurship at the University of Huddersfield. He has spent time as a Visiting Professor at Universities in Finland, Australia and New Zealand. As well as his books on entrepreneurs, he has written several strategic management texts. His *Strategic Management: Awareness and Change* is currently available in its 7th edition. He has written numerous papers on both strategy and entrepreneurship during his academic career but he has also been an active case writer and is a great believer in the power of both case teaching and storytelling. To this end he has always maintained active links with both large and small organisations to carry out his research. He has also worked with of a number of social enterprises and charities and helped with the start-up of several small businesses. In 2009 he was awarded the Queen's Award for Enterprise Promotion.